ONE NATION DIVIDED BY SLAVERY

# AMERICAN ABOLITIONISM AND ANTISLAVERY
### JOHN DAVID SMITH, SERIES EDITOR

# One Nation Divided by Slavery

*Remembering the American Revolution While*

*Marching toward the Civil War*

MICHAEL F. CONLIN

THE KENT STATE UNIVERSITY PRESS

*Kent, Ohio*

© 2015 by The Kent State University Press, Kent, Ohio 44242

ALL RIGHTS RESERVED

Library of Congress Catalog Card Number 2014049004

ISBN 978-1-60635-240-3

Manufactured in the United States of America

LIBRARY OF CONGRESS CATALOGING-IN-PUBLICATION DATA

Conlin, Michael F., 1968– author.

One nation divided by slavery : remembering the American Revolution while
marching toward the Civil War / Michael F. Conlin.

pages cm. — (American abolitionism and antislavery)

Includes bibliographical references and index.

ISBN 978-1-60635-240-3 (hardcover : alk. paper) ∞

1. Antislavery movements—United States—History—19th century.

2. United States—History—Revolution, 1775-1783—Influence. I. Title.

E449.C747 2015

326'.8097309034—dc23

2014049004

19  18  17  16  15          5  4  3  2  1

# Contents

# Illustrations

# Acknowledgments

I became interested in the antebellum era during my first year in graduate school at the University of Illinois when my housemate and political science graduate student Jim Sopp lent me his copy of David Potter's *The Impending Crisis*. I read it in a day and a half. From that time on, I have found the coming of the war far more interesting than the war itself or its desultory end in Reconstruction. While systematically reading the *Washington (D.C.) Daily National Intelligencer* for my dissertation, which charted how the Civil War influenced the research program of the Smithsonian Institution, I was intrigued by reports that antebellum Americans were erecting seemingly countless monuments to George Washington, Henry Clay, Daniel Webster, and other national figures in the late 1840s and throughout the 1850s—at the very time when Northerners and Southerners were supposed to be galvanized into separate nations on the brink of an inevitable war. At that time, Harry Liebersohn introduced me to recent work on the invention of European nationalism when I served as his teaching assistant in a survey class on Western Civilization. Although the idea that Europeans had created their national stories was surely lost on most, if not all, of the undergraduates, it dovetailed nicely with the "monument mania" that jumped out at me from the pages of the *National Intelligencer*. I resolved to begin researching that topic as soon as I defended my dissertation and that is what I have done over the following fourteen years.

Although researching a book, especially one based primarily on archival materials, is largely a solitary activity, the assistance of outstanding archivists is absolutely necessary. I would like to thank the staffs of the William L. Clements Library at the University of Michigan, the Filson Historical Society, the Historical Society of Pennsylvania, the Maryland Historical Society, the Massachusetts Historical Society, the Missouri History Museum, the New York Public Library, the Rubenstein Rare Book & Manuscript Library at Duke University, the Small Special Collections Library at the University of Virginia, the South Caroliniana Library at the University of South Carolina, the Southern Historical Collection at the University of North Carolina, and the Wisconsin Historical Society at the University of Wisconsin. While I worked with numerous outstanding archivists, a few individuals merit individual praise: Barbara DeWolf and Clayton Lewis at the Clements Library; Shirley Harmon, Becky Rice, and Mark Wetherington at the Filson; Anna Clutterbuck-Cook, Peter Drummey, and Elaine Grublin at the Massachusetts Historical Society; Marc Thomas at the Maryland Historical Society; Brian Cuthrell, Sam Fore, and Henry Fulmer at the South Caroliniana Library; and Laura C. Brown at the Southern Historical Collection. As finding economical lodging within walking distance of the archives was my greatest logistical challenge, I would like to thank those who solved that problem for me: Jennifer R. Hannah of the Filson for finding me lodging in the dorms of Spalding University; Brian Cuthrell for putting me in contact with Tom Lekan, who generously allowed me to house-sit; Bruce Hall for the use his row house in Fell's Point, Baltimore; and James Green of the Library Company of Philadelphia for getting me a room in the Mary Cassatt House. As researchers need good cheer as well as a place to stay, I greatly appreciated the Massachusetts Historical Society for inviting me to its Strawberry Festival; the Clements Library for taking the time to have tea every day; the repeated hospitality of Tracy and Tyler Batton, Scott Heyward and Tina Cavaluzzi, Jim and Tracey Sopp, which relieved me of the dreariness of hostels; and the tours of Manhattan and Brooklyn led by Matthew Friedberger.

I would like to thank the institutions that provided financial assistance for my research. The Filson Historical Society's C. Ballard Breaux Visiting Fellowship, the Gilder Lehrman Institute of American History's Fellowship in American Civilization, the Maryland Historical Society's Lord Baltimore Research Fellowship, and the North Caroliniana Society's Archie K. Davis Fellowship, as well as two summer research grants and a year of sabbatical from Eastern Washington University helped to defray the expense and time of traveling two or three time zones and residing for a month to read and transcribe archival manuscripts by day and read newspapers on microfilm by night.

As a scholar I have incurred many intellectual debts at the University of Illinois and Eastern Washington University. I am grateful for the outstanding mentors I had at the University of Illinois. By sending me to the Newspaper Library for twenty hours a week as his research assistant, Daniel Littlefield introduced me to newspapers as a rich primary source, the historical significance of colonial and early national slavery, and my wife Stephanie. I also served as research assistant for Winton Solberg and my Ph.D. advisor Robert Johannsen: from the former I learned to be careful in my research and writing and unstinting in my industry; from the latter I learned to love the mid-nineteenth century and to aspire to write simple, direct, and fluid prose. John Hoffmann offered historiographical assistance and unflagging encouragement. My students and colleagues in the History Department and the College of Social and Behavioral Sciences and Social Work at Eastern Washington University have been supportive. A few merit special recognition: Bryan Carter, Larry Cebula, John Collins, Kathleen Huttenmaier, Ann LeBar, Joseph Lenti, Joel Martin, Nicole Montgomery, Edward Slack, Vickie Shields, Paul Warden, Gerry Wilson, and Bill Youngs.

While writing this book I received valuable advice and constructive criticism from a number of scholars and editors. William Blair, Russell McClintock, Larry McDonnell, Alex Moore, John Neff, Kristen Oertel, and Manisha Sinha helped me organize and sharpen my arguments; Robert Dean, Thomas Hawley, Bruce Levine, and David May read portions of the manuscript; Robert Bonner, Dick Donley, and Michael Morrison read the whole thing. It is much improved by their comments and suggestions. Special commendation goes to Robert M. Owens, my sometime collaborator cum overqualified research assistant and always friend, for reading the entire book manuscript and transcribing some of the archival manuscripts, and to Liping Zhu, my mentor whose boundless enthusiasm, thoughtful suggestions, and critical eye have never failed me. I would also like to thank Joyce Harrison, acquiring editor at the Kent State University Press, John Hubbell, the Press's former director, and John David Smith, editor of the Press's "American Abolitionism and Antislavery" series, and Valerie Ahwee for their unflagging support, sharp criticisms, and patience. They have saved me from glaring errors, tedious digressions, and excessive examples. In short, they saved me from myself. Of course, I am responsible for what remains.

Finally, I would like to thank my family for tireless support of my academic pursuits. From my father Michael F. Conlin Sr. I learned the value of hard work; from my mother Carrie Conlin Royalty I learned to love learning. Their support and that of my brother John and my aunt and uncle, Mary Ann and Randy St. Clair, meant the world to me. My wife Stephanie and my sons Devin and Eamon have offered the greatest support and suffered the greatest hardships. In addition to reading the entire manuscript and offering her own editorial commentary, Stephanie endured my absence of seventeen months in the archives, making her a "research widow." After the auspicious arrival of Devin and Eamon she was also a "research single mom." Over the course of fourteen years, they kept my spirits up when I became homesick, welcomed me home from research trips, and cheerfully endured my seemingly endless transcribing, writing, and rewriting. Therefore, I dedicate this book to them.

# Abbreviations

UMich    Clements Library, University of Michigan, Ann Arbor, Michigan

FHS    Filson Historical Society, Louisville, Kentucky

HSP    Historical Society of Pennsylvania, Philadelphia, Pennsylvania

MdHS    Maryland Historical Society, Baltimore, Maryland

MaHS    Massachusetts Historical Society, Boston, Massachusetts

MHM    Missouri History Museum, St. Louis, Missouri

NYPL    New York Public Library, New York City, New York

DukeU    Rubenstein Rare Book & Manuscript Library, Duke University, Durham, North Carolina

UVA    Small Special Collections Library, University of Virginia, Charlottesville, Virginia

USC    South Caroliniana Library, University of South Carolina, Columbia, South Carolina

UNC    Southern Historical Collection, University of North Carolina, Chapel Hill, North Carolina

WHS    Wisconsin Historical Society, University of Wisconsin, Madison, Wisconsin

# A Note on Sources

Unless mentioned in the endnotes, all emphasis was in the original sources. I have expressed in italics what antebellum Americans underlined for emphasis in letters and diary entries. I have made a few silent changes to manuscript sources in the interests of clarity by adding or deleting commas and periods, capitalizing the beginnings of sentences, substituting commas for dashes, removing accidental repetitions of words, lowering superscription, and the like. I have included the city of publication for newspapers, magazines, and journals even if it is not part of the periodical's title. With the exception of the *New York Day Book,* all of the newspapers I have consulted were on microfilm, most of them at the Newspaper and Current Periodical Reading Room at the Library of Congress.

# Introduction:
# Slaves on Bunker Hill

Despite being just 221 feet tall, the Bunker Hill Monument loomed large in the antebellum American imagination. Because that short granite obelisk commemorated not just the North's greatest victory in the American Revolution but also the iconic battle for the United States, it towered over the North and the South. As construction of the Washington Monument had been interrupted in 1854 at just 150 feet (not to be resumed until 1877 nor completed for seven years after that), the Bunker Hill Monument was the American obelisk. It occupied the symbolic status that the Washington Monument does today. No trip to New England was complete without ascending the 294 steps to the top of the monument. The tourists' itinerary in Boston has remained remarkably constant in the 150 years since then and now: Harvard Yard, the USS *Constitution,* Boston Common, Faneuil Hall, and, of course, Bunker Hill. Another constant is vendors hawking patriotic trinkets to the tourists. Indeed, it was so emblematic of Boston—though it was actually in Charlestown—and so emblematic of the battle—though that conflict was actually fought on Breed's Hill—that visitors were disappointed when they were unable to see it. When time constraints precluded a visit, Julia Marsh Patterson, a Georgia teenager, salved her disappointment with "seeing it afar off."[1]

The Bunker Hill Monument was a powerful sectional symbol of Northern resistance to tyranny, whose effect extended well beyond the antebellum era. Abolitionists routinely invoked the battle as a talisman in their resistance to slavery. Some used it to galvanize public opinion against the

1

national reach of slavery, especially in the aftermath of the Fugitive Slave Act of 1850. Byron Paine, a young Milwaukee lawyer, denounced that piece of federal legislation because it prostrated Northerners' last vestige of honor by compelling them to assist federal marshals in the apprehension of alleged fugitives. The odious law required the lineal "descendants of those who fell at Bunker's Hill" to pursue fugitive slaves or at the very least to suffer slave catchers to make that pursuit. The thought of slave catchers roaming the streets of Boston—"in the very shadow of Bunker Hill"—in search of alleged fugitives disgusted Giles Richards, an Ohio textile manufacturer and abolitionist. If fugitives could not find refuge beneath the Bunker Hill Monument, then well and truly the North had not really ended slavery. Not all opponents of slavery used Bunker Hill as a negative symbol. Some used it as a positive example of brave resistance to oppression. By the "logic" of Concord, Lexington, and Bunker Hill, the *Liberator* reasoned that John Brown was a "hero" and his raid on the federal arsenal at Harpers Ferry, Virginia, analogous to those battles. Employing the "same logic," William Lloyd Garrison's strident but pacifist newspaper finished its syllogism by concluding that "every slaveholder has forfeited his right to live, if his destruction be necessary to enable his victims to break the yoke of bondage."[2]

During the sectional conflict that led to the Civil War, the Bunker Hill Monument served as a kind of shorthand for the North. After Congress repealed the Missouri Compromise in 1854 and the Supreme Court ruled in the *Dred Scott* decision three years later that Congress could not exclude slavery from the territories, conspiracy-minded abolitionists and Free-Soilers fretted that the Slave Power conspired to extend slavery to all the states as well as all the territories. To dramatically illustrate the spectacle of slavery being reintroduced to the North, they claimed that Sen. Robert A. Toombs, a Whig from Georgia, had declared his intention of demonstrating the nationalization of slavery by calling the roll of his slaves beneath the famous obelisk. That act in itself was highly symbolic. On tightly run plantations, overseers called the roll each day before assigning the slaves to their day's work. Bunker Hill was sacred. The *Providence Post* claimed that it was second in importance to Americans in their veneration of the Revolution to only the Declaration of Independence itself because it was the site of the "first pitched battle" in the War of Independence. Toombs's apparent desecration of what Philadelphia abolitionist William Morris Davis called "Freedom's holiest altar" predictably outraged Northern opponents of slavery. If the Northern states could not exclude slavery within their own boundaries, the *New York Tribune* reasoned in a rush of Southern iconoclasm at New England patriotic sites, then "slaves can be kept in Boston: Mr. Toombs can call the roll of his chattels on the slope of Bunker Hill; auctions of black men may be held in front of Faneuil Hall, and the slave-ship, protected by the guns of United States frigates, may land its dusky cargo at Plymouth Rock."[3]

Toombs's alleged prediction was widely printed in the abolition press and gained currency with each succeeding Southern outrage from the opening of the northern part of the Louisiana Purchase to the possibility of slavery in 1854 to the demand for a federal slave code for the territories six years later. Judge John K. Kane's notorious ruling in the William Passmore case (1855), the *Liberator* asserted, was part of the Slave Power's unrelenting campaign to impose slavery on the North. In 1855, Kane determined that the federal Fugitive Slave Act permitted Southerners to recover slaves they had voluntarily brought to Pennsylvania despite an 1822 ruling by that state's Supreme Court that any slave brought to the Keystone State by his or her master was ipso facto free. According to Kane's decision, the *Liberator* declared, the slaveholder "may call his roll, not only under the shadow of Bunker Hill, but [also] on the plains of Lexington, at Saratoga, and at Yorktown." Of course, since Yorktown was in Virginia, neither Toombs nor any other slaveholder would have had difficulty mustering their slaves there. The *National Era* had dismissed Toombs's prediction as "empty bravado," only to see the efforts of federal authorities to aid Southerners taking their slaves through the North as the "realization of Toombs' boast." Parker Pillsbury, an Ohio abolitionist, believed that Rep. Preston Brooks's 1856 assault on Sen. Charles Sumner was one of many signs that Toombs's "prophecy" was to be fulfilled. After the *Dred Scott* decision, Carl Schurz, a Wisconsin Republican, predicted that in addition to the extraordinary spectacle of Toombs lining up his slaves under the Bunker Hill obelisk, Northerners would soon see the everyday indignity of black slaves working beside free white men in corn and wheat fields across the free states. The canny fugitive slave-turned-abolitionist Frederick Douglass publicly dared Toombs to make good on his supposed threat, noting that Massachusetts law might well liberate the Georgian's slaves.[4]

Douglass notwithstanding, many abolitionists were worried that the law was on Toombs's side. In 1857, Ellen Grover, a Massachusetts abolitionist, wanted to know if the Massachusetts Supreme Court had affirmed that the *Dred Scott* decision applied to the Bay State. Grover believed such a ruling would finally settle whether Toombs's boast was a "vain one or not." Her interest was not academic. Grover was harboring a Kentucky slave, who had been taken north by her master. What the nervous abolitionist really wanted to know was whether or not she would face arrest if she sent the Kentucky bondswoman to Canada. Of course, the state courts did not have the final say on the application of federal law—the United States Supreme Court did. Other opponents of slavery believed that the Buchanan administration, with or without Congress, would make Toombs's prediction a reality. Increasing the symbolism, Ohio abolitionist Celestia R. Colby worried that the Georgia senator would celebrate Independence Day in 1858 by taking the roll of his slaves on Bunker Hill.[5]

Conservative Northerners added insult to the antislavery advocates' injury when they invited Sen. James M. Mason of Virginia, the author of the Fugitive Slave Act, to Charlestown to participate in the inauguration of a statue of Patriot martyr Joseph Warren near the obelisk in 1857. Abolitionists writhed in fury. Mason's presence at the base of the Bunker Hill Monument seemed to confirm Toombs's prediction even if he was a slavemaster, not a slave. The *Liberator* believed that the Virginian's presence made good on the Georgian's boast. At the very least, the *Liberator* reasoned, the presence of the most despised slaveholder in the United States at the quintessential celebration of freedom in the North only went to show how complete was the Slave Power's control of the United States. The symbolism was so powerful that Theodore Parker, a leading Boston abolitionist, conflated Toombs with Mason, believing that Boston had realized the Georgian's boast by hosting the Virginian. Even Free-Soilers took pause at the thought of the author of the Fugitive Slave Act consecrating a statue on the holy soil of Bunker Hill. The *St. Louis Missouri Democrat,* a Republican newspaper despite its name, decried the Virginian for not just being a pro-slavery propagandist but also for being a "disunionist" when he advocated secession in the event of Republican John C. Frémont's election as president in 1856.[6]

When they were not criticizing abolitionists for their rudeness, moderate Northerners rebuked opponents of slavery for allowing politics to rain on a patriotic parade. The *Boston Post* heralded Mason's speech for being "appropriate, eloquent, and national." Ignoring the Virginian's secession threats made just the year before, the *Post* believed that Mason's visit proved that the vast majority of Northerners and Southerners loved the Union more than agitating the issue of slavery. When Boston abolitionists took advantage of the Fourth of July to publicly decry Mason and those who invited

The obelisk at Bunker Hill was the antebellum equivalent of the Washington Monument today—it was the iconic patriotic monument of the United States in the 1850s. ("Bunker Hill Monument, Charleston." *Gleason's Pictorial Drawing-Room Companion*, July 12, 1851.)

him to Charlestown, the *Cincinnati Commercial* could only scold them for inappropriately allowing partisan harangues to intrude on not just one but two patriotic celebrations.[7]

For the most part, white Southerners ignored the controversy or were unaware of it. The local outrage amused William Cabell Rives Jr., a Virginia teenager attending school in Boston. Rives observed that a cartoon in the *New York Tribune* portrayed Rep. Robert C. Winthrop, a dough-faced Massachusetts Whig, as one of Toombs's slaves lining up with the others beneath the Bunker Hill obelisk. This silence is not surprisingly as most Southerners thought that abolitionists' fevered claims of a Slave Power conspiracy to foist slavery on the North were risible. The South, as a Georgian reminded readers of the *Boston Post* in 1856, never forced slavery on the North; rather it was the North that forced antislavery on the South. Privately, Southerners believed that the North's indulgence in pro-slavery conspiracy theories was, as Georgia rice planter James Hamilton Couper put it, "conclusive proof" of the North's wild-eyed abolitionism. Couper believed that the Slave Power conspiracy was cynically used by abolitionists to rally naive Northerners to wage political war against the South.[8]

It seems unlikely that Toombs made this prediction—even though he was certainly a slaveholder, possessing well over two hundred bondspeople at that time, and calling roll would be a plausible way to keep track of his chattels during a trip to the North. Toombs was, after all, a moderate among Deep South politicians, who did not advocate secession until after Abraham Lincoln's election in 1860. Moreover, when Toombs spoke in Boston on January 24, 1856, at the invitation of conservative textile industrialist Nathan Appleton, he was not asked about the matter—a glaring omission if he had in fact made the boast. In response to local newspapers hurling this already infamous quotation at Toombs, the dough-faced *Boston Post* corrected the record: "Senator Toombs never made any such boast." Instead, Toombs argued in Boston that the Constitution sanctioned and even protected slavery in the *Southern* states. The *Boston Herald* noted that Toombs's address was a "candid statement" of the standard Southern pro-slavery interpretation of the Constitution, which "commanded the respect of his auditors if it did not accord with their judgment." Besides, even fire-eaters realized that slavery could not be imposed on the North. One of Toombs's biographers dismissed the roll call boast as an "absurd report." For his own part, Toombs claimed to have issued three published "contradictions" in the newspapers. On February 20, 1860, on the floor of the Senate Chamber, Toombs indignantly denied that he ever made such a statement.[9]

Indeed, Toombs's mythical boast revealed more about Northern apprehensions than Southern ambitions. The *New Englander* extended the premise behind Toombs's alleged prediction to its logical end: "all legal barriers to the introduction of slavery into the free states must be repealed." In his memoirs, the aforementioned Winthrop seems to have made the most accurate appraisal: it was "one of those legends fabricated in the *ante-bellum* period in order to 'fire the Northern heart.'" It was a classic case of what historian Richard Hofstadter called the "paranoid style" of American politics. As the 1850s progressed, Republicans and antislavery advocates came increasingly to believe that the Slave Power conspiracy wanted to nationalize slavery. Although historian Eric Foner argues that that fear did not become widespread until after the Southern Democratic majority on the Supreme Court issued the *Dred Scott* decision, reports of Toombs's alleged boast came three years earlier.[10]

When Toombs declared that he had never made such a boast in a public speech, his antislavery detractors charged that he had done so in *"private conversation"*—yet another canard that the Georgian denied. Despite Toombs's protests, one of his colleagues in the Senate claimed to have heard him say something to that effect. John P. Hale, a Republican from New Hampshire and one of the leading opponents of slavery in the upper house, asserted that Toombs had privately said that he believed antislavery agitation had the unintended effect of strengthening Southern commitment to slavery and improving Northern opinion of slavery. "It was in connection with the growth of public opinion at the North, favorable to the institution of slavery," Hale recalled, that Toombs "made the remark that I should see the slave-holder and his slaves on Bunker Hill." In 1856, the embattled Georgian privately protested his innocence and charged Hale with willfully misrepresenting him. In 1879—when Northerners persisted in throwing this statement back at him a quarter century later—Toombs publicly declared that it was a "fancy lie" started by Hale.[11]

Few antislavery Northerners were aware of Toombs's protestations. Many of those who were in the know joined the *New York Times* in dismissing them. The *Times* sneeringly suggested that Toombs's denials were evidence of a guilty conscience rather than innocent conduct. Those who were not had no reason to doubt the veracity of Toombs's Bunker Hill boast. The *Lawrence Republican* believed that nationalizing slavery was precisely what a fanatical disunionist like Toombs favored, never mind that Toombs was a moderate Southerner and the incongruity of nationalizing slavery and then seceding from that nation to protect slavery.[12]

Although likely a fabrication, Toombs's Bunker Hill boast had remarkable reach and staying power. In 1863, during the middle of the Civil War, a sailor in the U.S. Navy lamented to his wife that his ship's crew had not received news for months so that for all they knew, the Confederate ships had shelled New York City or "Toombs may at this moment be calling the role [*sic*] of his slaves on the crest of Bunker Hill." In that same year, the *New York Times* mocked Toombs by making a prediction of its own: after the Emancipation Proclamation, the "Georgia rebel" would call the roll of slaves on *his plantation* and find that no one answered because they were all free. In 1880, George William Curtis, a Rhode Island Republican, alluded to it in a speech against "Machine Politics," noting that if the Northern Democrats had not resisted the national party's stance on slavery, "Toombs would long since have called the roll of his slaves on Bunker Hill." In an 1899 memoir vindicating Unionists in east Tennessee, Oliver P. Temple referred to Toombs's mythical prediction (without naming the Georgian) as evidence of the overweening confidence that prompted many Southerners to secede and rebel. "The [Bunker Hill] boast was universal," Temple remembered, and also the belief that "one Southern man could whip five Yankees." Indeed, it was a staple of postbellum accounts of the causes of the war written by opponents of slavery precisely because of the special role Bunker Hill and the obelisk that honored the battle played in the hearts and minds of Northern sectional identity. So grating was the image of Toombs lining up his slaves under the Bunker Hill obelisk that even in 2006, former Education Secretary William J. Bennett found the Georgian's alleged boast to be "wildly offensive."[13]

At least two black abolitionists used the Bunker Hill obelisk in more or less the same way as Toombs was alleged to have done. While slavery had not been imposed on the North per se, its reach extended all the way to Charlestown. In 1849, William Wells Brown, a fugitive slave and novelist, invoked the Bunker Hill Monument as a poignant symbol to show the national claims of slavery and the hollowness of the American boast of liberty to an enslaved person. Even though he could see Bunker Hill, Brown observed that he remained a Kentucky slave nonetheless, and nothing could protect him from capture by his master so long as he remained in the United States. In exactly the same fashion, Henry Bibb, a Kentucky fugitive who found liberty in Canada and established a stridently abolitionist newspaper, the *Voice of the Fugitive,* observed that the famous fugitive couple William and Ellen Craft could not hide from slave catchers even in the "shadow of the Bunker Hill monument," but were forced to flee to England.[14]

To say that the Founding Fathers and their American Revolution loomed large in the construction of national identity in the United States would be understating an obvious truth. However, since the realization of independence in 1783, Americans have argued over what the American Revolution really meant and who the Founders really were. Inevitably these quarrels involved more than just a debate over history. In a very real sense, they involved efforts to define or redefine the essence of the United States. During the antebellum era, Americans engaged in a thoroughgoing debate over the place of slavery in the United States. As all thirteen original states practiced slavery in 1776, the leader of the Continental Army was a tobacco planter, and the principal author of the Declaration of Independence was too, the role of slavery in the founding of the United States was impossible to ignore. At the same time, however, the Declaration of Independence justified the Revolution in terms of universal natural rights, the Northern states gradually emancipated their slaves, the United States banned the international slave trade and prevented slavery from expanding into the Northwest Territory, and the leading slaveholding Founders took antislavery actions ranging from eloquent denunciations of bond labor to voluntary manumission of their own chattels. The ambiguous legacy relating to slavery that the Founders bequeathed to antebellum Americans provided opponents and proponents of slavery alike with plenty of evidence to support their preferred image of the United States.

In the two decades preceding the Civil War, Americans engaged in what might be called "history wars" every bit as ferocious (and in some ways analogous) to those that have been waged by contemporary Americans over the proposed National History Standards and the commemoration of the atomic bombing of Hiroshima in the Smithsonian Institution's National Air and Space Museum.[15] Like their descendants in the 1990s, Americans in the 1850s did not agree on the essential nature of the United States. To put a fine point on it, antebellum Americans tried to resolve the ambiguities relating to slavery that still haunted the republic some eight decades after its founding. In the 1850s, the United States was poised to be a great industrial democracy, but at the same time, it had become the center of the Atlantic slave system, surpassing Brazil and Cuba in gross number of slaves and staple crop production.[16]

The centrality of the Revolution in American nationalism makes it and its leaders the ideal starting place for the study of antebellum national identity. While many historians have cast the sectional struggle between the South and the North during the two decades before the Civil War as a quarrel over the true legacy of the American Revolution,[17] no one has yet made a sustained analysis of this subject.

In contrast to the numerous studies treating the period immediately following the Civil War, there have been few studies on nationalism during the period immediately preceding it. What little work that has been done on antebellum nationalism has tended to focus on ideas, elites, and the North. Implicitly, these historians assumed that the North articulated the "American" nationalism or a national nationalism, while the South, if they treated it at all, was engaged in mere sectionalism or a regional nationalism.[18] Their approach was based on the erroneous premises that Northern nationalism has been well studied and that it was easily distinguished from the Southern variety. This trend was reinforced by "Southern historians and southerners in general," as Carl Degler noted in a 1987 address before the Southern Historical Association, who "dwell[ed] on southern differences from, and southern conflicts with, the North."[19] Most of the work on Southern nationalism in the Civil War era treats the South in isolation in an attempt to explain Southern secession,[20] the Confederacy's spirited resistance,[21] or the Confederacy's devastating defeat.[22] While there are recent studies of a distinctly Northern nationalism,[23] of the distinctly Southern variety,[24] and how Northern and Southern nationalisms were influenced by the "age of revolution" in the nineteenth-century Atlantic world,[25] the historiographic pattern remains.

Although there are a few honorable exceptions, such as Charles Sellers and Edward Ayers, most historians regard the South as having what Wilbur Zelinksy calls an "alternate nationality" rather than being part of the mainstream of American nationalism. Indeed, Susan-Mary Grant argues that antebellum Northerners used the South as a "scapegoat" to define American identity based on an "antisouthern ideology." Larry Griffin and Don Doyle note that many Americans have regarded the South as being so at "odds" with the values and behavior of the United States as to constitute a "special problem." James Cobb observes that the North's tendency to view the South as an exotic and barbarous "other" dates back to the 1770s. Liah Greenfield believes that the "nascent Southern ideology bears unmistakable resemblance to the Romantic ethnic nationalisms such as the German and Russian ones" rather than American nationalism per se.[26]

In contrast to scholars who assert that the South developed its own distinctive nationalism, I argue that slavery was fundamental to the attempts of *both* Northerners and Southerners to fashion a common national identity in the antebellum era. Indeed, it was the pivot around which the entire debate turned. It is impossible to understand how antebellum Americans fashioned their national identity without a focus on slavery and the Founding Fathers. Nationalism is not simply the positive act of defining what a nation is or who a people are. It is also the negative act of defining what it is not or who they are not. This essential tension between inclusion and exclusion underlines the history wars of the antebellum as well as the contemporary era. In the case of history it is particularly the processes of forgetting and remembering even if what it is remembered never happened and what is forgotten was essential, e.g., abolitionists claiming the slave-driving Founders were opponents of slavery or even crypto- or proto-abolitionists and fire-eaters holding up the same anxious slavemasters as the archetype of paternalistic slaveholders. Benedict Anderson's brilliant definition of the nation as an "imagined political community" and Eric Hobsbawm's apt phrase the "invention of tradition" indicate just how nationalism is actively constructed and how it is often built on mythical foundations.[27]

I demonstrate that the differing notions of antebellum national identity turned on the place of slavery in the American Revolution, the lives of the Founders, and ultimately the antebellum United States. As late as 1861, most Americans, even most Northerners, agreed that the United States was, at least in part, a slaveholding republic. "In a society in which slavery was a well-established institution and in which slaveholders clearly had a privileged position," Leonard Richards observes about the pro-slavery orientation of the antebellum Democratic Party, "one did not have to be a blatant apologist for slavery to be a defender of slavery." His point applies equally well to moderates of all political persuasions in the North and the South. For them, the crucial issue was whether slavery would expand with the territorial domains of the nation or be contained in the Southeast. These moderates regarded the half-free, half-slave division of the United States as natural as breathing even if they disagreed on its relative importance. Whereas the place of slavery in the United States was crucial to Southern moderates, it was secondary to Northern moderates. Abolitionists and fire-eaters were shunted to the periphery of this pan-sectional nationalism. From the margins, these sectional extremists attempted to place slavery in the center of American identity: the one regarded slavery as pernicious and subversive, while the other regarded it as beneficent and essential.[28]

If we accept this antebellum consensus and isolate slavery from the analysis, it is clear that the United States was not being pulled apart by distinctive sectional nationalisms in the 1850s. Instead, there was remarkable agreement among most antebellum Americans in the North and the South as to what civic virtues they valued and who displayed them. In other words, excepting slavery, a majority of Americans agreed on what was patriotic and who was a patriot. Even when they disagreed, antebellum

Americans made their criticisms in the common language of American nationalism. In short, there was a shared national culture; where the sections differed was limited to the issue of slavery. The United States was one nation divided by slavery.

Throughout this study, I will divide antebellum American opinion on the political and moral issue of bond labor into three broad categories: opponents of slavery, moderates, and advocates of slavery. The construction of what might be called antebellum *mentalités* is an effort to get at the complexity and nuance of the shifting views of millions of Americans on the most vexing issue of the day. Of course, this tripartite division is simply shorthand, providing markers along the spectrum of opinion on what was politely called the "slave question" or the "Negro question," what one Cincinnatian grimly labeled the "desperate folly of the Negro feud," what the *Memphis Appeal* tellingly termed the "abolition question," or what Thomas Carlyle bluntly described as the "Nigger Question." The Scotsman's use of this distinctly American epithet showed that he was a careful observer of the conflict.[29]

To be sure, this sectional taxonomy is imprecise. On one end, it elides the differences between the various defenders of slavery, ranging from "positive good" apologists to "necessary evil" practitioners, from Southern poor whites to Northern conservatives. On the other, it blurs the distinctions between the various opponents of slavery, ranging from colonizationists to Garrisonians, from fugitive slaves to Free-Soilers. No doubt, the most troublesome category is the one that fills the largest area on the continuum: the moderates. They range from one end of the extreme to the other: from Southern whites who had no stake in the slave system to Northerners who worried more about Catholic immigrants than the Slave Power conspiracy, from planters who clung to the Union in the face of Lincoln's election to opponents of slavery who were willing to compromise with slavery to placate white Southern fears. At any rate, these categories are flexible and overlapping. They can accommodate dynamism of real people who resist rigid and precise categories. Over time, some individuals moved along the spectrum in one direction or another; others oscillated back and forth. A few remained in place. What this division lacks in precision it compensates with convenience and accuracy.

Each part of the sectional trinity emphasized distinctive aspects of antebellum American nationality, demonstrating the dynamic nature of nationalism and self-identity. Abolitionists believed that slavery was fundamentally incompatible with the ideals of the Founders. To them, slavery was an aberration, a regrettable colonial legacy. They were confident that the natural rights ideology that animated the American Revolution would end slavery in the United States. They regarded the Founding Fathers, even those who were slaveholders, as proto- or even crypto-abolitionists, who tried to limit the spread of slavery or end it altogether. While acknowledging that George Washington's antislavery feelings were not strong enough for him to "free himself of [slaveholding] during his lifetime," the *National Anti-Slavery Standard* lauded him for posthumously freeing his slaves.[30]

At the same time, fire-eaters, emphasizing America's origins as a slaveholding republic as well as the pro-slavery provisions of the Constitution, argued for the expansion of slavery westward into the Mexican Cession and southward into Latin America. Their radical vanguard theorized that slavery should be nationalized, that the institution should be peculiar to the United States and the Western Hemisphere, not just the South, Cuba, and Brazil. They contended that slavery was the sine qua non of the American republic. Accordingly, they claimed the slaveholding Founders as exemplars of the American ideal. The *Richmond Whig* adverted to "Washington, the slaveholder" to ridicule the notion that the United States was established on principles antithetical to slavery. Either these pro-slavery advocates ignored the antislavery impulses of the Founders, explained them away, or repudiated them. As far as they were concerned, slavery was inseparable from the founding of the United States.[31]

In between the sectional extremes were the moderates, who tried to bridge the slavery divide. They acknowledged that the United States was composed of "Slaveholding states" and "non-slaveholding states." Moderates looked less to the text of the Declaration of Independence than to the "spirit" of the Constitution and the tenor of North-South relations in the subsequent seven decades. They regarded the spirit of compromise that marked the nation from independence as the essence of the United States. They believed it was the Spirit of '76 in practice. They asserted that the Founders' legacy was to make sectional compromises that maintained the slavery status quo. They demanded that the compromises that time and time again relieved sectional pressures—in 1787, 1820, and 1850—be renewed. In fact, a special sort of Northern moderate, the doughface, specialized in just this sort of compromising. Indeed, doughfaces were christened with their inscrutable name during the Missouri Crisis. In 1820, Rep. John Randolph, a Democrat from Virginia, described the eighteen Northerners who ensured the passage of the Missouri Compromise in the House as "dough faces." Fourteen of them had voted for the Missouri statehood bill without slavery restriction, the key concession to the South, and four more had conveniently absented themselves rather than vote against it. While they were lauded in the South, the first doughfaces were scorned in the North. Only five of the eighteen were returned to Congress in the next election. While this cryptic name—no one really knows what Randolph meant by the epithet—was applied originally to the eighteen Northerners who made the Missouri Compromise possible, it soon was applied to any Northerner who supported the South on sectional matters. In fact, Southerners came to count on doughfaces for moral support and political votes in the sectional controversy. I argue here and elsewhere that doughfaces made common cause with Southern moderates because they shared a common vision of American society and wanted to protect it from radical challenges from abolitionists and fire-eaters. Four months premature, David Outlaw, a North Carolina Whig, rejoiced upon learning "all parties" supported the Compromise of 1850. Outlaw was not surprised by the support of many Northerners. Indeed, it was what he expected due to their "good sense and patriotism." In saying that "all" supported the Compromise, he deliberately excluded the abolitionists of New England and the "Hotspurs" of the Deep South. These two extremes joined in op-position to the Compromise, forcing him to conclude that they opposed any "settlement" of the sectional conflict over slavery.[32]

Of course, abolitionists and fire-eaters rejected this understanding of American nationality. Unlike the mass of Free-Soilers and proto-Republicans, abolitionists did not mourn the Kansas-Nebraska Act's repeal of the Missouri Compromise in 1854. It was, after all, a "compromise with crime." Instead of praising them, they wanted to bury all "compromises with slavery"—even ones that restricted slavery. The first half of Garrison's famous motto for the *Liberator* put it in terms, simple and direct: "NO COMPROMISE WITH SLAVERY!" It finished by placing slavery beyond the borders of the United States through Northern secession: "NO UNION WITH SLAVEHOLDERS!" At the same time, advocates of Southern secession dismissed any sort of compromise with Northern "fanaticism." Ruing the Missouri Compromise as a well-intentioned error and arguing against compounding it with the

Compromise of 1850, the *Charleston Mercury* observed, "compromise, compromise, has got to be a great word. What on God's earth have the South got to compromise?" George M. Dallas, a Pennsylvania Democrat and doughface in good standing, put it best in an admonition to the North and the South to turn to the Constitution to settle the slavery dispute. Elevating slavery to the center of American nationality, Dallas noted, there were "matters compromisable and matters uncompromisable."[33] If there was one thing on which fire-eaters and abolitionists could agree, it was that slavery was in the latter category.

Chapter 1 covers the different ways antebellum Americans in the North and the South celebrated the anniversary of independence, a topic that is only beginning to receive attention from historians.[34] Although they shared many common practices, Americans developed distinct ways of commemorating the national Sabbath. White Southerners downplayed the Declaration of Independence because its natural rights ideology might inspire their slaves to resist or even rebel against bondage. Instead they emphasized the Constitution, which explicitly protected the property rights of slavemasters, as the founding text of the nation. As the sectional crisis deepened, fire-eaters began to use their Fourth of July speeches to liken the federal government to George III and themselves to their patriotic forebears, hinting or even threatening that they might have to resort to the Lockean right to revolution. Like a lash on their back, enslaved people felt the painful irony of celebrating a day devoted to natural rights in a slaveholding republic. Indeed, fugitive slaves, free blacks, and abolitionists dedicated the Fourth of July to demands for the universal realization of the natural rights hailed in the Declaration. In between the two sectional extremes, moderates reminded all Americans that not so long ago, Northerners and Southerners in the thirteen states had worked together to win independence by force of arms. These Unionists, scorning all who made sectional appeals on the national holiday, held up their half-free, half-enslaved republic as the "model" for oppressed people the world over to follow on the path of liberty.

Chapters 2 and 3 look at how Americans remembered Jefferson's and Washington's ambiguous legacies regarding slavery, compromise, and the Union with particular emphasis on the former's Declaration of Independence and the latter's Farewell Address. While Merrill Peterson has done a fine job of studying how Americans remembered and used Jefferson throughout the century and a half after his death, his study lacks my focus on the sectional conflict.[35] One historian has shown that Republicans' interpretation of the Declaration shaped their political rhetoric in the late 1850s,[36] but does not consider how fugitive slaves, abolitionists, and doughfaces read the document let alone white Southerners as I do here and elsewhere.[37] Another scholar considers how Americans remembered Independence Hall.[38] There is no such overarching study of Washington's image. Instead, there has been a flurry of studies on how Americans remembered him immediately after his death in 1799 and in the Early Republic.[39] Abolitionists and fire-eaters rehearsed the arguments made about Washington's slaveholding when debating Jefferson's. While opponents of slavery proudly asserted that Jefferson would have been an abolitionist if he had been alive in the 1850s; defenders of slavery ignored the Declaration or asserted that Jefferson had erred in stating that "all men were created equal." Antebellum Americans revered Washington above any other Revolutionary. Abolitionists credited the American Cincinnatus for condemning slavery in life and for freeing his slaves in death, while white Southerners noted that American independence had been won by a slavemaster. Moderates placed Washington above the sectional contest. They adduced his Farewell Address, which warned of the dangers of sectionalism, and his general advocacy of national rather than sectional interests as general and president.

Chapter 4 looks at the ways antebellum Americans remembered the struggle for independence against the British. Historians have begun to study how the Revolutionary generation and the following generation remembered their sacrifices,[40] but with four honorable exceptions they have not considered how mid-nineteenth-century Americans remembered their grandfathers' sacrifices.[41] Of course, they realized that independence was impossible without military victory. Americans made a few battles into sectional icons: Bunker Hill (June 17, 1775) for the North, and King's Mountain (October 8, 1780) and Cowpens (January 17, 1781) for the South. These battles served as a kind of ideological formula, conveying the hardships and sacrifices borne by the Patriots during the Revolutionary War. In addition, Americans lionized the military leaders and heroes of the war: the minutemen, Joseph Warren, Francis Marion, and so forth. In the mid-1850s, Northerners and Southerners quarreled over the military contributions of their respective sections to the Revolutionary War. Sensitive to Northern claims that they shirked their duty, Southerners decried Northern histo-rians and history books, returning the charges to their senders.

Chapter 5 illustrates how these competing ideas of American national-ity boiled over under the heat of the sectional conflict in the late 1850s and early 1860s. As the United States started to fracture under the strain of being half free and half slave in the middle of the nineteenth century, abolitionists, moderates, and fire-eaters remembered that seven of the origi-nal slaveholding thirteen had either freed their chattels or had begun the process of doing so by the beginning of the century. During the Secession Crisis, all three members of the sectional triumvirate invoked the symbols of the American Revolution. Fire-eaters attempted to preserve slavery by exercising their Lockean right to revolution, moderates in the North and the South struggled to fashion yet another grand sectional compromise on slavery to maintain the Union, and abolitionists came to accept war as the price for emancipation or welcomed the split. After the Civil War began, many Northerners and Southerners attempted to secure their understand-ing of American nationality through force of arms. Several Confederate states drafted Declarations of Immediate Causes to justify secession, which invoked the Declaration of Independence to protect the natural right to hold bondsmen. Confederate Southerners wanted to forge their own slaveholding republic without the antislavery impurities that weakened the American alloy. Initially, most Americans countered with the preservation of the half-free, half-slave Union. Only a few immediately saw the conflict as a continuation of the Revolutionary quest to achieve natural rights for all Americans and end slavery. Over time, however, more and more Americans accepted that slavery would be a casualty of the war. After the war began, the number of moderates shrank considerably in the North and the South. Nonetheless, they condemned the bloodshed and called for an armistice so that the North and the South could resort to the spirit of compromise that had marked the United States since its beginning.

# 1

# The Fourth of July

## *Independence for and from Slavery Day*

Although there were many constants—the reading of the Declaration of Independence, the exploding of fireworks, and so forth—antebellum Americans developed distinct ways of commemorating their common Independence Day. White Southerners downplayed the Declaration sometimes to the point of ignoring it altogether because its natural rights ideology might prove instructive to their chattels. Instead they emphasized the Constitution (with its protections of property held in humans) as the iconic document of the day. As the sectional crisis worsened, fire-eaters began to invoke the Lockean right to revolution that animated their patriotic forebears to take up arms to secure their rights against a distant tyrant, serving notice that they might have to make the same resort vis-à-vis the federal government. More than any other antebellum Americans, enslaved people fully appreciated the irony of celebrating a day consecrated to natural rights in a slaveholding republic. Indeed, fugitive slaves, free blacks, and abolitionists used the Fourth of July to call for the full application of the natural rights touted in Thomas Jefferson's Declaration. In between the two sectional extremes, moderates in the North and the South asserted that the thirteen states, i.e., the North and the South acting in concert, achieved independence by mutual sacrifice, common consent, and combined force of arms. These Unionists scolded those who tried to make sectional hay out of a national holiday and held up the United States as the tribune of liberty in the world.

From the top of the Upper North to the bottom of the Deep South, all Americans—black and white, men and women, young and old, free and enslaved, native-born and immigrant—throughout the antebellum era commemorated the anniversary of American independence. While some flouted cultural norms and social elites by drinking heavily, quarreling, and carrying on, most reserved Independence Day as a time for reflection on those qualities that distinguished the United States from other countries around the world, especially the despotic regimes of the Russian czar and the Ottoman sultan. James R. Doolittle, an antislavery Democrat in upstate New York, claimed, with characteristic hyperbole, the Declaration of Independence's assertion in its "first sentence [that] all men are equal sounds the death knell of Tyranny. At one blow it levels all distinctions." The *Richmond Whig* agreed. Americans fancied, the *Whig* editorialized, that the Declaration's decree that "all men were created equal" made despots the world over "tremble" on their thrones. Of course, many Americans, such as "free" blacks and women, were not entirely free; others, such as enslaved people, were not free at all. Accordingly, these words—at least when spoken by certain Americans, such as slaves—also made other Americans, such as slavemasters, tremble. Reflecting a characteristic Southern ability to harmonize the conflicting notions of slavery and liberty, the *Whig* observed that the time for the tyrants of Europe to oppress "millions upon millions of slaves" was fading, while eliding the fact that the United States enslaved over three million people and disfranchised the female half of its free population.[1]

On the Fourth of July, Americans reflected on their Revolutionary heritage of freedom and equality. On this day, Northerners and Southerners celebrated by listening to the Declaration read aloud. But as the sectional conflict intensified, Americans in the North and the South emphasized different aspects of the Founders' legacy, indicating the dynamic quality of American nationalism and the constant construction and reconstruction of American identity. White Southerners muted the Declaration's appeal to natural rights and focused on the rights accorded to them and the institution of slavery by the Constitution. Abolitionists and enslaved people did exactly the opposite to the point of making Jefferson, the author of the Declaration, into a crypto-abolitionist. Trying to preserve the sanctity of the Fourth of July from sectional appeals, moderates emphasized British tyranny over the whole nation, remembered the national struggles of the Patriots North and South, and called for compromise for the sake of the Union.

Independence Day was the quintessential American holiday. Antebellum Fourth of July celebrations followed an almost universal pattern. A minister offered a public prayer for the United States, its leaders, and its citizens. Then a local dignitary read the Declaration of Independence in its entirety. Next, another person—a local minister, a venerable citizen, a politician on the make, or an invited guest—gave an extended address on the American Patriots and their successful struggle against British tyranny. Finally, thirteen formal toasts and a series of "volunteer toasts" were offered to the Fourth of July, the Founding Fathers, local and national political leaders, and so forth. There were, of course, sectional and local variants to this national theme.

The reading of the Declaration of Independence was the sine qua non of a Fourth of July celebration in the antebellum era. After all, Americans chose that day to celebrate because it was the day that the Declaration was accepted by the states and given to the American people. To supplement the universality of the Declaration, celebrations often incorporated local figures and events in the War for Independence. Not satisfied with noting their participation in the American Revolution, many locales asserted that their ancestors played a crucial role in the conflict. Of course, the people

Public celebrations of the "glorious Fourth," like this one in Boston in 1853, featured a series of patriotic toasts. ("Fourth of July Festivities at Faneuil Hall, Boston." *Gleason's Pictorial Drawing-Room Companion,* July 30, 1853.)

"The 'Car of Liberty' in the Procession as it Passed Logan Square, Philadelphia." *Gleason's Pictorial Drawing-Room Companion,* May 29, 1852.

of Charlottesville, Virginia, could point to Jefferson, the principal author of the Declaration, as their contribution. In recognition of his service, local patriots celebrated the anniversary of the Declaration's adoption by gathering at Monticello and reading it aloud. William C. Preston, a South Carolinian politician and scholar, observed such a celebration in 1858 and found it to be a particularly appropriate way to commemorate the day. Likewise, Philadelphians took great pride in the fact that Jefferson and the Second Continental Congress promulgated the Declaration in their city. (They also basked in the reflected glory of the Constitution, which was also a product of the City of Brotherly Love.) Accordingly, they held their Fourth of July celebrations (and commemorations of the signing of the Constitution) in front of Independence Hall.[2]

After the reading of the Declaration of Independence, an oration followed. Politicians used Independence Day celebrations as a festive opportunity to appear before their constituents. Although this was a time of heated political debate and sectional polarization, nonpartisan patriotic platitudes were the order of the day for Fourth of July orators. In 1849, before the sectional crisis reached the tipping point to secession and civil war, the *Charleston Courier* praised an address given in Columbia for being "wholly free" of partisan or sectional sentiments.[3]

The themes of Independence Day orations tended to be formulaic, relating the sacrifices borne and privations endured by the Revolutionary generation to a contemporary issue. They usually began by tracing the broad outlines of the epic contest between liberty and tyranny, both in North America and Britain, as well as in Europe and around the world. Most Fourth of July orators believed that this struggle climaxed, with liberty as the victor, in the founding of the United States. The *North American Review,* a stodgy Boston periodical, lauded an 1859 oration that engaged in Whiggish history writ large, outlining the memorable events in the historic struggle between freedom and repression in world history that culminated in the Revolutionary War and the advent of the United States. In an 1842 address, John C. Bullitt, a Kentucky college student, praised the "glorious deeds of [our] ancestors" in winning the independence of the United States. Lionizing the distinctive American legacy of freedom of speech, religion, and conscience, the collegiate orator contrasted Eurasian monarchies' religious bigotry and political repression with the American republic's religious tolerance and political freedom.[4] To be sure, American tolerance had limits. While Bullitt spoke, the House of Representative maintained its infamous "Gag Rule," which tabled abolition petitions without reading them. Such a solipsistic view of the world and the place of the United States within it, of course, was not unique to the antebellum period. Nor was the hypocrisy.

As sectional tensions wound ever tighter in the 1840s and 1850s, however, Americans gradually worked political asides and sectional appeals into Fourth of July orations and toasts. The whole conceit of a nonpolitical Fourth of July celebration was absurd on its face. After all, independence was a political act—the political act that began the United States. Independence Day was then an annual political rite that allowed Americans the leisure, if not always the sobriety, to take stock of the progress made and the distance traveled since the Second Continental Congress had adopted the Declaration of Independence. As such it was a star-spangled moment for Americans along the entire sectional spectrum to adopt the mantle of the Founding Fathers and cast their opponents as traitors à la the Loyalists or tyrants à la George III. In the 1850s, Southerners and Northerners used rival Fourth of July celebrations to castigate their rivals as un-American. During the Crisis of 1850, Southern communities in Georgia and Alabama celebrated Independence Day by endorsing the Nashville Convention—a gathering of Southern delegates that implicitly threatened secession if slavery was not extended to at least a part of the Mexican Cession. The next year, an Ohio abolitionist raised a glass of cold water to an equally radical disunionist toast in opposition to the possibility of slavery in the Mexican Cession: "God speed the day of dissolution to this slaveholding confederacy." Showing the fluidity of antebellum nationalism, these fire-eaters and abolitionists used the celebration of the formation of the Union to announce their intention to dissolve it rather like alluding to the possibility of divorce during a wedding. Indeed, the grandiloquent patriotism that pervaded the day pressed fire-eaters and abolitionists to the sectional extremes while at the same time pushing moderates to counterbalancing Unionism.[5]

Just as the Fourth of July celebrations highlighted the virtues of an American patriot, they also showed in bold relief the vices of dissenters. Southern "ultras" and Northern "fanatics" used Independence Day as the occasion to attack un-American radicals in the other section. In much the same way as some scholars, politicians, and jurists today claim that their own interpretations of the Constitution conform to the "Founders' Intent," both fire-eaters and abolitionists employed the symbols of the American Revolution to underscore how their position on the great sectional question of slavery was the Founding Fathers' one true heir. Emphasizing the spirit of compromise that marked the Union from its founding, moderates attacked the extremists. Of course, the moderates also claimed that their position was *the* Revolutionary legacy.

In their Fourth of July speeches and toasts, Southern fire-eaters had an aversion to the Declaration and its natural rights ideology, choosing instead to emphasize the protections for slavery secured in the Constitution. Just as the text of the Constitution employed euphemisms for slaves—"other persons," "person[s] held to Service or Labour," and so on—most Southern orators spoke of defending "Southern Institutions" or "Southern Rights" instead of explicitly acknowledging that preserving slavery was their goal. While the drafters of the Constitution employed these circumlocutions to appeal to Northern public opinion in 1787—and the drafters of the Confederate Constitution explicitly used the term "negro slavery" over and over because it did not worry them in 1861—it seems that antebellum Fourth of July orators in the South used them to appeal to moderates in their section and in the other.[6]

At the same time that Southern ideologues called for a defense of slavery on Independence Day, they linked the plight of the oppressed colonists with their own, using the occasion to call for Southern unity or, failing that, separate state action in the face of what they regarded as Northern tyranny. Characteristically, South Carolina took the lead. The partygoers at an 1849 celebration of the national birthday in Charleston raised their glasses to "The Union of South—The best means of preserving the union of the States." During the Crisis of 1850, a South Carolina periodical threatened to cease celebrating the "National Anniversary" if Southerners submitted to the North's neocolonial subjugation because they would have disgraced their Revolutionary forebears. The Compromise of 1850 did not mollify the fire-eaters. On July 4, 1851, the Charleston '76 Association toasted South Carolina twelve times. One of the members succinctly asserted their position in a toast—"South Carolina, right or wrong"—anticipating the classic expression of American nationalism that is used today, but with a state's rights twist. A year later, advocates of secession in Beaufort cheered a Fourth of July address on the Palmetto State's "conflicts with the General Government."[7]

So great was the alarm felt by some white Southerners with regard to the abolitionist threat that they rejected the idea that democracy was America's gift to the world—a cliché of Fourth of July orations for generations. Instead of lauding the Revolutions of 1848 as an attempt by Europeans to challenge monarchs just as Americans had done some three-quarters of a century ago, conservative Southerners disdained these democratic outbursts, which they regarded as European analogues to American abolitionism. At an 1849 Independence Day celebration at Orangeburg, South Carolina, the orator traced the origins of the American Revolution to the dim recesses of European history only to show how each successive development advanced democracy, culminating in the United States. But unlike traditional addresses, which emphasized the untrammeled advance of the sovereignty of the people, the South Carolina speaker emphasized the "checks and safeguards necessary" to prevent the "excesses" of unrestrained democracy. He pointed to the Revolutions of 1848 as a cautionary tale of democratic "perversion and abuse" that undermined republican government in the North. Ultimately, he predicted that simple democracy would "prove fatal to *free institutions*," by which he meant (with unintentional irony) slavery in the South.[8]

Despite the fact that the reading of the Declaration was de rigueur during antebellum Fourth of July celebrations, some Southern orators seemed allergic to Jefferson's magnum opus, which unequivocally stated that "all men were created equal." Accordingly, white Southerners downplayed the Declaration, clinging to the Constitution and the protections it gave to slavery against what they regarded as the tyranny of the Northern majority. Some explained away the Declaration. At an 1857 celebration in Arkansas, Corydon E. Fuller, an itinerant Northern bookseller plying his trade in the South, derisively paraphrased a Southern Fourth of July orator as saying, "*we was weak when them men signed the Declaration.*" Some ignored it. A South Carolina state's rights advocate enjoyed the 1844 Independence Day orations at Pleasant Grove, which emphasized the "constitutional restrictions" placed on the federal government vis-à-vis slavery in the states. Although Jefferson's Declaration was conspicuously absent, the hotspurs hoped that a "Declaration of Southern Independence" might soon be penned to fill the awkward gap. Others furnished substitutes. On July 4, 1849, instead of listening to the Declaration, several Southern communities celebrated the day with a recitation of the "Address of the Southern Delegates in Congress," John C. Calhoun's manifesto demanding that Southerners be given the opportunity to take chattels into the Mexican Cession. Others found supplements. On July 4, 1845, numerous Georgians and South Carolinians lauded James Henry Hammond's recently published pro-slavery tract, *Two Letters on Slavery.*[9] As we shall see in Chapter 2, several Southerners revised the Declaration and a few repudiated it.

During a telling 1849 Fourth of July address at Charleston, William Porcher Miles, a Palmetto hotspur, referred to the Constitution seven times as well as George Washington twice, the Wilmot Proviso twice, and the Missouri Compromise once, but did not once mention Jefferson or his Declaration. The closest he came was to say that the "spirit of '76" was "embodied" in the Constitution. Indeed, the Declaration was not read aloud during that Independence Day celebration—a striking departure from protocol. In similar fashion, even though the South Carolina Forty-niners aboard the *Thomas Bennett* celebrated the Fourth of July with a public reading of the Declaration, they balanced this by making a toast for "Our Constitution." Of course, this was not a universal trend in the antebellum South, even in South Carolina, even in 1859. In that year, just two years before the outbreak of civil war, the arrangements committee of Hazelwood invited an orator to join them in "celebrating" the Declaration.[10]

When reflecting on the importance of the national anniversary, a few fire-eaters invoked the Founders' resort to the Lockean right to revolution to overturn a tyrannical government and used the anniversary of the formation of the Union of American states to openly advocate its dissolution. Feeling increasingly besieged by an intolerant and aggressive Northern majority, which threatened the South's "cherished institution" of slavery, Southern extremists deployed the tropes and symbols of the American Revolution, casting themselves in the role of the oppressed colonists and the antislavery North as the tyrannical George III. In 1850, a South Carolina community tasked its Independence Day orator with speaking on the topic of "A Republican Government cannot exist without Slavery." The title neatly illustrated the South's view that slavery was not incompatible with but rather crucial to American liberty. In short, black slavery supported white liberty. One year later, a Kentuckian charged that the practice of "latitudinous construction" of the Constitution gave abolitionists license to effectively repeal the Fugitive Slave Act. If these worrisome trends continued, he believed the United States would become a "consolidated republic," i.e., one without "checks and balances." If that happened, the United States would be transformed from the model republic to the "most tyrannical and oppressive government" on earth. In 1859, the Fourth of July oration delivered before Charleston's '76 Association was provocatively entitled, GOVERNMENT AND THE RIGHT OF REVOLUTION. As might be expected, the *Mercury* praised the effort as "eminently southern."[11] Such sectional appeals were not unprecedented. By the late 1850s, however, they increased in frequency and were made by speakers far from the fire-eating fringe and far beyond South Carolina.

Instead of making the Founders into states' rights advocates and slave-masters on Independence Day, some white Southerners commemorated the day with little enthusiasm, others ignored it, and a tiny minority repudiated it. In 1855, William Henry Holcombe, a Natchez physician, observed that in Mississippi the Fourth of July had been reduced to a "commonplace and plebian affair." Burdened by this desultory feeling and the intensification of the sectional crisis, several Southern communities did not host public celebrations of the national jubilee. In 1859, a New England schoolteacher in central Louisiana informed her mother that there were "no *public performances*" to honor the Fourth of July because white Southerners had soured on the American experiment in self-government. In the following year, the *Memphis Appeal* admitted that Memphians went through the motions of celebrating the day. A few hotspurs went so far as to not celebrate the anniversary of American independence, a correspondent to the *Mercury* explained, because Northern outrages on Southern rights had "sapped" enthusiasm for the day (and the Union) below the Mason-Dixon Line. Corydon E. Fuller, that traveling book salesman from the North, was astonished to meet a pro-slavery Arkansan who informed him that "liberty is a humbug; [and] the fourth of July [is] a day of blasphemy and wickedness." These boycotts were a fire-eater analogue to Massachusetts abolitionist William Lloyd Garrison's repudiation of the Sabbath to protest the pro-slavery orientation of Southern churches and the vacillating position on slavery taken by Northern churches. Misrepresenting these rare instances as the norm in the South, Cassius M. Clay, a Kentucky abolitionist, charged that most white Southerners regarded celebrating the Fourth of July as tantamount to "treason" to the South.[12]

It is impossible to separate white Southerners' feelings regarding the Fourth of July, the Declaration, and Jefferson himself from those of their bondsmen. Many slavemasters felt the contradictions of slaveholding more acutely on a day dedicated to celebrating oppressed people's violent assertion of their natural rights against their oppressors. Those few Southerners who defied local custom as well as economic self-interest and liberated their slaves often chose that day, following the practice of New York and other Northern states that had enacted their emancipation laws on the day. This was especially the case in Delaware, a slave state that had almost completed its transmutation into a free state. Realizing the power and danger of a day dedicated to honoring the violent assertion of natural rights, some white Southerners prohibited slaves and free blacks from attending Independence Day celebrations. Others held explicitly apolitical midsummer holidays on the day as a safe alternative. A few masters tried to reserve Independence Day as an exclusively white holiday by forbidding their slaves from acknowledging, let alone celebrating, it. The mundane oppressions of slavery obscured the transcendent glories of the Fourth for many bondsmen. On July 4, 1854, William H. Tripp, a yeoman farmer and slaveholder, attended the jubilee at New Hope, North Carolina, while his bondsmen (and his wife) toiled on his modest farm in Beaufort County. In much the same way, two years later, Curtis W. Jacobs, a Maryland planter, marched thirty-eight of his chattels through rural Alabama en route to hiring them out, without stopping to celebrate the day. On Gabriel B. Shield's "Aventine" plantation in Adams County, Mississippi, the slaves did not celebrate the Fourth of July; it was just another long, hot day in the field.[13]

Despite these efforts, slaves frequently participated in Independence Day celebrations on the plantation and beyond. After all, the national Sabbath was a day of community-wide celebration, which interrupted the daily routine of plantations, farms, and villages across the South and attracted all Southerners, free and enslaved, black and white. Some paternalistic masters gave their slaves the day off, which was often capped with a "big party." Others simply let their bondsmen enjoy the day with family and friends. While a few masters used the Fourth as what one planter called a "powerful controlling power [sic] in the management of negroes," in practice, few did so because celebrating the Fourth was one of the "rights" slaves had seized for themselves. Some slaveholders brought their slaves to community-wide observances of the national anniversary. Revealing the ubiquity of enslaved people (and free blacks) at celebrations of the glorious Fourth, an orator noted in passing that his 1858 address at Abbeville District, South Carolina, was heard by a "mingled crowd of ladies, men, children, & negroes." In their efforts to pretend that the majority of American slaves were happy and content, some white Southerners used slaves and free blacks as patriotic props on that day. A South Carolina newspaper singled out "juvenile negroes" as the greatest fans of Charleston's impressive fireworks display in 1849. An article entitled "Fourth of July among the Slaves" from an Augusta, Georgia, newspaper—reprinted under the *National Anti-Slavery Standard*'s "Pro-Slavery" column—reported that a slave-driving Georgian allowed one of his slaves to give an address on July 4, 1858, to his peers. As might be expected under such circumstances, the slave orator praised his master and plantation in particular, and slavery in general, before condemning abolitionism.[14]

Such heavy-handed propaganda fooled no one—least of all enslaved people themselves. Although they appeared on the periphery of Independence Day festivities, their presence unnerved thoughtful whites. In the 1830s, a leading Charlestonian warned that the emphasis on "personal liberty" in Independence Day speeches might stir dangerous feelings in the hearts of slaves. Thoughtless whites did not share these concerns. During the 1850 celebration in Richmond, white celebrants made a point of stopping their parade and reading the Declaration in front of the "African Church."[15]

Like other antebellum Americans, enslaved people commemorated Independence Day in their own way and in light of their own experiences and concerns. More than any other antebellum Americans, slaves were aware of the limits of American liberty. This boundary was painfully evident on the Fourth of July. In a celebrated Independence Day address, Frederick Douglass, the leading black abolitionist and a former slave, told a crowd in Rochester in 1852 that Independence Day revealed to the slave, more than any other, the "gross injustice and cruelty to which he is the constant victim." Contrasting Americans' exceptional pretensions to liberty with the quotidian oppressions of slavery, Douglass asserted that it was a holiday of hypocrisy. Indeed, slaves realized the national Sabbath's ironies as well as the fact that it was a day when the white population was intoxicated, engorged, enchanted, or otherwise engaged. Accordingly, slaves reserved the day for acts of resistance, small and large. On the night of July 3, 1859, three slaves on a Virginia plantation stole a hog in anticipation of celebrating Independence Day in style. Sadly for them, they were found out and flogged harshly on that day instead. Although Nat Turner's Revolt began on August 23, 1831, the Virginia slave minister's original plan had called for the "work of death" to begin on July 4. A year later, an enterprising slave cook took advantage of the celebration itself by poisoning a feast at the national jubilee in Sumter, South Carolina, killing several celebrants and sickening two hundred others.[16]

Some abolitionists, including Douglass, came to accept this violence as a legitimate means for a bondsman to gain freedom—the right to revolution, sanctified by Jefferson in the Declaration. After all, violence was central to the establishment of the United States. Without irony, these opponents of slavery expressly linked leaders of slave rebellions with slaveholding leaders of the American Revolution, comparing slave rebels with rebellious slaveholders. They cast Gabriel Prosser, Charles Deslondes, and Nat Turner as modern-day patriots à la George Washington, Patrick Henry, and the Sage of Monticello. Rejecting the fire-eaters' emphasis on the Founders' determination to protect the right to own slaves consecrated in the Constitution, antislavery advocates relied on the Founders' determination to protect slaves' natural rights delineated in the Declaration. In his Fourth of July address, Douglass contrasted the current belief in the "infallibility" of the federal government with the Founders who denounced British tyranny as intolerable.[17]

Many opponents of bond labor were eager to claim the Fourth of July as their holiday. By staking an antislavery claim to Independence Day, they were trying to take it away from the slavemasters. Time and time again, they asserted that American slaves enjoyed natural rights just as the American colonists did. Time and time again, they asserted that slaveholders were oppressive tyrants just as George III was. Time and time again, they asserted that enslaved people had the right to revolution to claim these natural rights just as the colonists did. Nonetheless, some of them realized the irony of celebrating the triumph of natural rights in a nation where millions were in chains. They seized upon the Fourth of July as the day to indict and condemn that irony. Some redeemed Independence Day by claiming that it was really an antislavery holiday. Women, who comprised the majority of rank-and-file abolitionists, were also keen to attack slavery on Independence Day and to hold up the Declaration of Independence as the founding document of the United States. In 1837, female congregants pressured the pastor of a Providence church to make the pulpit available for a Fourth of July antislavery service, despite his personal opposition to the cause. In 1853, an abolition newspaper called on opponents of slavery, "above all others," to celebrate that day above all others. After all, abolitionists alone lived up to the Declaration's clarion call for universal "human rights."[18]

Six years later, William Wells Brown, an abolitionist and fugitive from Kentucky, asserted the Fourth of July was *the* day to discuss slavery because the issue of liberty was on every American's mind. After contrasting the Declaration with a Southern newspaper advertisement, which announced a slave auction on the Fourth of July, Brown observed that the coincidence of the "national birth-day" and the sale of a bondsman was a "fair illustration" of how the South practiced its understanding of Jefferson's declaration that *"all men are created equal."* Indeed, he claimed that Southern slavemasters regarded the anniversary of American independence as "especially adapted to the sale of slaves, and used to a great extent, because . . . the traffickers in human flesh found a larger market for their chattels" when white Southerners gathered to commemorate the day. Although Brown's claim is not confirmed by the historical record—New Year's Day was in fact the day for hiring out—it was a brilliant rhetorical flourish. Against all odds, Brown believed that soon the Declaration's injunction would be realized and he looked forward to the day when "all men are indeed free."[19]

Much as a few radical abolitionists refused to honor the Sabbath and join the mainline Protestant churches, pay taxes, or participate in the federal government because of the complicity of the churches and the government in the slave system, others declined to celebrate the founding of a slave-driving nation. In 1845, an abolitionist boycotted a Fourth of July celebration in Cincinnati—just across the Ohio River from the slave state of Kentucky—because the thought of "celebrating American Liberty" while three million Americans remained in bondage sickened him. On July 4, 1853, an Ohioan was discomfited by the "solemn mockery" of revelers who read the Declaration's preamble without any disquietude. In 1854, the *National Anti-Slavery Standard* could not get excited about "our bastard Independence Day." Instead, the *Standard* longed for the crowning glory of the American Revolution, a "true" Independence Day, i.e., the day when the United States declared independence from slavery. Free blacks and fugitive slaves in the North, who struggled under indignity, segregation, and discrimination, as well as constant threats of mob violence and kidnapping, appreciated the galling ironies of the celebration of a revolution justified on natural rights in a slaveholding republic. They reserved Independence Day for "humiliation, fasting, and prayer" when they asked God to break the "shackles of slavery" in the South as well as the restraints of halfway freedom in the North. African Americans in New York City commemorated the anniversary of Emancipation Day in New York State (July 4, 1827) on July 5 so that the Fourth of July would not lose any of its bitterness. Free blacks in the South also celebrated the Fifth of July, but without the irony or bitterness. Living in a slave state concentrated their minds and hopes. They hoped that the Empire State's example might have a salutary effect on the South.[20]

A few opponents of slavery, especially the free blacks of the North, celebrated alternative days in lieu of the Fourth of July. Some chose January 1. It was the day when in 1804 some 500,000 self-emancipated slaves declared the independent republic of Haiti, completing the largest slave rebellion in history. It was also the day when in 1808 Congress proscribed American participation in the international slave trade. The vast majority chose August 1, the day in 1838 when Britain gradually emancipated some 800,000 slaves in the West Indies. During the 1850s white and black abolitionists celebrated "West India Day" as far south as Cincinnati, as far west as San Francisco, and as far north as Racine, Wisconsin. In fact, that day was celebrated by American fugitive slaves in Canada and the United States and by abolitionists in Canada, the United States, and the United Kingdom, as well as by the freedmen and women in the Caribbean.[21]

Other opponents of slavery rewrote the American calendar of "freedom celebrations" so that it climaxed on alternate days, demoting or even ignoring the national jubilee. After a Syracuse mob rescued Jerry McHenry, a fugitive slave, on October 1, 1851, some abolitionists celebrated that day with the gusto that most Americans reserved for Independence Day. Showing resourcefulness, a few opponents of slavery managed to salve a bitter defeat in this way. After a federal judge in Boston rendered another fugitive, Thomas Sims, to Georgia on April 12, 1851, an antislavery coterie ironically commemorated his fate in "perpetual slavery." Several American communities inadvertently encouraged this practice by forcibly barring free blacks from Fourth of July commemorations.[22] This exclusion functioned the same way that forgetting the Founders' antislavery words and deeds did—it reinforced the notion that American liberty was for whites only.

To be sure, antislavery advocates were a tiny (and unpopular) minority in the antebellum North so their appropriation of the Fourth of July as an antislavery holiday was usually only an annoying diversion from the general tenor of celebrations in the United States. To a lesser extent, fire-eaters were not representative of the majority of white Southern opinion either. Indeed, moderates from the North and the South were irritated by what they considered to be sectional blasphemy on America's most high secular holiday. They were determined to celebrate their common Revolutionary heritage: the war that was successfully waged in the North and the South; the liberty enjoyed by adult white male Americans in all sections; and the Founders who hailed from all sections. Downplaying both the Declaration (and its explicit assertion of natural rights) and the Constitution (and its explicit protections of slavery), moderates emphasized the spirit of compromise between the sections in their Fourth of July orations and toasts.

Moderates tried to rescue Independence Day from Northern fanatics and Southern ultras by making pan-sectional nonpartisan appeals to the Revolutionary generation and the Union. They were dismayed when blatant partisanship and overt sectionalism desecrated observance of the national Sabbath. They tried to use public humiliation to shame the blasphemers into penitence. In 1851, the *Picayune* disapprovingly observed that South Carolinians celebrated the Fourth of July with an "unusual degree of ferocity." The New Orleans newspaper noted that the tone of the speeches and toasts there made it sound as if there was a worldwide conspiracy against that state's rights. Of course, such admonitions did not sit well with the hotspurs. The *Mercury* scoffed at the *Picayune*'s patriotic pretensions, indicating that criticism—even that from fellow Southerners—only reinforced the zeal of South Carolinians to assert their natural rights.[23]

Most Americans took the side of the *Picayune* in that dispute, believing that Independence Day celebrations should be free from sectional harangues as well as partisan quarrels. When Southern extremists violated this etiquette, moderates seethed with indignation. On July 4, 1851, Captain John Wolcott Phelps, a Vermont-born career officer in the U.S. Army, took offense at a political oration at a celebration in Brownsville, Texas. Phelps noted that the orator wanted his unit to fire a salute during the celebration, but the captain refused because of the politicization of the national jubilee. Not mentioning the political issues of the day was a political act as well. Apparently these ideals were inculcated in officers' training. Cullen Bryant, a cadet from Illinois, described a "grand" 1860 Independence Day celebration at the U.S. Army Academy at West Point, which was marred only by a cadet from Tennessee, who gave an oration that alluded to the "peculiar institution." Nonetheless, the Army's national orientation ensured that the Tennessean's defense of slavery was "rather moderate for one of his latitude." In fact, the superintendents of the academy carefully tamped down sectional feeling lest it undermine the esprit de corps.[24]

When Northern extremists violated this etiquette, moderates became belligerent. Although abolitionists faced greater danger in the South, they risked their lives when they spoke in the North as well. The delivery of a "regular abolition, disunion harangue," which denounced the dough-faced president Franklin Pierce as a "murderous villain" at an 1856 Independence Day celebration at Clarksville, Pennsylvania, provoked the crowd to threats of violence. If the orator had not retired from the platform—surrendering his constitutional right to freedom of speech—he would have been mobbed by the assembled patriots and quite possibly would have surrendered instead his natural right to life. It is likely that the members of this almost anti-abolition mob would have "self-consciously and self-righteously," as historian Leonard Richards described an actual one, identified with the Sons of Liberty, the minutemen, and other Revolutionary vigilantes. This was the attitude of a Philadelphia mob, which, in August 1835, seized abolitionist pamphlets, ripped them to shreds, and dumped them into the Delaware River à la the Boston Tea Party. A year later, a

Cincinnati mob destroyed James G. Birney's press in part because of their anger at the black community's celebration of July 3. Birney, a Free-Soiler, had been scheduled to address the celebrants but did not so the mayor would allow the commemoration to proceed. The mob, however, found another excuse to celebrate in its own way.[25]

In fact, some moderates believed that denouncing, if not assaulting, sectional extremists was their patriotic duty on Independence Day. This was the way to cheer patriots as the archetypal Americans and to alienate radicals as un-American. Elliot Crisson, a Pennsylvania philanthropist and colonizationist, privately decried the American abolition movement as a "deep plot" by the British to turn the North against the South and thereby dissolve the Union. On July 4, 1849, John B. Bynum, a North Carolina temperance advocate, publicly arraigned Northern extremists for spurning the "spirit of good will" between the states and instead fomenting "jealousy" between them. Bynum believed that disunion was their "hellish design." Of course, if the Union was sanctioned by God, then it followed that trying to dissolve it was demonic. An embarrassed *Charleston Courier,* a communicant to that church, apologized to its readers for erroneously using the word "friends" instead of "fiends" in a Fourth of July jeremiad against abolitionists.[26]

Just as the political parties used Northerners and Southerners to provide sectional balance to presidential tickets, so did moderates to drive home the point of intersectional harmony. The 1854 celebration of Independence Day in Philadelphia featured Unionist Democrats from the North and the South—Sen. Stephen A. Douglas of Illinois and Rep. James Lawrence of South Carolina—who took the occasion to preach a sermon of unity and to castigate extremists. These two members of Congress were supposed to represent trans-sectional moderation and bipartisan unity. Having just played a key role in the repeal of the Missouri Compromise with the Kansas-Nebraska Act, Douglas proved a controversial speaker in his own right. The "Little Giant" asserted that popular sovereignty, the guiding principle behind that piece of legislation, was the basis of the colonial protests against British tyranny ninety years earlier. Douglas attacked fire-eaters, Know-Nothings, Free-Soilers, and abolitionists, trying to claim the broad ground of the Union for himself and his fellow Democrats. Dennis F. Dealy, a twenty-one-year-old Philadelphia store clerk and a loyal Democrat, found Douglas's speech to be the "most eloquent and convincing" he had ever heard.[27]

. . .

The polarization of the sectional conflict revealed the differences between the ways black and white Americans, Northerners and Southerners, extremists and moderates commemorated the anniversary of American independence. The extremists in the North and the South fought over meanings of the Fourth of July. They alternated between claiming the day and its legacy as their own and distancing themselves from it. While some fire-eaters slighted, ignored, or even repudiated the Declaration of Independence—the raison d'être of the day—some abolitionists celebrated other days instead. Enslaved people honored the day by resisting tyranny in their own way. At the same time, moderates clung to the spirit of compromise that had seen the United States through repeated sectional storms over the eight decades of independence.

The sectional schism over the Declaration and the Constitution was dramatically revealed in William Lloyd Garrison's famous Fourth of July oration in 1854. At Framingham, Massachusetts, one month after the Bay State returned the fugitive Anthony Burns to slavery, Garrison honored the national jubilee in his own distinctive way. In the course of his remarks, Garrison contrasted the Declaration with the Fugitive Slave Act of 1850. Afterwards, he read the pro-slavery provisions of the Constitution—the three-fifths clause, the international slave trade clause, the fugitive slave clause, the clause that allowed the militia to suppress (slave) insurrections, and the clause that promised federal protection to the states against domestic violence—and then burned copies of the Constitution and the Fugitive Slave Act. After condemning the last document to the flames, Garrison announced, "so perish all compromises with tyranny." Most Northerners were not impressed. Indeed, the majority of his audience—expecting to hear slavery and the Fugitive Slave Act of 1850 denounced rather than their beloved Constitution—booed and hissed. Beyond Massachusetts, Garrison's political theater was largely ignored.[28]

Garrison's Independence Day attack on the Constitution outraged white Southerners. The *Picayune* reported that Garrison signaled his desire for disunion by "formally burning" the Constitution. Its editors reasoned that Garrison's doctrines would lead to miscegenation, noting with disapproval that men, women, and children of "all colors" had attended the event. The *Mercury* was so angry that it would not even mention Garrison by name. Its low expectations of abolitionists were confirmed by the arch-abolitionist's desecration of the civil holiday by burning the "sacred charter of our rights and liberties." Its fire-eating editors reproached the fact that it shared same national Sabbath with those "hell-hounds of fanaticism" like the Boston abolitionist who sneered at the Founders.[29]

While the *Boston Herald* worried that sectional appeals had sapped popular enthusiasm for observing the day, most Americans were heartened by Fourth of July celebrations even on the eve of the Civil War. Before Garrison had outraged the *Picayune* by burning the Constitution, the New Orleans newspaper dismissed reports that Providence had decided not to celebrate the Fourth of July to protest the repeal of the Missouri Compromise and the rendition of Burns to Virginia. The people of that Rhode Island port were reputed to have violated the day's sanctity by tolling church bells and dedicating this happiest of all days to fast, humiliation, and prayer. But the *Picayune* insisted that Americans there and elsewhere would heartily celebrate the national jubilee. Rising above the "sectional animosities" unleashed by the Election of 1856, *Frank Leslie's Illustrated Newspaper,* the *Life* magazine of the antebellum era, cheered the way Americans celebrated the day. Despite the fact that the Republican candidate, John C. Frémont, ran on an anti-South platform and fire-eaters threatened to secede if he won, the New York newspaper detected a "new spirit of patriotism," which crowded out demagoguery and fanaticism from all quarters. It delighted in "the noise and bustle—the crowded streets—the thronged edifices—the tramp of citizen soldiery—the bad orations—the worse liquor—the pistols—the firing of cannon—the consumption of lager-bier—the everything in fact, peculiar to 'Fourth of July.'" This evidence convinced the Gotham editors that most Americans remained proper patriots "sound" on the Constitution and the Union, though it conspicuously omitted the Declaration.[30]

# 2

# Thomas Jefferson

*Proto-Abolitionist and Paternal Slavemaster*

Antebellum Americans regarded Thomas Jefferson, in the apt words of
W. M. Corry, an adoring Ohioan, as the "civil chief" of the Revolution. *De
Bow's Review,* a leading Southern periodical, agreed, even though it qualified its praise with reservations about the Sage of Monticello's democratic
excesses. With the exception of George Washington, *De Bow's Review*
observed, "no man fills so large a space as Jefferson in American history."
But the *Review* acknowledged that Jefferson's legacy was not without its
blemishes: the "universal democracy, unrestrained by class, orders, customs
or usage, is the work of his hands." Although Jefferson played a minor
role in the American war of national liberation—as a member of the First
and Second Continental Congress, principal author of the Declaration of
Independence, and governor of Virginia—mid-nineteenth-century Americans placed him atop the highest niche of the civil side of the Founding
pantheon. The *Cincinnati Commercial* lauded him as the "Apostle of Human
Liberty." Enraptured by Jefferson, Northerners and Southerners visited his
mansion, celebrated his birthday, and venerated "his" Declaration.[1]

Jefferson's words and deeds over the course of a long career as a diplomat,
politician, and philosopher allowed Americans across the political spectrum
to claim him as their own. While Oscar J. C. Stuart, an emigrant from the
Old Dominion to the Mississippi Black Belt, resented the fact that ideologues quoted Jefferson to support "both sides of nearly every question,"
the transplanted Virginian conceded that the slavemaster of Monticello's
"published writings" could be fairly used in that way. Although Stuart

Thomas Jefferson was the leading civic hero of the American
Revolution. ("Civic Heroes of the American Revolution." *Ballou's
Pictorial Drawing-Room Companion,* July 1855.)

decried disunionists and abolitionists alike for appropriating Jefferson's
good name, his admonition applied equally well to colonizationists and
compromisers. No matter the answer they gave to the "Slavery question,"
antebellum Americans believed that Jefferson was on their side. As their
views on bond labor changed, their memory of Jefferson kept pace.[2]

In the mid-nineteenth century, Monticello was a tourist site. Unlike visitors today, who take guided tours of Jefferson's mansion, marveling at
its architectural brilliance, purchasing replicas of Jefferson's effects, and

Thomas Jefferson and his iconic mansion (and plantation) were inseparably linked in the public memory of antebellum Americans. ("Jefferson" and "Monticello." *Gleason's Pictorial Drawing-Room Companion,* April 8, 1854.)

collecting various bits of Jeffersoniana, antebellum visitors were unable to enter the building. At that time, Monticello was in private hands. It offered no tours. It had no gift shop. It had no food court. It was not open to the public. Unable to tour the interior of Jefferson's home, many consoled themselves with, as one South Carolinian reported, catching a "glimpse" from the road. More determined visitors traipsed through—or rather trespassed—the grounds and paid their respects at his grave. For many this was enough. In 1858, a venerable South Carolinian visited Jefferson's "Little Mountain" merely to enjoy the view.[3]

In the 1850s, some Americans fretted that Jefferson's mansion was falling into disrepair under the ownership of Uriah P. Levy, a naval officer from Philadelphia, who had purchased the estate in 1836. At the same time that antebellum Americans were engaged in a national campaign to raise funds to purchase Washington's Mount Vernon and save it from dilapidation (a topic treated in the following chapter), others worried that Jefferson's Monticello might suffer the same fate. In 1856, *Frank Leslie's Illustrated Newspaper* reported that Monticello had fallen into "decay." The following year,

William S. Pettigrew, a North Carolinian cotton planter, visited the estate and agreed, finding it "much neglected." Pettigrew repeated the widespread rumor that the absentee Northern owner suffered Monticello to decline to discourage tourists. Although that was not Levy's plan, perhaps it should have been. Visitors overran his property. While most simply poked around the grounds and enjoyed Monticello's Palladian architecture, some vandals took souvenirs and others left their marks. Pettigrew found that "lawless admirers" had desecrated the Jefferson family cemetery with graffiti. Of course, not all visitors were so destructive. Upon finding the fence surrounding Jefferson's grave locked and refusing to defile the place by climbing over, John Wheeler, a New Hampshire teacher, declined to even step on the "sacred ground." In fact, Levy, a Jew, had been restoring the famous building as soon as he had purchased it. The rumors to the contrary seem to have originated from local antipathy toward a non-Christian Yankee owning that iconic Southern building. Of course, while Jefferson was a Southerner, he was most certainly not a Christian.[4]

If Virginians resented being unable to properly visit Monticello, they commemorated the anniversary of Jefferson's birthday (April 13, 1743) with enthusiasm. Beyond the Old Dominion, Americans honored the day sporadically. Indeed, only in Jefferson's native state did the day rival Washington's birthday (another topic treated in the following chapter), let alone Independence Day. As William Fitzhugh Gordon, a Virginia planter, exclaimed in 1830, April 13 was the "advent of our great Star of Freedom." Without fail, the celebrants listened to a public reading of the Declaration of Independence followed by a speech. Although the Declaration was always read, it was not always read well. Virginians, having a proprietary interest, had rather exacting standards. At an 1859 celebration hosted by the University of Virginia's Jefferson Society, one of the orators lulled John B. Minor, a law professor, to sleep. At another celebration there, Louisa H. A. Minor, a young woman in attendance, complained that the Declaration was "*badly* read."[5] Perhaps its very familiarity soothed sympathetic ears and pricked critical ones.

Louisa H. A. Minor's criticism was noteworthy because in many ways, the defining celebration of Jefferson's birthday was conducted under the auspices of his eponymous society at the University of Virginia. Jefferson had not merely founded the university: he supervised its construction, selected its curricula, and screened its faculty. To a great extent, it was *his* university. Beginning in 1832, the faculty allowed a member of the society, a student organization, to give an address on what was called "Founder's Day." The first orator addressed the recent and unsuccessful attempt to add a gradual emancipation amendment to the Virginia Constitution, drawing the university into a political controversy. While the speaker chafed the Board of Visitors with this implicit link between Jefferson and emancipation, his thesis was not without merit. After all, Jefferson himself had privately endorsed (but offered no public support for) just such a scheme and his namesake grandson, Thomas Jefferson Randolph, had proposed a similar plan three months earlier in the Virginia Convention.[6]

In fact, the Founder's Day oration was frequently roiled by politics. Of course, the issue of slavery caused the most trouble for the university. In 1851, George W. Randolph, a concerned and influential alumnus, complained that the Jefferson Society's oration ought to be abolished because it invariably focused on "politics" and thus hurt the university. It was not just student orators or the April 13 oration that had this effect. One year earlier—as the Crisis of 1850 was vexing Congress—John C. Cabell, a member of the Board of Visitors, was outraged that Muscoe R. H. Garnett, a Virginia fire-eater and board member himself, delivered an address to the university's alumni that reeked of "Calhounism." That Garnett had the gall to defend slavery as beneficial to the bondsman and the slavemaster at the university established by the "Apostle of Equality" was too much for Cabell to bear. Although a slaveholder himself, Cabell detested pro-slavery apologists. These three Virginians almost covered the entire range of white Southern opinion on the solution to the problem of slavery: Cabell advocated gradual emancipation and African colonization; Garnett immediate secession; and Jefferson the status quo through practiced indecision.[7]

In their celebrations of Jefferson's birthday, Northerners showed similar ideological diversity, ranging from pro-slavery compromisers to abolitionists, from colonizationists to Free-Soilers. In 1851, John Bigelow, a New York Free-Soil Democrat, lamented the near coincidence of that day with the rendition of Thomas Sims, a fugitive slave, to Georgia under the auspices of the Fugitive Slave Act. Adducing Jefferson's private criticisms of and public misgivings about slavery, Bigelow observed that if the third president had lived to see the mid-nineteenth century, he would be "styled an abolitionist." In declining an invitation to speak at a celebration of Jefferson's birthday eight years later, Gideon Welles, a proper abolitionist, gave the outlines of the speech he would have delivered. Welles asserted that Jefferson's "hostility to slavery" was clearly expressed and consistently acted upon in his personal life and political career. Colonizationists, even those in the South, proudly claimed that the "very idea of African Colonization" originated with Jefferson and other Virginia slaveholders. The dough-faced *Boston Post* ignored Jefferson's antislavery views altogether. Instead the *Post* contrasted Jefferson's endorsement of compromise and concession on the issue of slavery with the traitorous agitation of Free-Soilers and abolitionists.[8]

In truth, Jefferson's perfectly ambiguous course on slavery left something for everyone. He was a lifelong slavemaster. He bought and sold chattels without compunction. He had a slave mistress and exploited the labor of their children. He took few concrete actions against slavery. And he publicly expressed a belief in the inherent inferiority of black people. At the same time, however, the Sage of Monticello made some of the most eloquent denunciations of slavery, implicitly in the Declaration and explicitly in *Notes on the State of Virginia* (1783). He discreetly supported gradual emancipation. He prevented the westward expansion of slavery into the Northwest Territory. As president, he signed into law the ban on American participation in the international slave trade. He expressed concerns about the immorality of slavery. And he worried about slavery's potential to dissolve the Union or precipitate civil war. Jefferson's words and deeds regarding slavery were well established by the 1830s. "Our wisest Statesmen disagree upon [the extent to which Jefferson held] those [antislavery] principles," James R. Doolittle, a nervous college student, explained in an April 13 oration at Hobart College in upstate New York so that he declined "to discuss them, within the hearing of persons experienced and renowned in all the walks of politicks [*sic*] and philosophy." Instead, the collegiate orator followed a time-honored strategy of piling on the platitudes and glossing over the controversy. "Upon almost every subject Literary and Philosophical, social and political," Doolittle insisted, Jefferson showed "him[self] to be universal in his genius and strong in his moral character."[9]

By the 1850s, Jefferson's views of slavery had ossified into two mutually exclusive sets of received wisdom that ran along parallel lines. Opponents of slavery seized upon Jefferson's good intentions and eloquent words to conscript the Sage of Monticello into their ranks. In 1848—seven years before the publication of *Leaves of Grass*—Walt Whitman, a Free-Soil Democrat, asserted that because Jefferson "hated slavery," the Virginia slavemaster was "in the literal sense of the word, an abolitionist." *Frederick Douglass's Paper* lauded Jefferson, "although born a Virginian" and a "Slaveholder," for being "superior to sectional prejudices" and for not allowing "self Interest to blind him to Conscience and Philosophy." Contrasting Jefferson's modest antislavery comments with the current pro-slavery apologetics, the newspaper pointedly observed that Jefferson's advocacy of liberty over slavery and nation over section contrasted with the pro-slavery shibboleths and disunion cant that Virginians bandied about in the 1850s. The fact that Jefferson's good intentions produced little in the way of results did not trouble that publication or the aspiring poet.[10]

For Southern admirers of slavery and the slavemaster of Monticello, Jefferson was an archetypal planter who looked after his charges with paternalistic care no matter what the Declaration of Independence or *Notes on the State of Virginia* said. Louisa S. McCord, a South Carolina slavemistress and pro-slavery polemicist, believed the stubborn fact of Jefferson's *"slaveholding"* to be sufficient to drown out the abolitionist chorus of his doubts, regrets, or second thoughts. In the same way, the *Richmond Enquirer* observed that Jefferson was a slavemaster when he drafted the Declaration and the *Notes,* and remained so all his life.[11]

These contradictions and contortions were neatly bound up in Henry S. Randall's three-volume *The Life of Thomas Jefferson* (1858). As a Northerner with antislavery antecedents writing a biography of a slaveholding Southerner in the tempestuous 1850s, Randall trod a narrow path. Not only did Randall rely on the graces of many of Virginia's great and good to locate manuscripts necessary for the work, he also coveted their endorsement. At the same time, Randall sought and received the help and imprimatur of Jefferson's family. Of course, a book on Jefferson panned by the Virginia elite would not sell. While Randall went out of his way to minimize the role of slavery in Jefferson's life, he could not avoid it altogether. *The Life of Jefferson* clearly revealed the American philosophe as a Chesapeake planter from cradle to grave. Indeed, Randall noted that Jefferson's first memory was of being carried on a pillow by a bondsman as a two-year-old boy. Tipping his hat to Southern opinion, Randall presented Jefferson as a paternalistic master. Tellingly for both biographer and subject, Randall followed Jefferson's practice of listing his chattels as part of his "family." Randall praised Jefferson for "raising the best crops, without in any way abusing or harassing his slaves." Nor did he praise only Jefferson. Without irony, Randall described Jefferson's wife Martha as "practically the busiest slave on the plantation" due to her tireless care of ill slaves. At the same time, Randall played up Jefferson's modest antislavery acts in the Virginia legislature, including his introduction of a voluntary manumission bill and his verbal support of the gradual emancipation of slaves.[12]

It would be unfair to say that Randall avoided slavery. In the last volume, Randall included a two-page appendix on "Jefferson's Views on Slavery, etc." It helpfully explained that while Jefferson was "wholly opposed to slavery on *all* grounds, and desired its abolition," at the same time he opposed abolition agitation, gradual emancipation without colonization, efforts to restrict the western expansion of slavery, and black citizenship. To the much-asked question of whether Jefferson changed his views on slavery, Randall refused to answer. "His 'consistency' is a matter of opinion," the author maintained without giving his own well-informed one. Had Randall himself been asked that question, he would have had to answer in the affirmative. Randall's own take on slavery changed over the course of *The Life of Jefferson:* Jefferson's biographer went from writing the antislavery platform of the Free-Soil Party in 1848 to supporting pro-slavery Southern Democrat John C. Breckenridge in 1860. In just twelve short years, Randall went from one side of the slavery divide to the other. It was almost as if Jefferson's temporizing on bond labor had convinced his biographer.[13]

Despite this appendix, Randall did not exhaust the subject. He discreetly treated the most controversial episode in Jefferson's role as a slavemaster— his prolonged sexual relationship with his bondswoman Sally Hemings. Randall relegated James T. Callender's charge in 1802 that "Jefferson's daughters weep[ed] to see a *negress* installed in the place of their mother" to a footnote in a section on how Callender had turned against Jefferson and the Democratic-Republicans after having been passed over in the award of patronage. Randall noted that the scurrilous editor had made similar attacks on John Adams when in the employ of Democratic-Republicans a few years earlier, implying that it followed that the unscrupulous political mercenary would revert to form once in the employ of the Federalists. Indeed, Randall refused to dignify Callender's attack by delving into the details. Dismissing the whole episode as "pseudo 'history,'" Randall did not even mention Hemings by name. Randall's strategy was a brilliant success. Not only did Randall effectively put the matter to rest in the mid-nineteenth century, he also ensured that it did not awaken until well into the twentieth century.[14]

Randall's discretion was not surprising. Sexual activity was not a subject fit for polite company then. The fact that this matter involved intimate relations between people of different races made it all the more uncomfortable for the biographer. Randall found the "story of 'Dusky Sally'" to be so off-putting that he cringed as he wrote a private letter about it, punctuating the phrase "African Venus!" with an ironic exclamation mark and following that with almost audible "(Ugh!)." Although Randall was embarrassed by the allegation, he was confident that Jefferson was not the father of Hemings's children because they were born when Jefferson had not been "within a hundred miles of their mother, for upwards of a year!" Randall implied that Peter Carr, one of Jefferson's nephews, was the father of Hemings's children. On this delicate matter, Randall took the word of Jefferson's eponymous grandson, Thomas Jefferson Randolph. In 1968 this assertion was proven false by historian Winthrop Jordan, who found that the Sage was in fact resident at Monticello nine months before the birth of *each* of Hemings's children. Recent DNA analysis and statistical models suggest that it is highly likely that Jefferson fathered the children. Historians routinely accept "facts" with far less corroborating evidence and the principle of Ockham's Razor established beyond any reasonable doubt Jefferson's paternity.[15]

It was not just the race-mixing of the Jefferson-Hemings sexual congress that disgusted Randall; it was also the fact the relationship involved a degree of coercion insofar as he was her master and she was his chattel. Indeed, this was a common trope of abolitionist attacks on slavery—one that infuriated male Southerners and mortified females. The *Southern Literary Messenger* fulminated against Harriet Beecher Stowe's *Key to Uncle Tom's Cabin* (1853) for its scenes of "habitual prostitution" on Southern plantations. The charges stung because they had the ring of truth. A planter's wife confided to her journal that all Southern women were "at heart abolisionists [*sic*]" for that reason. That this abolitionist cant was leveled against an iconic Southerner made it all the more galling. The *Charleston Courier* believed that Theodore Parker, a Boston abolitionist, should have been expelled from the pulpit for "such vulgar and indecent talk" about Jefferson. Just as Southerners touted Jefferson as an archetypal planter for his paternalism, so his dalliances with Hemings suggested to opponents of slavery that the corrupting power of slavery could vitiate even a statesman of the first order. As the British abolitionist Frances Trollope scornfully observed, Jefferson "taught young females to obey his nod, and so became the father of unnumbered generations of groaning slaves." Although Jefferson did not sell any of Hemings's children—in fact, he either manumitted them or let them escape—the

Just the thought of Jefferson having sexual relations with Sally Hemings disgusted Henry S. Randall so much that he wrote, "(Ugh!)." (Letter from Henry S. Randall to Theodore Parker, Apr. 18, 1856, Theodore Parker papers, Massachusetts Historical Society. Not to be reproduced without permission.)

belief that he did so proved irresistible to a few opponents of slavery. The *National Anti-Slavery Standard* used that apocryphal story to highlight the routine practice of breaking up slave families to settle the debt owed by a slaveholder's estate. The *Standard* claimed that after Jefferson's death, a creditor had taken one of Jefferson's slave children from her mother in Virginia and sold her in Mississippi "as if she had been a cow or a horse."[16] The idea of Jefferson being the beau ideal of a slaveholder cut both ways and it hurt both fire-eaters and abolitionists.

On the issue of slavery, Randall's *The Life of Jefferson* struck just the right balance between paternalistic practitioner and conflicted theorist. It was praised in both the North and the South by moderates and pro-slavery advocates. W. M. Corry, an Ohio Democrat, was delighted by all the hitherto neglected sources Randall used, believing that the New Yorker had literally given Americans a "new life of Jefferson." Arthur P. Hayne, a South Carolina hotspur, complimented the book as able, honorable, and enduring. Publications ranging from the venerable *North American Review* to the fire-eating *Memphis Appeal* lauded the work. In particular, the reviewers appreciated Randall's portrayal of Jefferson as a devoted husband and loving father.[17]

Jefferson's convoluted legacy regarding slavery confounded a few, but it appealed to most. Americans had (and continue to have) an irresistible urge to make Jefferson a stand-in for all the Founders on the issue of slavery. As a slavemaster critical of slavery whose writings on the subject spanned five decades, Jefferson was claimed by polemicists across the entire spectrum of the slavery controversy: immediate abolitionists and gradual emancipators, Free-Soilers and colonizationists, slavery restrictors and slavery expansionists, doughfaces and compromisers, as well as necessary evil defenders and positive good advocates.[18]

Abolitionists, even of the Garrisonian stripe, held up Jefferson as proof of the Founders' hostility toward slavery. To do so they tended to focus on Jefferson's famous lament in Query XVIII of *Notes on the State of Virginia* that history and God were turning against slavery: "I tremble for my country when I reflect that God is just; that his justice cannot sleep forever. . . . The spirit of the master is abating, that of the slave is rising from the dust, his condition mollifying, the way I hope preparing, under the auspices of heaven, for a total emancipation . . . with the consent of masters, rather than by their extirpation."[19] Abolitionists quoted this famous passage as proof that Jefferson was an opponent of slavery, if not a proper abolitionist. In much the same way, John Boynton, an earnest New England schoolteacher, paraphrased Jefferson's famous lament: "alas! I tremble for America."[20]

Some abolitionists discreetly began quoting Query XVIII *before* Jefferson noted that slavery was morally wrong. In this passage, Jefferson fretted that slavery hurt masters, especially their children, more than slaves: "The whole commerce between master and slave is a perpetual exercise of the most boisterous passions, the most unremitting despotism on the one part, and degrading submission on the other. Our children see this and learn to imitate it. . . . The man must be a prodigy who can retain his manners and morals undepraved by such circumstances."[21]

Although Jefferson's main concern there was about slavery's injurious effects on slavemasters rather than on their bondsmen, a few abolitionists found this Jeffersonian gem useful in combating the pro-slavery idea that slavery *benefited* master and slave. As early as 1846, a correspondent to the *National Anti-Slavery Standard*—a Northerner living in the South—quoted that passage, coming to believe its truth only after watching slavery in action. In a critical review of George Fitzhugh's pro-slavery *Cannibals All!* (1857), the *Liberator* triumphantly cited that part of Query XVIII, invoking one Virginian to refute another. The *Liberator* summoned Jefferson as a "true" witness of slavery on the ground. Two years later, the *Chicago Tribune* did much the same when it referenced Jefferson, "himself a Virginian," to this same effect.[22]

With all due "respectful deference" to the Sage of Monticello (but presumably contempt to the *Liberator,* the *Standard,* and the *Tribune*), *De Bow's Review* dismissed the concerns about the deleterious effects of slaveholding on masters that Jefferson had raised in Query XVIII. Reducing Jefferson's apprehensions to the absurdity that the master constantly exercised the "most odious tyranny," *De Bow's* asked, "Is not this master sometimes kind and indulgent to his slaves? Does he not mete out to them, for faithful service, the reward of his cordial approbation? Is it not his interest to do it?" After satisfying itself that the answers to these questions were affirmative, the New Orleans periodical concluded that the children of slaveholders learned those qualities.[23]

If antebellum Southerners were not convinced by Jefferson's worries, it was not for a want of effort by Garrison and other opponents of slavery. Northerners across the antislavery spectrum lauded Jefferson as an opponent of slavery. Indeed, Bigelow, the New York Free-Soil Democrat, counted Jefferson as an antislavery ally based largely on the part of Query XVIII that Garrison had neglected to quote. It was, Bigelow thought, a telling and prophetic warning. Anticipating modern commentators, Bigelow believed Jefferson was too much a man of thought and not enough a man of action in the application of his antislavery beliefs.[24]

Bigelow was not the only Free-Soiler to claim Jefferson. As opponents of slavery's westward expansion rather than slavery per se, Free-Soilers were keen to highlight Jefferson's efforts to contain slavery in the South rather than his moral qualms about its practice there. Accordingly, they relied upon Jefferson's 1784 draft of the Northwest Ordinance, which would have excluded slavery from that territory by 1800. They gave Jefferson too much credit. Jefferson the theorist was not novel and Jefferson the politician was not successful. Jefferson was not the first to make such a proposal. Moreover, Jefferson failed to get his proposal enacted into law by the Confederation Congress. Three years later, Congress approved a slavery exclusion provision, which immediately ended slavery in the Northwest Territory. In fact, Free-Soilers routinely called it the "Jefferson Ordinance" even though Jefferson had nothing to do with the one that the Congress passed in 1787. The introduction of the Wilmot Proviso in 1846, which explicitly drew on the language of the Northwest Ordinance to exclude slavery from the Mexican Cession, put Free-Soil support of Jefferson on the boil. Although the Wilmot Proviso passed the House of Representatives several times, it failed in the Senate. Nonetheless the Proviso brought the issue of slavery expansion to the fore. It also allowed slavery restrictionists to cast Jefferson as a Free-Soiler. In a speech advocating its passage, Byron Paine, a Wisconsin Free-Soiler, hailed the Founders for shielding the Northwest Territory from the "blighting curse" of slavery. Mixing his documents (if not his metaphors) during the buildup to the Election of 1848, Anthony B. Cleveland, another Free-Soiler, lauded the Wilmot Proviso as a "new declaration of independence" that freed Americans from the tyranny of the Slave Power.[25]

Unfortunately for opponents of slavery, Jefferson's long career and vacillating path offered other interpretations of his legacy. Pro-expansion Democrats noted that Jefferson had no objection to annexing the slaveholding Louisiana Territory. Nor did he insist on emancipating the enslaved people there. In fact, Jefferson opposed such efforts during the Missouri Crisis (1819–21), arguing that slavery should be diffused widely to soften its rough edges. Jefferson's volte-face on slavery expansion was due to the Constitution's three-fifths clause, which rewarded the slaveholding South with disproportionate political power in the House and the Electoral College. In some ways, Jefferson was the ultimate beneficiary of that part of the Constitution as the extra votes given to the South tipped the presidency to him in 1800. *De Bow's Review* dismissed the "Jeffersonian Ordinance" as having had "no practical effect whatever" on excluding slavery from the Northwest Territory. Just as environmental forces excluded slavery from that region, the *Review* reasoned, so they imposed slavery on the South. Instead the New Orleans periodical trumpeted the Louisiana Purchase as evidence that both Jefferson and nature itself supported the expansion of slavery.[26]

During the run-up to the Election of 1848, Edward Coles, former private secretary of President James Madison and former neighbor of Thomas Jefferson, sent a copy of a letter he had received from Jefferson on the "subject of slavery" to John Van Buren, a Free-Soiler, for publication. Van Buren's father, former President Martin Van Buren, was running for president as a Free-Soiler on a platform that advocated the congressional exclusion of slavery from the Mexican Cession. Although the letter had been published ten years earlier, Coles insisted on its republication when antislavery forces were making their most significant foray into presidential politics yet. On July 31, 1814, Coles, then a twenty-eight-year-old Virginian who harbored antislavery designs even though he had inherited his father's slaves and plantation, wrote a letter asking Jefferson to publicly support a gradual emancipation law that would have ended slavery in the Old Dominion. Jefferson replied 26 days later in a letter giving qualified support to gradual emancipation as an "expedient" solution to the problem of slavery. While Jefferson admitted that emancipation was advancing (and slavery retreating), he counseled Coles against emancipating his own chattels at that time because neither the slaves nor the nation were ready for such a bold move. While Jefferson's rhetoric sounded antislavery, it really supported the slaveholding status quo. Opponents of slavery did not quibble. The *New York Tribune* took Jefferson's words at face value and enlisted him in the efforts to gradually emancipate Kentucky's slaves. Jefferson's eloquence fooled even some hardheaded abolitionists. Citing that letter, the *National Anti-Slavery Standard* proudly counted Jefferson as a lifelong "opponent of African Slavery" despite his slaveholding. Dismissing Jefferson's advice, Coles freed his bondsmen in 1819 and moved to Illinois. Three years later, Coles was elected governor of Illinois and led the fight to end the tolerance of slavery in the Sucker State, triumphing in an 1824 referendum, which rejected a pro-slavery constitution.[27]

Of course, it was Jefferson's endorsement of gradual emancipation—halfhearted and qualified as it was—that allowed advocates of gradualism and colonization to enlist him in their cause. In 1837—just as the positive good defense of slavery was gaining traction—George Tucker, a Virginian who was appointed by Jefferson himself as a professor of philosophy at the University of Virginia, reminded his fellow Southerners that the Sage of Monticello "always regarded emancipation, accompanied with colonization, as practicable." In the weeks preceding the 1849 convention that considered a gradual emancipation amendment to the Kentucky constitution, the *Louisville Courier* invoked the antislavery example of Jefferson to dismiss the pro-slavery dogma then in vogue in the Bluegrass State. John C. Bullitt, a Kentucky hemp planter, also counted Jefferson as a supporter of gradual emancipation. There was some truth to their protestations. As an old man, Jefferson advocated federal support for the American Colonization Society. Despite Bullitt's advocacy of gradual emancipation, his wife noted that he refused the label of abolitionist. Nor did the hemp planter free his own bondsmen. In those respects at least, the ordinary Kentuckian was very much a true heir of the great Virginian.[28]

Jefferson was not the only Founder that opponents of slavery claimed. They were so keen to liken abolition to the Revolution (and themselves to the Revolutionaries) that they hailed the "anti-slavery feeling" of nearly all the Founding Fathers. In their haste, they did not distinguish between dithering slavemasters, such as Jefferson, Patrick Henry, and Washington, and active opponents of slavery, such as the Marquis de Lafayette, Alexander Hamilton, and John Adams. James M. Lucas, an Indiana Democrat, lauded the Founders for declaring, "slavery was an evil" that should be abolished by the states and credited the end of slavery in the North to their appeals for the exercise of this state's right. They had a ready explanation for why the South did not also follow the path of gradual emancipation. Eliab P. Mackintire, a Massachusetts Free-Soiler, attributed the volte-face whereby subsequent Southern statesmen went from decrying slavery as a necessary evil to justifying it as a positive good to the "amazing stimulus" that the cotton gin provided to bond labor.[29]

Despite the very real doubts that Jefferson had regarding gradual emancipation, many white Southerners conceded that he was an abolitionist at
least in the sense they understood the term. They did the same for many of
the other Founders, even the slaveholders from the South. The *Charleston
Mercury* acknowledged that abolitionists were correct in observing that
Jefferson, James Madison, James Monroe, and others "deplored and condemned" bond labor. The *Mercury* dismissed this as a trite historical fact.
It believed that the glory of the South's herrenvolk democracy trumped
Jefferson's squeamish humanitarian concerns. A few white Southern intellectuals did more than disregard Jefferson. They disdained the American
philosophe for taking the "folly of democracy" so far as to allow the "li-
centious Northern mob" to imperil the "great conservative institution" of
slavery. These Southern savants believed that Jefferson had recklessly set
dangerous "precedents" that permitted the "tyranny" of the Northern majority to oppress the Southern minority. Taken to its logical end, Jeffersonian
democracy would allow the non-slaveholding majority in the South—white
and black—to overthrow the slaveholding minority. Making Jefferson into a
sort of American Socrates, others condemned his loose talk about universal
natural rights for its tendency to corrupt the "young Southern mind."[30]

Moderates in the North and the South adduced Jefferson's example for
all to follow. Fearing the realization of Jefferson's prediction that the "vexed
question" of slavery would imperil the Union, H. H. Hite, a Virginia Whig,
hoped that Northerners would step back from the precipice. John Durant
Ashmore, a South Carolina cotton planter, explained that as a member of
the "Jeffersonian School of Politics," he reproached Southern secessionists
and Northern abolitionists in equal measure. Another Southerner lamented
that Northerners had strayed from the Jeffersonian path and instead had
impudently attempted to interfere with slavery in the Southern states. In
much the same way, Northern moderates, such as Massachusetts Democrat Benjamin F. Butler, extolled Jefferson as just the sort of slaveholding
Southerner for whom they could vote for president.[31]

While some Southerners forthrightly claimed Jefferson as a slave owner,
others did so obliquely, discreetly placing his slave-driving in the background.
A sympathetic Georgian lauded him as the "modle" [*sic*] Southern statesman
whose only recent intellectual heir was John C. Calhoun. The Georgian complained that no living Southerners were fit to pick up their mantle in 1859. In
much the same way, a North Carolina tobacco farmer, who owned a modest

number of bondsmen, pledged his fealty to the "state's right doctrines" of Jefferson and Calhoun. Fire-eaters shrank from Jefferson as a talisman of Southern weakness on slavery. A South Carolinian hotspur lamented to a like-minded Virginian that the failure of the Upper South to join the Lower South in taking a hard line against the North was because Virginia and South Carolina could not agree on a joint course of action. Rather than seeing Calhoun as an extension of Jefferson, he saw the two as polar opposites, whose divergent approaches divided the South at its moment of crisis.[32]

Of course, Jefferson's authorship of the Declaration of Independence was the main source of his antebellum renown (and current infamy). Virtually all Americans, aside from the fire-eating fringe, revered the Declaration. Unlike the origins of most nations—such as the twins who founded Rome—that were based on mythic events demoted to the mundane,[33] the real beginning of the United States—the adoption of the Declaration—was an ordinary event that was elevated to mythos. Convinced that they lived in the greatest nation in the world, Americans lauded the Declaration as well as its author and signatories with hyperbolic praise. With typical grandiosity and enduring solipsism, *Ballou's Pictorial Drawing-Room Companion*—the *Life* magazine of antebellum America—asserted that the signing of the Declaration was the "most important event of modern times" because this symbolic act had been followed by the concrete realization of American natural rights. Overlooking the very real limits of American freedom, which excluded poor white men, all women, most African Americans, and all Amerindians in the 1770s, *Ballou's* rhapsodized the Declaration as the "great charter of universal liberty." This overblown rhetoric was not reserved for editors. Americans from all walks of life believed that the Declaration had achieved a sort of transcendent perfection.[34]

Americans thronged the Patent Office in Washington, D.C., to catch a glimpse of the fading manuscript. In 1856, a correspondent for the *United States Magazine* described viewing the Declaration with an almost ecstatic intensity: "The sheet of paper has felt the pressure of the hand of each patriot, who, by signing it, consigned himself to the gallows or immortality." He observed, "the breath of each has fallen upon it; can you not almost feel the presence of those great and noble sponsors of freedom and liberty?" His account would have been breathless were not for his observation that the Founders had breathed while drafting the document. In that same year, American newspapers trafficked the rumor that the "original MS" of the Declaration had been stolen. The report was false. The "immortal state paper" remained in the Patent Office. In fact, the Declaration had not been touched since it was put on display fifteen years earlier.[35]

Descendants of the signatories of the Declaration of Independence claimed and received special status. One proud grandson bragged to his diary that he had seen the "original" document complete with his grandfather's John Hancock scrawled at the bottom. Another immodestly reminded George Bancroft, the leading American historian, that his grandfather, George Read of Delaware, had not only signed the Declaration but also the Constitution. This reverence was not limited to succeeding generations. In 1856, with a shaky hand and an almost unintelligible script, Zachariah Green, then a ninety-seven-year-old veteran, claimed that the highlight of his three years' service in the Continental Army was hearing the Declaration read for the first time in New York City on July 4, 1776. Green believed that hearing those magical words on that great day transcended his participation in battle under the command of Washington. In fact, the majesty of the event and the lapse of eighty years' time clouded his memory as the Declaration was first read in Gotham on July 9, 1776. In the construction and reconstruction of the antebellum popular memory of the Declaration, such details were beside the point.[36]

Washington was not the only holy city for American pilgrims. Others made a hajj to Philadelphia, the site of the Declaration's composition and adoption. With a slave in waiting, Jefferson had drafted the document in fifteen days, in June 1776, in a rented room of a house on the corner of Seventh and Market streets. Although the building had not been commemorated in any formal way, a few, hoping to share his muse, visited the place anyway. Most, if not all, of these patriotic tourists went to Independence Hall, what *Ballou's* called the "shrine of American Liberty," or, putting a finer point on it, the "Mecca" for liberty-seeking pilgrims. Despite this lofty rhetoric, their actual experiences were not much to write home about. After visiting Independence Hall, Girard College, and the U.S. Mint in rapid succession, W. T. Allen, an overwhelmed South Carolina tourist, found that the details of each site crowded each other out. In a letter home, Allen lamely reported that the birthplace of American independence had a "great many interesting relics." Some struggled to keep the historic buildings straight, despite the efforts of the Philadelphia city council to make Independence Hall a tourist attraction. George W. Patton, a harried visitor from central Pennsylvania, summarized his day-trip to Philadelphia: "visited the State House, all the Halls, Independence Hall, &c."[37]

It was only natural for Americans to erect a monument in Philadelphia to honor the Declaration, its author, and its signatories. The proposal began in 1852 when the Pennsylvania legislature passed a resolution in favor of an Independence Monument. By 1859, the legislatures of ten of the original thirteen states had endorsed the idea of building such a monument in Philadelphia's Independence Square and pledged funds for its construction. The three laggards—Virginia, North Carolina, and South Carolina—were below the Mason-Dixon Line. Employing a divide-and-conquer strategy, *Ballou's* tried to shame them into compliance. Confident that Virginia and North Carolina would participate, it observed that it would look very bad indeed for South Carolina to abstain. The *Chicago Tribune* sneered that the Palmetto State would devote its monies to purchasing "disunion [gun] powder" rather than a Union statue. Those Southern stragglers did not attend a meeting, held in the summer of 1860 in Philadelphia, to select a design for the monument. Their absence did not permit the ten states in the vanguard to unite. As late as October of that year, the reverent ten states had not yet even agreed on a design. The political fallout from the Election of 1860 smothered the necessary goodwill for such an ambitious project.[38]

It was fitting that the sectional conflict prevented the erection of a monument to the Declaration of Independence and its signers. By necessity, the friction caused by the different understandings of American nationality was focused along several fault lines, including the Declaration. While abolitionists lauded the Declaration as the natural rights touchstone for American liberty for men and women of all races, conservatives in the South and the North read it as applying exclusively to native-born white males. During the fourth Lincoln-Douglas debate at Charleston, Illinois (September 18, 1858), Sen. Stephen A. Douglas dismissed Abraham Lincoln's claim that the Declaration, in Douglass's paraphrase, proclaimed that the "negro is the equal to the white man" because it led to the slippery slope toward "negro citizenship." Lincoln, keen to refute charges that he was a "Black Republican," i.e., an abolitionist, did not deny that he read the Declaration's "all men" expansively, but repudiated the idea that the Founders made African

Americans citizens. In this regard both Lincoln and Douglas agreed with Chief Justice Roger B. Taney's assertion in the *Dred Scott* decision that blacks ipso facto could not be citizens of the United States.[39]

Going beyond Lincoln's Free-Soilism, proper abolitionists were quick to apply Jefferson's natural rights formula to the condition of African Americans, free and enslaved. They appropriated the Declaration, Independence Hall, and the Liberty Bell to their cause. Quoting Jefferson's maxim of "inalienable rights," William Wells Brown, a fugitive slave turned abolitionist, indicted the United States for professing to believe in natural rights while profiting from the "child-robbing, man-stealing, woman-whipping, chain-forging, marriage-destroying, slave-manufacturing, man-slaying" system of bond labor. Henry Bibb, another fugitive turned abolitionist, paraphrased the Declaration to denounce slavery. Going well beyond Jefferson's pithy "life, liberty, and property," Bibb expanded the Declaration's catalog of natural rights, asserting that "every man has a right to wages for his labor; a right to his own wife and children; a right to liberty and the pursuit of happiness; and a right to worship God according to the dictates of his own conscience." Even if we ignore Bibb's abolition section, his view of natural rights went further than even the French Revolutionaries did in the Universal Declaration of the Rights of Man and of the Citizen (1789).[40]

Julia Griffiths, a correspondent for *Frederick Douglass's Paper,* was one of the pilgrims who went to the Patent Office to view the Declaration in its moldering transcendence. Just seeing that glorious document, Griffiths believed would transform even the most cynical dough-faced congressman into an abolitionist. Her fellow abolitionists in Philadelphia believed that Independence Hall and its bell would have a similar effect in that city. Of course, not everyone read the same message from these icons. Although abolitionists made the bell in Independence Hall an antislavery symbol—the "Liberty Bell"—many white Southerners nevertheless regarded it as a symbol of American resistance to British oppression. It was, after all, the bell that announced the first public reading of the Declaration on July 8, 1776. Samuel Wells Leland, a South Carolina physician who visited Independence Hall in 1858, enjoyed seeing (if not hearing) the famous "old crack[ed] bell." Leland was untroubled by—and seemingly unaware of—its abolitionist symbolism.[41]

That South Carolinian notwithstanding, the Declaration of Independence was a powerful symbol for opponents of slavery, who explicitly identified themselves with the Founders. In 1845, Massachusetts abolitionist Wendell Phillips noted that Frederick Douglass had written his famous *Narrative* as a fugitive who could have been consigned to slavery at any time just as the signers of the Declaration did so with the "halter about their necks." In much the same way, the Washington, D.C., *National Era* urged all American citizens to implement the principles the Founders had "risked their lives to disseminate." Of course, the worthies in Philadelphia had risked more than that—they also risked their "Fortunes" and their "sacred Honor."[42]

Some Americans made the Declaration more radical than it actually was by adding two or three words that were not in the original, but perhaps should have been. Although most Americans joined the *Louisville Democrat* in "tak[ing] it for granted [that] all have read" the Declaration, the evidence clearly proves otherwise. Or at least, the evidence proves that antebellum Americans read the Declaration's Preamble in such a way as to have it confirm their hopes for or (in the case of Southern slaveholders) fears about the future of the United States. In 1855, Melissa Bryant, a Massachusetts abolitionist, invoked the Declaration to justify her opposition to the Fugitive Slave Act, asserting that she "would sooner loan the last drop of life blood than acknowledge that all men were not 'created *free and* equal.'" Bryant was anticipating the improved wording that was used in Massachusetts's Declaration of Rights (1780) and the French Republic's Declaration of the Rights of Man and of the Citizen (1789), as well as the United Nations' Universal Declaration of Human Rights (1948).[43]

This reformulation of Jefferson's aphorism was not unique to Bryant. Indeed, antebellum Americans from across the political spectrum on the issue of slavery—from William Lloyd Garrison to John C. Calhoun—gratuitously added the words "born free and" to the Declaration's Preamble, making their public understanding of the founding document of the United States more expansive than it actually was. While the "created equal" in Jefferson's version took aim at the white supremacy that was at the base of the system of racial slavery in the United States (and perhaps made an implicit attack on slavery itself), the revised edition of "born free and equal" undercut both white supremacy and black slavery. Although the Preamble of the Declaration of Independence consists of what historian Joseph Ellis rates as "the best known fifty-eight words in American history," antebellum Americans routinely misquoted them, adding two or three extra words that transformed America's founding document into an abolitionist treatise.[44]

While opponents of slavery ranging from the gradual emancipationist Cassius M. Clay to the Free-Soiler Abraham Lincoln were guilty of this wishful thinking, it was most pronounced in Garrisonian circles. For every time that the gradualist *National Era* alluded to all men being born "free and equal," the immediatist chorus of the *National Anti-Slavery Standard,* the *Pennsylvania Freeman,* the *Anti-Slavery Bugle,* and, of course, the *Liberator* boldly asserted this self-evident truth.[45] At the same time, many of the most ardent defenders of slavery conceded this significant point (and fallacious reading) to their antislavery adversaries. Edmund Ruffin and Louisa S. McCord were among the pro-slavery advocates who also quoted the Declaration to the effect that all men were "born free and equal." They were joined by leading Southern periodicals, including the *Southern Literary Messenger.*[46]

In fact, countless opponents of and advocates for slavery made this mistake, as did neutrals. When abolitionists radicalized the Declaration by adding three words, slaveholders literally trembled at the thought of slaves hearing it read out loud. It was the added "born free and" that allowed the *Cincinnati Commercial* to mock Southern fears of a "stray copy" of the Declaration sent through the mail, fomenting a slave revolt.[47]

To be sure, some antebellum Americans realized that they were expanding or improving Jefferson's text. In response to the State Department's refusal to issue passports to free black men because they were not citizens, the *Liberator* sarcastically referenced a "foolish clause in a foolish document to the effect 'that all men are born free and equal,'" declaring it should be revised with the proviso "negroes excluded" to reflect the discriminatory practice of the federal government. But many others did not realize they were interpolating the document and exaggerating its scope. This added to the bitter irony abolitionists felt that the United States remained a slave-driving nation despite the Declaration's Preamble. Speaking for the Free-Soil Party in the heat of the Election of 1852, James G. Birney, a Kentucky slavemaster turned Michigan abolitionist, observed that the Declaration asserted a "truth which [sh]ould have liberated every human being held as a slave." Few appreciated this better than enslaved Americans who sought refuge in Canada. These American expatriates found their independence in the very nation against which the Patriots had rebelled. In 1840, Joseph Taper, a fugitive slave from Virginia, observed that he preferred the "Queen's dominions" to the model republic because in Canada "all are born free & equal" unlike in the United States. In *The Voice of the*

*Fugitive,* the newspaper he established in what became Ontario, Henry Bibb, the fugitive slave from Kentucky with an expansive understanding of natural rights, declared that on British soil African Americans could realize the abstract truth that "all men are born free and equal."[48]

Even white Southerners who read the Bible and the Constitution literally to defend slavery, did exactly the opposite when interpreting the Preamble of the Declaration. Not only did many Southerners include those gratuitous two or three words but a coterie of Southern intellectuals also explained away the "all" and "created" not to mention the "equal" and the "free." They made this restricted reading as early as the Missouri Crisis (1819–21), anticipating the pro-slavery apologetics that appeared in the following decades. In fact, they made rejection of Jefferson's aphorism a branch of pro-slavery political and moral philosophy. Although there were earlier efforts in this vein, the heyday for pro-slavery treatises was the 1850s. In 1851, *De Bow's Review* dusted off William Harper's classic "Memoir on Slavery" (1838), which ridiculed abolitionists for claiming that the United States was founded on the notion that "all men are born free and equal," when in truth, "no man was ever born free" and "no two men were ever born equal." In that same year, Louisa S. McCord, the South Carolina plantation mistress cum pro-slavery polemicist, regretted that Jefferson's Declaration was marred by "six unlucky words," which she specified as *"all men are born free and equal."* Luck, of course, had nothing to do with it. Like other Southern critics of natural rights, McCord asserted, "no man is born free, and no two human beings, perhaps, were ever born equal." Like other Southern apologists for slavery, McCord tried to explain away Jefferson's qualms about slavery by observing that the great Virginian was a lifelong slavemaster and all of the thirteen original states were *"slaveholding* States" in 1776. In 1855, the *Southern Literary Messenger* almost chortled at abolitionists' appeal to the Declaration. The interpretation of the Declaration made by these naive abolitionists, the *Messenger* observed, implied that the slaveholding Founders were "so ignorant of the purport of their own language as to write themselves down as asses in the face of the civilized world!"[49]

In 1857, William S. Grayson, a Mississippi Methodist divine, haughtily paraphrased the Declaration as maintaining that "all men are naturally free; and equal in that freedom," and then gave the tag line "very good, but what does it amount to?" In his view, not very much. Grayson then proceeded to decry "natural freedom" as the freedom from the "restraints" of morality, justice, and religion. In 1851, Samuel W. Cartwright, the Louisiana physician who had famously diagnosed slave-specific mental illnesses to account for enslaved people's seemingly inexplicable habits of resisting slavery by doing shoddy work and running away, dismissed Jefferson's aphorism as a "false Jacobinical French hypothesis, asserting the negro's right to liberty and equality." In a pithy summary of the Southern intelligentsia's rejection of Jeffersonian natural rights, Cartwright scolded, "*the negro is not a white man painted black.*"[50]

Edmund Ruffin, a Virginia disunionist and connoisseur of pro-slavery tracts, made the refutation of Jefferson's "indefensible" aphorism that "all men are born free & equal" the acid test for slavery apologetics. In fact, Ruffin faulted Albert Bledsoe's *An Essay on Liberty and Slavery* (1857) because it defended Jefferson's odious notion "instead of admitting it to be both false & foolish." Bledsoe, a mathematician at the University of Virginia, made the aphorism agreeable to some white Southerners by making its least common denominator the abstract natural right of each person to occupy his or her appropriate place in the hierarchy, thus reducing a radical attack on the status quo of the 1770s into a reactionary defense of the status quo of the 1850s. Anticipating Ruffin, a reviewer in Louisiana had written a similarly critical review of Bledsoe's treatise for *De Bow's Review,* but had not published it because such a nuanced criticism would have caused more irritation and confusion than edification. Bledsoe eased his burden by quoting the Declaration properly and leaving off the gratuitous "born free and," perhaps irritating Ruffin all the more. In contrast to Ruffin and the *De Bow's* reviewer, the *Southern Literary Messenger* appreciated Bledsoe's efforts to redeem the Declaration by exploding the facile and fallacious reading that abolitionists made of the phrase with the "ingenious" argument showing that chattels had only the natural right to be enslaved. Corydon E. Fuller, a Northern bookseller, bluntly described how this abstraction was practiced on the ground in Arkansas. Many slavemasters, Fuller found, believed in the "divine right of nigger-drivers" rather than the natural rights of black people.[51]

Bledsoe was not the only pro-slavery theorist to quote Jefferson more or less properly before rejecting him. Indeed, the three most famous slavery apologists—James Henry Hammond, George Fitzhugh, and Calhoun—got the Declaration's Preamble right. Hammond, a South Carolina politico and cotton planter, repudiated as "ridiculously absurd, that much lauded but nowhere accredited dogma of Mr. JEFFERSON, 'that all men are born equal.'" To be sure, Jefferson did not write that all men were born equal, but Hammond reasoned that one must be created before one is born. Fitzhugh, a Virginia lawyer and the most famous pro-slavery theorist, accounted for both steps in the sequence. In his *Sociology for the South* (1854), Fitzhugh explained away the Declaration's natural rights ideology in a pro-slavery flourish. "Men are not created [n]or born equal," Fitzhugh contended, "and circumstances, and education, and association, tend to increase and aggravate inequalities among them, from generation to generation."[52]

Then and now, the most notorious Southern denouncer of Jeffersonian natural rights was Calhoun, the great statesman, political philosopher, and cotton planter from South Carolina. During the debate over approving a government for the Oregon Territory on June 27, 1848, Calhoun famously dismissed the "most false and dangerous error" that "all men are born free and equal." In fact, Calhoun believed that Jefferson's "hypothetical truism" had misled the "vast majority on both sides of the Atlantic." Because of its ubiquity and its threat, Calhoun believed that he had a "duty" to refute this insidious doctrine. "There is not a word of truth" in the expanded version of Jefferson's proposition, Calhoun lectured:

It begins with "all men are born," which is utterly untrue. Men are not born. Infants are born. They grow to be men. And concludes with asserting that they are born "free and equal," which is not less false. They are not born free. While infants they are incapable of freedom, being destitute alike of the capacity of thinking and acting, without which there can be no freedom. Besides, they are necessarily born subject to their parents, and remain so . . . until the development of their intellect and physical capacity enables them to take care of themselves. They grow to all the freedom, of which the condition in which they were born permits, by growing to be men. Nor is it less false that they are born "equal." They are not so in any sense in which it can be regarded.[53]

Unlike the others who added the extra three words, the South Carolinian knew the correct wording of the Declaration—that "all men are created equal"—but he liked it no better than the expanded popularized version. Jefferson's "form of expression, though less dangerous, is not less erroneous," Calhoun observed. "All men are not created. According to the Bible, only two, a man and a woman, ever were, and of these one was pronounced subordinate to the other. All others have come into the world by being born, and in no sense . . . either free or equal. But this form of expression being less striking and popular has given way to the present, and under the authority of a document put forth on so great an occasion, and leading to such important consequences, has spread far and wide, and fixed itself deeply in the public mind."[54]

Calhoun regarded both versions of the axiom—"all men are created equal" and "all men were born free and equal"—as dangerous abstractions whose "disorganizing effects" led to abolition, socialism, and ultimately anarchy. Calhoun asserted that Jefferson had unnecessarily radicalized the Declaration and this doctrine's baleful effects unsettled both Europe and the United States, i.e., that it was the driving force behind the Revolutions of 1848 in Europe and the slavery extension controversy in America. In his posthumous *Disquisition on Government and a Discourse on the Constitution of the United States* (1851), Calhoun returned to these themes, rejecting the "prevalent opinion that all men are born free and equal."[55]

Calhoun's belief that the expanded version of Jefferson's Preamble was more dangerous to the conservative slaveholding regime than Jefferson's original formulation was undoubtedly correct. While Calhoun's fears vis-à-vis the abolitionized Preamble were widespread among Southern intellectuals, his understanding that these radical words were an expansion of Jefferson's original was limited. That so many antebellum Southerners believed that Jefferson himself had declared that "all men were born free and equal" is indicative of their belief that the great Virginia slavemaster was soft on the issue of slavery. Despite the very real doubts that Jefferson had regarding gradual emancipation, some influential Southerners conceded that the Sage of Monticello was an abolitionist, at least in the sense that they understood the term.

Southern periodicals bristled with attacks on the Declaration's Preamble in the late 1840s and throughout the 1850s. The *Southern Quarterly Review* dismissed it as a "humbug" and a "dogma." The *Southern Literary Messenger* remonstrated that it was an "infidel production." For its part, *De Bow's Review* merely observed that Jefferson was mistaken. After noting that the "faculties of adult individuals vary indefinitely," *De Bow's Review* reformulated Jefferson's turn of phrase into its antithesis: "all are alike, but unequal." Regardless of the tone of their admonitions, Southern periodicals regarded natural rights as an insidious doctrine. They believed that a broad democracy based on even a narrow reading of the Declaration's Preamble, i.e., one that included just poor white men—would undermine not just bond labor in the South but also republican government in the United States.[56]

Southern periodicals argued that Jefferson had been led astray by his dabbling in Locke, Hume, Voltaire, Fourier, and Rousseau. After Virginia enacted a new constitution in 1851, which apportioned seats in the House of Delegates on the "white basis" rather than counting whites and slaves, they feared that Jefferson was leading the Old Dominion down the path of universal democracy that would end in general emancipation or servile insurrection. The *Southern Quarterly Review* attributed this unsettling privileging of population at the expense of property to the dangerous effects of Jefferson's egalitarian words. Rather than all men being created equal, the *Review* argued that the "very reverse of this proposition is the truth, namely, that all men are by nature unequal." The *Southern Quarterly Review* denounced Virginia's new constitution (and its premise of Jeffersonian democracy) for placing "power over the property of the East in the hands of the West." The *Southern Literary Messenger* also worried about the "leveling doctrines" found in the Declaration. In a pique of gallows humor, Alfred Huger, a venerable South Carolina planter, quipped: "[George] Washington bequeath'd us a 'Republic'; Mr. Jefferson swap'd it off for a 'Democracy.'"[57]

It was not just Southerners who had a restrictive view of natural rights in the antebellum era. During the debates over the Kansas-Nebraska bill, Sen. John Pettit, a Democrat from Indiana, stated the Declaration's assertion that "all men were created equal" was a "self-evident lie" rather than a "self-evident truth." Pettit believed that "it is utterly false that men are, either mentally, morally, physically, or politically, created equal." Two years later, in the partisan frenzy of the Election of 1856, Rufus Choate, a conservative Massachusetts Whig, dismissed the Declaration's Preamble as overblown rhetoric from the heat of the Revolutionary War, which was improperly appropriated by opponents of slavery. Choate believed that Republicans had foolishly made the Declaration's "glittering and sounding generalities" of natural rights as the foundation of their platform of slavery containment. Although the document had indeed figured prominently in their efforts in 1856, some Republicans tried to distance themselves from the Declaration to defuse Democratic claims that they were "Black Republicans" who favored equal rights for blacks and whites.

On December 8, 1859, Lyman Trumbull, an Illinois Republican, explained that when members of his party quoted the Declaration's Preamble, "we do not mean that every man in organized society has the same rights. We do not tolerate that in Illinois." In other words, Trumbull argued that the Republican Party was not founded on the abolitionist premise of the innate equality of all people. This restricted view of natural rights was not just a conceit of politicians and philosophers. The idea that the natural rights adumbrated in the Declaration applied only to white people was commonplace in the North as well as the South. Indeed, Henry Ashworth, a Briton who toured the United States in 1857, found this sentiment to be common among the "generality of the people of America." Some of the Americans this affable traveler from Lancashire interrogated regarded the notion that "all men are to be deemed alike at birth" to be a "mistake" or even an "abominable lie."[58]

Harper, Grayson, Cartwright, Ruffin, Hammond, and Calhoun, as well as Pettit and Choate, took an extreme position—one rejected by many Southerners (and most Northerners). Calhoun, the leading exponent of this doctrine, came in for special criticism. Logan McKnight, a Kentuckian transplanted to New Orleans, thought that Calhoun's "metaphysical discussion," which found that the Declaration's sweeping assertion of universal natural rights did not apply to African Americans, was a "sad proof" of the degradation of the South Carolinian's great intellect. The *Louisville Courier* mocked Calhoun's "great discovery" that while all children were made in God's image, all "babies are not born equal." William Henry Brisbane, a South Carolina slavemaster turned Ohio abolitionist, was so infuriated by Calhoun's sophistry on this matter that he wrote a letter to the editor of the *Cincinnati Herald* to rebut it.[59]

In particular, Pettit's criticisms outraged many Northerners. Pettit dismissed Jefferson's soaring rhetoric as "glittering generalities" that sparkled but did not illuminate. Even more galling, Pettit had transformed Jefferson's self-evident truths into equally clear lies. Perhaps it was the fact that Pettit was a Northerner that stung the most. Theodore Parker, a Boston abolitionist, fumed that the "Democrats" who thought the self-evident truth of the Declaration was a "self evident lie," lustily celebrated Democrat James Buchanan's victory over Republican John C. Frémont in the Election of 1856—what Parker believed was really the "victory of Slavery over Freedom." The *Lawrence Republican* derided those who reduced the Declaration into "glittering generalities" or, even worse, scorned as "self-evident lies." Samuel Breck, a venerable Philadelphia merchant and Whig, denounced orators who reduced Jefferson's "sublime truths" to mere "GLITTERING GENERALITIES!!!!" Breck, a first-wave abolitionist who had introduced a bill for the final emancipation of the bondsmen remaining in the Keystone State in 1821, believed this to be tantamount to a repudiation of the Declaration itself. Lydia Maria Child, a leading second-wave abolitionist, lamented that some had dismissed Jefferson's "genuine, practical *belief* in *Freedom*" to a "mere abstraction." To the contrary, Child asserted it was a "glittering generality" to most Americans. Ralph Waldo Emerson, the great Transcendentalist, famously rejoined that the Declaration did not contain glittering generalities, but instead "blazing ubiquities that will burn forever and ever." Eliab P. Mackintire, a Massachusetts Free-Soiler, marveled at how the Declaration could be so easily transformed from a clarion for freedom to an "instrument of oppression." William Morris Davis, a Philadelphian who pursued the seemingly contradictory vocation of sugar refiner cum abolitionist, could only nod his head in sad agreement at how "Slave[o]crat[s]" and their doughface allies had reduced Jefferson's noble intentions to a mere "Rhetorical Flourish."[60]

Despite the controversy, Jefferson's words inspired. In the early 1790s, four states had enacted new constitutions that proclaimed that all men were born equal while at the same time outlawing slavery. Several newer states also incorporated those words into their constitutions. For example, the Illinois Constitution of 1818 declared that "all men are born equally free and independent, and have certain inherent and indefeasible rights; among which are those of enjoying and defending life and liberty, and acquiring, possessing, and protecting property and reputation, and of pursuing their own happiness." Although these states did not always live up to their constitutions' color-blind credo, opponents of bondage repeatedly invoked these words, confident that they were slavery's last rites. Rallying before the Election of 1848, Free-Soilers in upstate New York declared, the "true foundation of civil government is the equal, natural, and inalienable rights of *all men*" and determined that the entire community was obliged to secure the "life, liberty, and the pursuit of happiness to each individual."[61]

Inasmuch as the Declaration continued for another twelve hundred words after the beginning of its famous Preamble, we must ask what antebellum Americans made of the rest of it. Opponents of slavery buttressed their abolitionist reading of the document by adducing the fact that in the draft of the Declaration, Jefferson charged George III with carrying on the international slave trade and foisting slavery on the unwilling American colonies. In this curious passage, Jefferson likened British oppression of colonial whites to Africans enduring one of the most brutal practices of the slave system. Untroubled by such rhetorical excess, abolitionists lamented the fact that the Second Continental Congress had removed the paragraph during the editing process at the demand of South Carolina and Georgia. Henry C. Wright, a New England abolitionist, claimed that had the condemnation of the slave trade been sanctified in the Declaration, American slavery would have not lasted a decade—i.e., that there would have been no need for the protections given to slaveholders in the Constitution because there would be no slaveholders to protect. Antislavery advocates liked to pretend that Jefferson had not been edited. For example, at an Independence Day celebration in Belleville, Illinois, opponents of slavery read the Declaration as "originally prepared by Jefferson" with that deleted paragraph included, trumping South Carolina and Georgia's pro-slavery editing.[62]

Even some Southerners adduced Jefferson's opposition to the international slave trade, albeit for different ends. In the 1850s, moderate Southerners invoked Jefferson's example to undercut fire-eaters' efforts to revive American participation in that infamous commerce. William Campbell Preston, a South Carolinian living in Virginia, denounced the slave traders as "demagogues" who would disrespect the Founders to increase the number of slaves in the South. Preston was a late-blooming moderate. As a young man he had helped provoke the Nullification Crisis, but as a sexagenarian he saw the virtues of compromise. An antislavery Virginian reminded his fellow Southerners that Jefferson as president had "prohibited the slave trade after [the] year 1808," apparently forgetting that Jefferson had also attacked the infamous traffic in the Declaration.[63]

More to the point, Southerners brandished the fact that Jefferson's Declaration actually indicted George III for fomenting slave rebellions. "He," the Declaration complained, "has excited domestic insurrection among us." Of course, George III, or rather his minions, had done just that. On November 7, 1775, Virginia's Royal Governor, John Murray, Earl of Dunmore, offered freedom to all slaves who would bear arms against the rebellion. Four years later (June 30, 1779), Sir Henry Clinton issued a similar proclamation on the eve of his campaign into Georgia, South Carolina, and North Carolina. Just like white Southerners in the 1850s, Jefferson in the 1770s used euphemisms to describe this great, pervasive, and usually unmentioned but nonetheless universal fear of all slaveholding societies. While the Declaration denounced the British king for "excit[ing] domestic insurrection," antebellum Southerners favored the phrase "servile insurrection." Most white Southerners did not worry about the apparent contradiction between the antislavery beginning of the Declaration and its antislave rebellion conclusion. They denied, ignored, forgot, or were unaware of Jefferson's antislavery rhetoric. Southerners' selective remembering and forgetting of Jefferson's qualms about slavery was mirrored by abolitionists vis-à-vis the Preamble and Jefferson's slaveholding. As Sen. Robert Toombs of Georgia pointedly observed in 1856, British incitement of slave rebellions was "one reason for [the Southern colonies] withdrawing from the mother country." Of course, Toombs and other Southerners believed that fomenting servile insurrection posed an existential threat to the South and was just cause for secession in the 1850s as well as the 1770s. To be sure, Lord Dunmore and Sir Henry had actually encouraged slaves to rebel by offering them freedom to fight their rebellious masters in 1775 and 1779, but so did John Brown in 1859 (and Nathaniel Bacon in 1676). Long before John Brown's Harpers Ferry Raid, Southerners had made this argument. "Read over the declaration of independence," the *Southern Quarterly Review* counseled in 1851, "and compare the wrongs recited there to those [we] now endure."[64]

Ultimately, Southerners emphasized the latter part of the Declaration's Preamble, the resort to the Lockean right to revolution. During the Crisis of 1850, DeWitt C. Greenwood, a Mississippi newspaper editor, wrote his former law professor about the theoretical legality of state nullification of a federal law, state secession from the Union, and federal coercion of a seceding state. Greenwood cautioned that his query did not question the "right of Revolution" because every oppressed person could resort to that right. The *Richmond Whig* concurred. In a paroxysm of sectional indignation, the *Whig* declared that the "right of revolution" had been "consecrated" by the Revolutionary generation. *De Bow's Review* noted that the Declaration was a "solemn act of disunion" by an "oppressed minority." At the 1852 Democratic national convention, Henry A. Wise, a Virginia lawyer and politico, counseled that Southerners must insist on the "Inalienable rights to the Individual" against all governmental oppression. In their penetrating study on the "mind" of the South's "master class," Elizabeth Fox-Genovese and Eugene Genovese find that the idea "that the Revolution justified the South's own 'right of revolution' against tyranny became a common theme during the 1850s."[65]

Southern slaveholders were not the only antebellum Americans to invoke the Declaration's Lockean right to revolution. Northern opponents of slavery turned the tables by using it to justify abolitionist violence and even slave resistance. An Indiana abolitionist paraphrased Jefferson to argue that patriotic Americans ought to break the Constitution to be true to the Declaration. Quoting Jefferson, the Hoosier thundered that "Nature's God" demanded that fugitive slaves in particular and Northerners in general violently resist the "robbers, murders, assassins, and pirates" who would take self-liberated slaves back to bondage in the South. In much the same way, Samuel J. May, a Unitarian minister from Syracuse, rallied local antislavery forces to violently rescue the arrested fugitive Jerry McHenry on October 1, 1851. Paraphrasing the Declaration's inspirational concluding sentence, May exhorted Syracusans to pledge their "lives, their fortunes, and their sacred honor, to protect the trembling fugitive in his distress." In commemoration of the second anniversary of McHenry's rescue, Theodore Parker, the Massachusetts abolitionist, likened the Fugitive Slave Act to the Stamp Act: both were so unjust that the only ethical response was to violate them. Six years later, Parker defended his financial support of John Brown's raid on the federal arsenal at Harpers Ferry in Lockean terms: "Slaves have a *natural Right to destroy their oppressors*."[66]

Enslaved people resorted to the Lockean right to rebellion as well even if they did not always allude explicitly or in a form that is extant to the Declaration of Independence or John Locke. Historian Kenneth Stampp famously described as a "personal Declaration of Independence" a letter written by a self-emancipated slave named Anthony Chase to the man his former mistress had hired him out to, which explained his reasons for running away. Like Jefferson's justification for American independence, Chase's justification for his personal independence was rational, measured, and justified. Just as Jefferson submitted facts of George III's tyranny to a "candid world," so Chase wanted to "prove to the world" the justness of his cause. Just as Jefferson outlined the colonists' "patient sufferance" of British tyranny and their petitions for redress, so Chase noted that his mistress had spurned his request to purchase his freedom. Just as Jefferson promised to treat the British with due respect after independence, so

Chase promised to pay her "every cent" that he thought his "servaces [*sic*] is worth." Chase's eloquence was exceptional, but his method was not. A surprising number of self-liberated slaves wrote their former masters, explaining and justifying their actions. Thousands of others used their feet instead of a pen when the Spirit of '76 moved them. Of course, millions more desired their independence, but were not bold enough to declare or achieve it. Their distress was palpable. In 1848, a missionary from New York's Burnt-Over District could not help but hear that in Kentucky there were "many poor oppressed beings sighing for liberty."[67]

Over the course of his long and eventful life, Jefferson took various positions on the important matters of the day. At times, he was a Unionist, a gradual emancipator, and a centralizer; at other times, he was a Southerner, a paternalistic slavemaster, and an advocate of states' rights. In between those times, he tacked to and fro. After his remarkable coincidental death on July 4, 1826 (along with John Adams)—the fiftieth anniversary of the adoption of the Declaration of Independence—antebellum Americans were free to pick and choose what parts of the Jeffersonian legacy appealed most to them. They did so with relish. This frenzy of selective quotation and misquotation allowed Americans from across the entire political spectrum to claim Jefferson as an abolitionist, a colonizationist, a Free-Soiler, a Unionist, a conflicted slaveholder, a pro-slavery defender, a secessionist, or a mixture of some of these. While hotspurs emphasized the Jeffersonian legacy of self-determination and resistance to encroachment on individual rights, especially the right to hold other people as property, enslaved people, abolitionists, and some Free-Soilers looked to the Jeffersonian legacy of natural rights for all; and moderates in the North and the South took pride in the notion that Jefferson's Declaration had bestowed a legacy of freedom that made the United States the most free nation on earth even though millions of Americans toiled in bondage. In the early 1850s, fire-eaters and fugitive slaves invoked the right to rebellion—to different ends—while at the same time moderates tried to keep the fire of the old Revolution alight while smothering that of the new.[68]

Jefferson's protean legacy as a natural rights advocate qua slaveholder permeated tourist trips to Monticello, celebrations of his birthday, and, of course, remembrances of the Declaration. Despite the seeming contradictions, Jefferson's mild brand of antislavery appealed to abolitionists. In the span of three years in the 1840s, the *National Anti-Slavery Standard* reflected this ambivalence. While the *Standard* counted Jefferson as a bold advocate of emancipation and the father of slavery restriction, it also circulated the story that Jefferson fathered at least one child with one of his chattels and allowed his own flesh and blood to remain in bondage even after his death. Nonetheless, most abolitionists most of the time were happy to enlist Jefferson—the "great apostle of Democracy"—and his Declaration—often with a "free and" added to its Preamble—to their cause.[69]

For their part, white Southerners found in Jefferson a fellow slaveholder who bought and sold slaves, worried about their proper management, and treated them as black members of his family. As James D. Davidson, a Virginia Democrat, noted with pride, Old Dominion's slaves had nursed Jefferson, "whose inspired words, made tyrants quail & taught our fathers how to be free." Slaveholders read his Declaration, if they bothered to read it at all, as applying only to white men. Many more *knew* what the Declaration really said even if that was not what it actually said. A few dismissed the Declaration's call for universal natural rights, as the *Southern Quarterly Review* did, as "cant" that was futile, fallacious, and hypocritical. Some sympathized with Jefferson's colonizationist impulses and his misgivings about the peculiar institution, while others dismissed them as the sentimental excesses of an earlier time. Most ignored his antislavery musings in *Notes on the State of Virginia*. They believed that Jefferson's purchase of the Louisiana Territory (1803), a vast slave region, trumped his efforts to restrict slavery from the Northwest Territory. The *Southern Literary Messenger* dismissed the abolitionist canard that Jefferson was an "emancipationist" as so absurd on its face as to be self-refuting—to coin a phrase, it was a self-evident lie.[70]

Moderates in the South and the North found in Jefferson's words and actions an unshakable love of the Union of slave and free states, a willingness to compromise the issue of slavery, and an aversion to radical solutions to the problem of bond labor. The dough-faced Philadelphia *Pennsylvanian* derided Free-Soilers' claim that were Jefferson alive in 1848, he would cast a vote for their presidential candidate Martin Van Buren. Not only was Jefferson a partisan Democrat, but he was also a steadfast advocate of national parties fielding tickets balanced between Northerners and Southerners with national platforms. The *Memphis Appeal* derided Republicans' claim that were Jefferson alive in 1856, he would cast a vote for John C. Frémont. The *Appeal* noted that Jefferson was aghast at the sectional agitation over the admission of Missouri as a slave state in 1819 and feared that the political controversy over slavery might lead to the "immediate dissolution of the Union." As that would be the result of Frémont's victory in 1856, the *Appeal* reasoned that Jefferson would have rejected the Republicans' "sectional candidate." Indeed, moderates noted that time after time, Jefferson advocated making sectional compromises to preserve the Union. In 1847, Hopkins Holsey, a Georgia Whig, pleaded for his fellow Southerners to endorse another sectional compromise by noting that no less a Southerner than Jefferson acquiesced to the Missouri Compromise. Twelve years on, W. M. Corry, an Ohio Democrat, lamented to a Kentuckian that Jefferson had opposed the "desperate folly of the Negro feud" that divided the nation in two rival sections.[71]

Jefferson did not just support making concessions to the North to assuage the political dispute over slavery: he also favored placating the South as well. Indeed, his acquiescence to Georgia and South Carolina's demand to remove the denunciation of the international slave trade (and implicitly bond labor itself) from the Declaration proved to the *Southern Quarterly Review*'s satisfaction that if compromises must be made on the issue, they should follow the precedent of Jefferson and the other Founders and favor the South. Whether it was his willingness to drop the indictment of the international slave trade from the Declaration or his acceptance of the Missouri Compromise's limited slavery expansion, moderates in the North and the South found numerous examples to back up their claim. Indeed, it could be argued that Jefferson's career as a mildly antislavery slaveholder perfectly embodied this sentiment because ipso facto any Unionist in the 1850s would have to accommodate slavery to a certain degree.[72]

# 3

# George Washington

## *Father of a Slaveholding Republic and Revolutionary Emancipator*

Antebellum Americans divided the Founders between civilians and soldiers, in effect, between Thomas Jefferson and George Washington. Of course, some worthies participated in the Revolution as statesmen and warriors, but most fell neatly into one category or the other. It was, after all, one thing to declare independence by the stroke of the pen and quite another to win it by the force of arms. The veneration of Washington began during the Revolution itself, gained momentum and intensity after his untimely death in 1799, and has never stopped. Washington knew full well that he was a powerful symbol of the new American republic and he consciously crafted an appropriate image. Americans in the 1770s, the 1850s, and the 2010s have delighted in making that image into a larger-than-life myth. In 1858, William C. Preston, a moderate South Carolinian, went to visit the grave of his grandfather, Patrick Henry. Preston was moved by the sight, but he concluded that the statue of Henry at the base of Thomas Crawford's recently erected equestrian statue of Washington on the capitol grounds in Richmond was the "best monument" for his forbear. That the orator stood in the shadow of the neoclassical monument to the general was an apt demonstration of their relative places in the Revolutionary pantheon. It also neatly encapsulated the elevation of the soldier over the statesman, a pattern that was repeated countless times. Regrettably, this "gunpowder popularity," as one disgusted North Carolina Whig called it, retains its sway even today.[1]

"Representation of the Equestrian Statue of Washington, at Richmond, Virginia."
*Gleason's Pictorial Drawing-Room Companion,* April 16, 1854.

Washington towered above all the other Founders in the antebellum American imagination. In 1853, a Boston periodical proclaimed that no other statesman rivaled Washington's integrity and virtue. Those who followed Washington in the White House just did not measure up. In 1851, Pennsylvanian John Doyle wrote a Virginian, paying Millard Fillmore what was the highest compliment possible for subsequent presidents: the New Yorker was the "very best President" since Washington. At the 1858 celebration of Washington's birthday in Charlestown, Eliab P. Mackintire, a Massachusetts Free-Soiler weary of the sectional wrangling over slavery, articulated the de facto credo of many Americans to solve national problems: ask what Washington would do and act accordingly.[2]

Washington's dual role as victorious general and precedent-setting president gave him claim to both sword and pen, though most antebellum

Americans thought of the former first. Schoolchildren were inculcated with the image of the American Cincinnatus from an early age. The *North American Review* noted that it was a truism that Washington's biography ranked as one of the first things every American child learned in school. As Cleland K. Huger Jr., a South Carolina boy, noted with juvenile matter-of-factness: "not long afterwards [the battle of Trenton] Cornwallis surrendered to Washington his army of 7000 men [at Yorktown]. This closed the war." The boy concluded: "Washington resigned the command of the army, and

"Group of Portraits of the Presidents of the United States."
*Gleason's Pictorial Drawing-Room Companion,* June 11, 1853.

retired to Mount Vernon, but he was soon called [to] assume the office of President, and continued in his office, being elected 2 [times]." Washington's transition from military commander to private citizen to chief executive and back to private citizen cemented his preeminent position above the other Founders in the minds of his Revolutionary contemporaries, as well as antebellum Americans (and their modern compatriots).[3]

Antebellum Americans projected their passions onto Washington, tying him to the procrustean bed of sectionalism, making him by turns a disinterested Unionist, a crypto-abolitionist, and a dedicated slavemaster. Washington's words and actions toward his slaves provided grist for all of these mills. Washington owned a large number of bondsmen and profited from their labor throughout his life. He believed that he treated his slaves well and did not want to use violence to maintain discipline, but he frequently resorted to the lash because his slaves resisted via petty theft, indolence, and truancy. Washington realized that his chattels were humans, but he exercised his property rights over them. Nonetheless, Washington had serious misgivings about bond labor and he wished that it would be abolished by state action. In the 1780s, he resolved not to buy or sell additional slaves to prevent the breakup of families. In the early 1790s, he devised a plan to slowly manumit his slaves without financial loss by superior management of their labor. It failed. Although Washington did not liberate his 124 slaves during his lifetime, his will did so after his death and his wife's. While Washington's will made provisions to support his slaves who were too young or too old to support themselves at the time of their emancipation—the last payment on this account was made in 1839—it had no effect on the 153 "dower" slaves on his plantation who were owned by Martha's family. Thus, Washington was a conflicted slaveholder: he exploited his slaves' labor, but did not trade slaves; he attempted to treat his slaves gently, but was compelled to coerce them; he knew slavery was wrong, but he wanted the state to force emancipation on him; he tried to free some of his slaves, but wanted to do so without economic hardship; and he manumitted all of his slaves, but only after he could no longer profit from their labor.[4]

Beginning in the early nineteenth century, American textbooks portrayed Washington's slaveholding as either an example of the Founders' qualms about slavery or the ideal of a paternalistic slaveholder. In fact, modern textbooks still resort to the former by holding up Washington as representative of the Revolutionary generation's concerns about slaveholding. Although Washington was a lifelong slavemaster and a native Southerner, most Northerners (and even a few Southerners) regarded him as an American first. Washington was the "American hero," the *North American Review* declaimed, precisely because he was representative of the nation. Unlike Alexander the Great, Caesar, and Napoleon, Washington did not achieve his greatness because of genius, but because of hard work and "moral consistency." The *New York Herald* agreed. The *Herald* doubted that France's Revolution of 1848 would follow the trajectory of the American Revolution of 1776 because Napoleons were in ready supply, but a Washington was rare indeed.[5]

Sectional ideologues held up Washington as an exemplary slave owner. Whereas pro-slavery proponents saw Washington as a model master lifting up his charges from heathenism and indolence, antislavery activists saw a good man debased by an evil institution. The *Memphis Appeal* lauded Washington for governing his bondsmen with the "mild and patriarchal authority of a Christian master." Not only was Washington "the Father of

Junius Brutus Stearns, *Life of George Washington: The Farmer*. Paris: J. B. Stearns, 1853 (Library of Congress).

Nathaniel Currier, *Washington at Mount Vernon 1797*. New York: N. Currier, 1852 (Library of Congress).

His Country," he was also the father of the slaves of Mount Vernon. George Tucker, Jefferson's handpicked philosopher at the University of Virginia, reversed the abolitionist proposition, arguing that Washington was a typical slavemaster whose exemplary conduct toward his chattels proved slavery to be a virtuous rather than a vice-ridden practice. In an article addressing the planter's perennial problem of managing overseers, *De Bow's Review* adduced Washington's instructions to his overseers as salutary examples for other slavemasters to follow. Like many planters, Washington found that his overseers did not follow his instructions when he was away from his plantation on other business—in his case, leading the Continental Army and then the United States. The tension between the theory and the practice of bond labor also bedeviled Washington's management of his chattels. As with most Southern slaveholders, Washington believed that he treated his bondsmen with characteristic paternalism. However, the systemic and prolonged resistance of his slaves indicates otherwise.[6]

At any rate, a few abolitionists effectively turned this picture on its head. If even so great and virtuous a man as Washington could not manage his chattels in a moral way, they asked, how could the mere mortals of the antebellum South hope to do so? In 1846, a correspondent of the *Liberator* visited one of Washington's slaves, Oney Judge Staines, a chambermaid, who put the lie to Washington's paternalism as a slavemaster (and his piety as a Christian). He reported that Staines "never received the least mental or moral instruction, of any kind, while she remained in Washington's family" so that she converted to Christianity only after freeing herself by running away. Half a century after she had effectively emancipated herself—legally she and her children remained enslaved as she was one of Martha's "dower" slaves—Staines remembered that Washington, a nominal Anglican with De-istic tendencies, did not observe the Sabbath, but instead entertained visitors with "card-playing and wine-drinking." The devout *Liberator* correspondent attributed Washington's lapses to slaveholding rather than disbelief.[7]

Staines was not a disinterested observer of Washington's slaveholding: her dislike of Washington as a master was exacerbated by the fact that he made efforts, legal and extralegal, to enslave her when she served Martha in the Executive Mansion in the temporary federal capital of Philadelphia and to re-enslave her after she had freed herself in 1796 and married a free black man in New Hampshire. As president, Washington had circumvented Pennsylvania's gradual emancipation act, which allowed nonresidents to keep slaves in the Keystone State for up to six months but freed slaves who resided for a longer period, by cynically transferring his slaves out of state for a day to prevent them from establishing a six-month residency. As many others had exploited this loophole, Pennsylvania had amended the gradual emancipation act in 1788 to close it, but Washington ignored this change to the law and improperly kept the slaves he took to Philadelphia in bondage. In addition to violating the Pennsylvania law, Washington also violated the federal law in his pursuit of Staines. The Fugitive Slave Act of 1793 required that the slave's owner or the owner's representatives produce evidence of enslavement (and ownership) to a federal or state magistrate before trans-porting a fugitive slave to another state. On two occasions, the president sent representatives to New Hampshire to entice Staines to return to Virginia (or possibly to kidnap her), but as Martha was Staines's owner, these actions violated the statute that Washington himself had signed into law.[8]

In fact, the factious abolitionist movement debated the virtues of Washington's misgivings about slavery and the vices of his slave-driving. Many abolitionists proudly cited him as an opponent of slavery, implicitly or explicitly exonerating his slaveholding. Some did so innocently. John Bachelder Pierce, a Massachusetts abolitionist working the gold mines of

California, extolled the Founders, especially Washington, for establishing the "Ark of Liberty" in the United States, while at the same time dismissing slavery as a regrettable colonial legacy. The fact that the United States had been a slaveholding republic from its inception was lost on him. Others adduced Washington strategically and a few did so cynically to win support for their unpopular doctrines or to insulate themselves from Southern claims that they attacked Washington as a hypocrite. The pragmatic Frederick Douglass, a fugitive slave cum abolitionist, put the best possible spin on the fact that Washington chose to free his chattels only after he could no longer exploit their labor. The Father of his Country, Douglass poetically explained, "could not die till he had broken the chains of his slaves." Douglass misleadingly implied that Washington was fighting death to free his slaves when, in truth, every breath he took prolonged their bondage. Even William Lloyd Garrison, editor of the *Liberator* and no stranger to controversy or inflammatory language, regretted abolitionist criticism of Washington (and Jefferson) because the pro-slavery press would circulate them to discredit the antislavery movement.[9]

Indeed, anti-abolitionists in the North and the South exaggerated the rare abolitionist criticism of Washington, transforming the exception into the rule. Southern newspapers routinely published poorly sourced accounts of abolitionists denouncing Washington in the most outrageous terms. The *Louisville Courier* claimed that the notorious British abolitionist George Thompson, during an American visit, called Washington a "humbug," while the *New Orleans Picayune* quoted a free black woman as denying that Washington was a "virtuous man" because he was a slaveholder. The *Memphis Appeal* attributed to Massachusetts Sen. Charles Sumner the ridiculous notion that if Washington sought the presidency in 1856, he would have to renounce slavery. Dough-faced newspapers also amplified the few abolitionist attacks of Washington's slaveholding. The Philadelphia *Pennsylvanian* ridiculed abolitionists for being "horror-struck" at the slaveholding of Washington and the other leaders of the Revolution. After all, the *Pennsylvanian* observed, the Founders lived their lives "upon the labor of their slaves." In an effort to whip up anti-abolitionist antipathy and racist rage, the New York *Day Book,* a Democratic newspaper second to none in the North in its abuse of abolitionists, claimed that Charles Lenox Remond, a leading black abolitionist, had said that he would *"spit upon Washington,"* were he still alive, for his slaveholding.[10]

Nonetheless, even a few Southerners took such inspiration from Washington's example as a liberating slaveholder that they manumitted their bondsmen. The *Louisville Courier* routinely adduced Washington (and Jefferson) as advocates of gradual emancipation in its lobbying campaign to get Kentucky to adopt such a provision at its constitutional convention of 1849. On Washington's birthday in 1850, a Louisianan took his thirteen chattels to Cincinnati, just across the Ohio River from the slave South, and set them free.[11]

Other white Southerners were not willing to allow abolitionists to claim Washington for good or ill. Indeed they heaped derision on the idea. The *Southern Literary Messenger* scorned abolitionists for citing Washington (and Jefferson) as "emancipationists" when they were first and foremost Southern planters. *De Bow's Review* agreed. The *Southern Quarterly Review* noted that while the South claimed both the "author of the Declaration of American Independence and the Father of the Republic," that section generously shared them with the North. A year later, the *Review* sneered at those who regarded Washington (and Jefferson) as "good *Unionists*" because they were really good Southerners. In eulogizing John C. Calhoun, William L. Yancey, an Alabama fire-eater, noted that the gravely ill South Carolinian had designated Washington as the "illustrious Southerner" in his last speech in the Senate (March 4, 1850). Yancey took delight that Calhoun's phrase had offended Northerners' patriotism. In his haste to emphasize that Calhoun had claimed Washington for the South, the Alabamian neglected to mention that the South Carolinian had also described the Virginian as "one of us—a slaveholder and a planter," which no doubt pricked sensitive Northern ears as well. Louisa S. McCord, a pro-slavery theorist and slavemistress from South Carolina, asserted that Washington was "a great and good man, a true patriot, a pure man, and, withal, a *slaveholder.*" Indeed, the *Charleston Mercury* faulted Virginia for disgracing Washington's legacy by lagging far behind South Carolina in the defense of the state's right to hold slaves.[12]

Moderate Northerners accepted Washington's slave-owning as a matter of course. In an 1837 Independence Day oration in the Burned-Over District, James R. Doolittle, a New York Democrat, tried to blunt abolitionists' criticisms of the South by asking: "[Who was] first to enter & last to leave the battlefield, who led your fathers shoulder to shoulder & in phalanx . . . [to] victory?" With a sense of irony given his earlier paean that "our government is the freest government on Earth," Doolittle answered, a "Southern

Slaveholder." Trying to silence the chorus of complaints in the North about the Fugitive Slave Act of 1850, the *New York Herald* considered how the first president acted with regard to the issue. While ignoring the very personal stake Washington had in the matter of the fugitive Oney Staines, the *Herald* noted that the "father of his country" had approved of the fugitive slave clause at the Constitutional Convention and signed the Fugitive Slave Act of 1793 into law. Accordingly, the dough-faced newspaper reasoned that he would have supported the 1850 statute as well.[13] It made a convincing case.

While many Northerners excused or ignored Washington's slaveholding vice, at least one abolitionist tried to make it into an antislavery virtue. Theodore Parker, a Boston divine, observed that though Washington was "born a slaveholder," he knew it was "wrong, wicked" and he freed his slaves after his death. In that act, Parker declared, Washington was "superior to his age" and to his section. Most abolitionists could not go that far. The *Pennsylvania Freeman* and the *Liberator* rejected efforts to explain away Washington's slave-driving. The *Freeman* believed that Washington's posthumous manumission of his chattels had hurt rather than helped the antislavery cause. Had Washington liberated his slaves "*in his own life time,*" the *Freeman* reasoned, his salutary example would have "done much to break down the system." The *Liberator* could only scorn Parker's portrayal of the Virginian as a hater of slavery. "If he '*always* disliked slavery—thought it *wrong,* wicked,'" the *Liberator* sneered, "why did he not emancipate [his slaves] as soon as he came of age" rather than waiting until he died? It is a fair question. Between the passage of the Manumission Act of 1782 and its repeal in 1806, Virginia slaveholders freed some ten thousand of their chattels. Although it had been forgotten by the 1850s, one of Washington's (and Jefferson's) neighbors, Robert Carter III, had freed over 450 slaves. While voluntary manumissions were not unusual in the Chesapeake at the turn of the century, when Washington freed his bondsmen, by the 1850s, this was an uncommon practice.[14]

In addition to Washington, a few abolitionists held up another man who also led his nation to independence through force of arms, but whose legacy as an emancipator was less ambiguous than the Virginian's. If, as we have seen in Chapter 1, some opponents of slavery celebrated the First of August instead of the Fourth of July—i.e., Britain's emancipation of some 800,000 slaves in the West Indies instead of the victory of American slaveholders in the Revolutionary War—then others lauded Toussaint Louverture instead of Washington. At first blush, the two Fathers of their Countries were quite similar. They were slavemasters. They led rebellions based on natural rights ideology against the leading military powers of the world. They helped to establish the first two republics in the Western Hemisphere. In an 1825 address, John B. Russwurm, an African American student at Bowdoin College, lauded Toussaint in tones that most Americans reserved for Washington: "He never imitated the conduct of the other leaders in flattering the multitude, encouraging them in crimes, or urging them to revenge and slaughter: on the contrary, mercy, modesty, and order were always inculcated by his words, recommended by his example, and enforced by his authority. . . . That *he never broke his word* was a proverbial expression common in the mouths of the white inhabitants of the island [of Hispañiola], and the English officers employed in hostilities against him."[15]

But Toussaint was no Washington. Or rather Washington was no Toussaint. Where Washington owned slaves, Toussaint had been a slave.[16] Where Washington established a slaveholding republic, Toussaint established a republic of freed slaves. Where Washington defeated the British with the help of the French, the Spanish, and the Dutch, Toussaint defeated the French, the Spanish, and the British with minimal foreign assistance. Where Washington served as an elected officer, Toussaint ruled as a military dictator. Where Washington retired to Mount Vernon to die a peaceful death confident of his success, Toussaint languished in a French cell to die a lonely death before independence was won. Indeed, rather than portraying Washington as a paternalistic master, Russwurm noted that Toussaint was a generous former slave. Indeed, Toussaint had saved his master from certain death at the hands of other revolutionaries and allowed him to immigrate to the United States with his family.[17]

Other abolitionists lauded Toussaint as well. More than three decades later, Wendell Phillips, a Boston lawyer, praised the "patriot-chieftain" of Haiti to much applause in Kingston, Massachusetts. Explicitly making the Haitian liberator the equal—if not the superior—of Washington, the Salem, Ohio, *Anti-Slavery Bugle* asserted that Haitians could justly take pride that no other nation had a leader more noble than Toussaint. If the starry-eyed abolitionists had paused for a moment of reflection, they might have realized that Washington himself would have found the comparison ludicrous on its face. Indeed, so concerned was the first president that American slaves would take inspiration from their brothers in arms (and bondage) on Hispañiola that his administration lent almost $750,000 to the French settlers there to purchase arms, munitions, and supplies to help suppress the rebellion.[18]

Surprisingly, white Southerners were not outraged by the comparison of Toussaint to Washington. Abolitionists and fire-eaters agreed that Toussaint was a great man, just as they both used the misnomer "Santo Domingo" when referring to the French colony of Saint-Domingue. Southerners regarded Toussaint as a moderating influence on the Haitian Revolution. After all, Toussaint believed that Saint-Domingue's economic future (and its political autonomy from France) depended on a return to plantation agriculture. Accordingly, Toussaint welcomed white planters back to their plantations. At the same time, Toussaint compelled ex-slaves to work on the plantations for wages. Toussaint had proved to the satisfaction of Southerners the necessity of coercive labor regimes. Ironically, they transformed the leader of the greatest slave revolt in history into a symbol for the necessity of slavery in the Western Hemisphere. Southerners blamed the excesses of the Haitian Revolution—the destruction of the plantation system, the indiscriminate massacre of whites, the bloody slave insurgency, and so forth—on Jean-Jacques Dessalines, Toussaint's lieutenant and successor. The distinction was invidious as Dessalines continued Toussaint's coercion policy of the freedmen and almost certainly carried out the atrocities against whites with the knowledge—if not on the order—of Toussaint.[19]

While Southerners lauded Toussaint, they were aghast at his revolution. They regarded praise of Haiti as tantamount to a call for servile insurrection in the South. Indeed, Southerners and Southern periodicals routinely warned that the South would be leveled to the status of Haiti—with the "horrors" of razed plantations, exiled whites, and indolent blacks—if the abolitionists succeeded in ending American slavery. In 1860, after the election of a Republican president, Napoleon Lockett, an Alabama slaveholder, predicted that if the Southern states did not secede, the South would be "reduced to the condition of St. Domingo [*sic*]."[20] Seven decades earlier, Washington had shared these concerns.

Although a few Southerners proudly adverted to Washington's slaveholding as yet another proof of slave labor's superiority to free labor, others were sensitive about any criticism of their peculiar institution or their Founding

Father. In 1857, William Buell Sprague, one of the leading ministers in the North, found that even mild criticism of Washington could prick Southern sensibilities. By his own count, Sprague had alluded to Washington's slave-owning in a "single sentence" in one of the dozens of sermons he had published. He found to his surprise (and amusement) that this offhanded remark—a throwaway line—had outraged a Southern gentleman who happened to read it. When the Southerner expressed "kindly" his resentment to Sprague, the famous Northern minister politely apologized for the offense in a letter, but he defended the sermon's obvious (and understated) truth. The "odious sentiment" of Washington's slaveholding provoked a "terrible [epistolary] explosion" from the Southerner, ending all further correspondence.[21]

Even some Northerners resented public criticism of Washington's slaveholding. Isaac Mervine, a Philadelphia policeman, claimed that antiabolitionist rioters had burned that city's "Abolition hall" on May 17, 1838, because of "some inflam[m]atory [pun unintended] speeches made" by the abolitionists—white and black, male and female—that were "derogatory to the character" of Washington. The *Boston Post* claimed that abolitionists had routinely indicted the Father of His Country as the "chief of criminals" for owning slaves, promulgating a pro-slavery Constitution, and presiding over a slaveholding republic.[22] Their successful efforts to smear abolitionists show how powerful the antebellum veneration of Washington was.

Washington's birthday was the only civil (and secular) holiday that rivaled Independence Day on the antebellum calendar. They were ideological bookends of the civil year. Although the contemporary United States has ceased celebrating Washington's birthday in favor of the generic, anodyne, and department store-inspired "Presidents' Day," antebellum Americans reserved the day solely for the Father of His Country. As the *Charleston Courier* observed, the American people, "from Maine to Georgia, from the Atlantic to the Pacific," celebrated the day more or less in the same way. In the morning, cannonade announced the dawn of his birthday. In the afternoon, citizens watched a parade composed largely of militiamen and veterans and then attended an oration that was preceded or followed by a reading of Washington's Farewell Address. In the evening, a gala ball concluded the festivities. Just as pious American Christians displaced Independence Day when it fell on Sunday, so they celebrated Washington's birthday one day earlier when it conflicted with the Sabbath. On Sunday, February 22, reverent Americans went to church, having honored Washington on Saturday, February 21, in the words of a South Carolina planter, in "anticipation of tomorrow." Unlike the Fourth of July, however, the weather tended to be inclement for Washington's birthday, so much so that a Pennsylvanian noted, "unfortunately for the patriots it rains and hails." Indeed, the antebellum era occurred at the end of what climatologists call the "Little Ice Age," which brought frigid temperatures to Europe and North America from 1300 to the 1850s, so there was often snow and ice as well as rain and hail.[23]

Perhaps the most notable feature of antebellum celebrations of Washington's birthday was its overt militarism. Militiamen marched. Veterans paraded. Cannon roared. Some found them amusing. Julia Lord Noyes, a Connecticut woman, chuckled at the sight of local militiamen mustering in her parlor. Some found them tiresome. Josiah Gorgas, an artillery officer in the U.S. Army, was chagrined by the military pomp at an Alabama celebration, especially his participation. Some found them inconvenient. Caroline A. Dunstan, a wealthy New Yorker, was annoyed that the parading soldiers made it difficult for her to use mass transit. Some found it alarming. Margaret Cabell Rives, a student at a Virginia academy, was so frightened by the dawn cannonade that announced the day that she feared some natural catastrophe had occurred. William Johnson Taylor, a Pennsylvanian who was attending school in Alabama, noted that Washington's birthday was celebrated in Mobile by a "show of military law."[24]

The festivities climaxed with an oration and the reading of the Farewell Address. Just as most Fourth of July speakers studiously avoided partisan topics as we saw in Chapter 1, so did February 22 orators. Instead they favored platitudes. The *Charleston Courier* lauded Washington as a "solitary instance" of military genius sans cruelty and patriotism sans ambition who placed the United States "foremost among the nations of the earth." In a comment that applied equally well to most February 22 speeches, *Frank Leslie's Illustrated Newspaper* observed that *"love of country"* powered the Virginian's every move. In 1858, a lyceum in rural Massachusetts considered a question that neatly encapsulates the mood of these celebrations: "Was Washington greater in the camp than in the cabinet?" Thomas B. Drew, an antislavery dentist who participated in the proceedings, noted in his diary that the question was "Decided in the Aff[irmative]" without indicating where the Virginia slavemaster was greatest. Such rococo praise was not just the domain of speakers or lyceums. The students of the Limestone Springs (South Carolina) Female High School successfully petitioned their principal to cancel classes so they could properly honor the "*immortal* and unequalled WASHINGTON" on his birthday. The formulaic speeches became too much for some auditors. With some sympathy, the *Charleston Mercury* noted that the sheer number of "22d of February" addresses made it almost impossible for an orator "to say anything which has not been already said a thousand times." Others were not so forgiving. Matthew J. Williams, professor of mathematics, natural philosophy, and astronomy at South Carolina College, groaned that he "never heard a worse public reading" of the Farewell Address than the one made by one of his students. His grade-sheet for the student's address on February 22, 1853, left little room for praise of any sort: "It was bad in every sense: the points, the pronunciation, the accents, the emphases were miserably conjured & mangled."[25]

Antebellum speakers thought all aspects of Washington's public service were remarkable. In descending order, most of the speakers focused on Washington's military exploits, his refusal to become a king or military despot, his role at the Constitutional Convention, and his precedent-setting presidency. The *North American Review* pronounced Washington as "at least the equal" of Caesar and Napoleon on the battlefield. (Modern historians make far more modest claims for Washington, though there is a lively debate over whether he was an offensive-minded strategist, a defender intent on waging a war of attrition, or even a daring commander who gambled in hopes of winning a decisive victory.) A Southern schoolboy's essay described what was perhaps Washington's greatest virtue: despite possessing "almost absolute power" as the victorious American general, he retired to his plantation in Mount Vernon, "presenting to the world the rare example of a great military chief descending voluntarily to the rank of a private citizen." For this reason, the *Charleston Courier* lionized Washington as the "Father of Constitutional Liberty and Equality" even though he played a largely symbolic role at the Constitutional Convention.[26]

All February 22 orators, except a few abolitionists, ignored Washington's driving (and manumitting) of slaves. They seemed to follow the advice that the *Richmond Whig* offered to defuse sectional wrangling over the slavery issue. Washington understood that the "best way to secure harmony among brothers," the *Whig* observed, was to avoid "irritating topics of discussion." In their haste to denounce British tyranny and American suffering, some

February 22 orators unintentionally broached the subject of slavery. Much as the slaveholding Founders routinely complained about George III enslaving them in the 1760s and 1770s, so slaveholding Americans in the 1840s and 1850s boasted that their forebears had thrown off shackles of British slavery and established the freest country in the world. In 1848, the *National Intelligencer* lauded Washington for achieving the "emancipation of his country from foreign thralldom." Speaking at an 1855 celebration, James D. Davidson, a Virginia Democrat and slaveholder, worried that sectional agitation threatened what he called without irony America's "free institutions," which Washington had established. Thanks in large part to Washington, Davidson extravagantly claimed, a slaveholding republic exhibited an "unprecedented example of liberty & equal rights" in the annals of human history.[27]

Many Americans used the day to decry sectional extremists. David Outlaw, a North Carolina Whig, was so distressed by congressional wrangling over the proposed Compromise of 1850 that he had little enthusiasm for celebrating the day. In a pique of pessimism, Outlaw privately wondered whether February 22, 1850, would be the last time that Americans celebrated Washington's birthday as a "united People." Southern orators denounced secessionists to some extent, but saved most of their vitriol for abolitionists. Declining an invitation to speak at a February 22 celebration in Georgia, shortly after passage of the Compromise of 1850, Howell Cobb, a Georgia Democrat, attacked both the Northern fanatics who made war upon the Constitution that Washington presided over and Southern disunionists who hated the Union that Washington helped create. Cobb echoed many Southerners in warning that to preserve the Union and ensure that compromise was the "final" one, the North must respect its provisions, especially the Fugitive Slave Act of 1850. The *Picayune* agreed. The New Orleans newspaper was appalled that many Northerners denounced the law and a few mobbed to resist it, abusing the very civil liberties for which Washington had fought so long and so hard to secure for the American people. Not only did these Northerners reject the spirit of mutual forbearance that Washington himself embodied on slavery and other contentious political issues, but also their actions imperiled Washington's Constitution, the Union, and the very nation itself. To remedy these evils, the New Orleans newspaper recommended that Americans "return" to the great Virginian's "principles." Although the *Picayune* meant only that Northerners should abide by the compromises that undergirded the Union, it was more accurate than its editors realized.

After all, Washington had pursued a fugitive of his own and he had signed the Fugitive Slave Act of 1793.[28]

The question "What would Washington do?" was a common theme in February 22 orations. Hearing it left Eliab P. Mackintire, a Massachusetts Free-Soiler, nonplussed. In what seems to be a veiled reference to Washington's posthumous emancipation of his bondsmen, Mackintire noted that it was much easier to ask what Washington would do than to actually do as Washington did. Unlike the vast majority of American slaveholders, Washington had manumitted his chattels, significantly diminishing the estate he bequeathed to his heirs. Of course, a tiny few did better than the national patriarch. Rather than profiting from the labor of their slaves their entire lives as the Virginian had, they liberated their slaves during their lifetimes and personally endured the economic consequences. Of course most Southerners and even many Northerners believed that Washington's legacy involved keeping the Union of free states and slave states together rather than liberating slaves. Hannah Robie, a Boston abolitionist, attended a celebration of Washington's birthday that featured Sam Houston, a Texas senator and slavemaster. Despite Houston's reputation for moderation on sectional issues, Robie was unconvinced by his words about Washington's deeds. Indeed, the Yankee thought that the Texan's speech would "make more converts to [the] antislavery [cause] than Garrison."[29]

Many Americans either forgot or ignored the day. In 1855, William Henry Holcombe, a Natchez physician, initially thought the dawn cannonade heralded the arrival of a new steamboat or the departure of filibusters for Cuba, but the "recruiting drum and fife" reminded him that it was Washington's birthday. In 1849, William P. Taylor, a Philadelphia carpenter who was working outside, took more notice of the day's inclement weather than its historical significance. Ten years later, the crew aboard a ship sailing from Philadelphia to San Francisco passed February 22 in the way they had done the day before and the day after. Others perfunctorily acknowledged the day and went about their daily business. In 1850, Frederick Henry Wolcott, a Gotham dry goods merchant, noted: "Washington's Birthday—the usual ceremonies."[30]

As part of the usual ceremonies Washington's Farewell Address was read at celebrations of the anniversary of his birthday. At the same time, Americans from all walks of life and political persuasions invoked it throughout the year. A telling indication of Washington's stature is the high regard antebellum Americans had for his Farewell Address, which appeared in many newspapers on September 19, 1796. In the nineteenth century, it occupied a place next to the Declaration of Independence and the Constitution as one of the iconic founding documents of the United States. Today, of course, the Bill of Rights claims that spot and Washington's Farewell Address has been largely forgotten—the analogue of modern celebrations of "Presidents' Day" instead of Washington's birthday. Ironically, Washington was one of the few distinguished Americans who never delivered the Farewell Address in public. This six-thousand-word document was really an open letter from the retiring president to the American people. In it, Washington warned against letting sectionalism undermine the Union, allowing the military to dominate the civilian government, and forming permanent military alliances. Although Washington never read it, some antebellum Americans celebrated the "anniversary" of its publication or rather, as a New York City newspaper put it, the day it was "dated." A supporter of the Compromise of 1850 advocated compulsory reading of the Farewell Address in every American classroom complete with mandatory rote recitation because its principles were an antidote to disunion.[31]

Indeed, moderates believed that the Farewell Address had an almost magical power to calm passions and ease tensions. Contending that the Farewell Address "cannot be too highly praised," the *Boston Herald* then tried to do exactly that. The *Boston Herald* observed that Washington had presciently warned of the likely dangers to the republic so that Americans might avoid them. Its editors believed it would do Congress good to hear the document read at the beginning of each session. In 1893—thirty-seven years after the Boston newspaper made its suggestion—the Senate made this an annual event and the practice still continues. During the Crisis of 1850, a Connecticut reader suggested that the *New York Herald,* a Northern newspaper famous for its Southern sympathies, adopt part of the Farewell Address as a "standing motto." However, the phrase he selected—"it is of infinite moment that you should properly estimate the immense value of the National Union to Your collective and individual happiness"—lacked pithiness. At any rate, the *New York Herald* did not adopt it.[32]

While the Farewell Address's admonition against "permanent alliances" is the best remembered today and its admonition against "overgrown military establishments" is the most relevant today, it was its admonition against sectionalism that was most often thought of by antebellum Americans.

While Washington was just as worried by East-West tension as by the North-South variety, by the 1850s it was clear what direction the fault lines ran. During the Crisis of 1850, William S. Pettigrew, a moderate North Carolina planter, regretted that his fellow Americans discounted the Farewell Address. Inferring from Americans' "disregard" of Washington's advice, Pettigrew believed that his compatriots thought of the Father of His Country as an antediluvian who held obsolete or even "erroneous" opinions. Alarmed at the disunionist sentiment in his state, Gilbert Lafayette Strait, a young and surprisingly moderate South Carolinian, took solace that there were a few in the Palmetto State who remembered the selfless sacrifice of Washington and the rest of the Founders for the good of the whole nation. Especially after the rise of the Republican Party in 1854, Northern Democrats and Southerners were quick to note that Washington had warned against the "fatal tendency" of a sectional political party.[33]

Both fire-eaters and abolitionists made efforts to invoke the Farewell Address, but it is clear that neither their (nor Washington's) heart was in it. Attacking the Wilmot Proviso in a Fourth of July oration, William Porcher Miles, a South Carolina hotspur, transformed the Farewell Address's attack on factions—i.e., abolitionists—into a defense of slavery. Observing the coincidence of the passage of the Kansas-Nebraska Act and the rendition of the fugitive slave Anthony Burns to slavery in the summer of 1854, James Kendall, a Massachusetts abolitionist, predicted that as long as the South practiced slavery, there could be no true union between the sections. Kendall then adverted to Washington's dread of disunion, observing that the Father of His Country had not only hoped for the "end of slavery" in the United States, but had also manumitted his own slaves.[34]

Even when antebellum Americans referenced other parts of the Farewell Address, sectionalism was usually lurking nearby. Southerners quickly took offense to Lajos Kossuth's efforts in 1851-52 to rally support for American intervention on behalf of Hungarian independence from the Hapsburg Empire in the aftermath of the Revolutions of 1848. Although Kossuth was a sympathetic figure—he had been imprisoned for advocating democratic reforms—and he had purposefully alienated abolitionists by not taking a position on American slavery, his tour alarmed white Southerners. His call for foreign intervention on behalf of the oppressed unsettled Southern slave owners. They had long feared that Britain had designs on intervening in the South to "Africanize" their section, i.e., to place the South "under Negro domination." At the same time, they worried about establishing any sort of precedent in this regard. If the United States intervened on behalf of the Hungarians, they realized, why not Britain on behalf of their chattels? Indeed, Southerners were cool at best to the Revolutions of 1848, and at worst they feared that the doctrines of "red republicanism" in Europe would lead to "black republicanism" in the South. While sympathizing with the oppressed of Europe and desiring the triumph of democracy over monarchy there, Rep. Thomas S. Bocock, a Virginia Democrat, promptly invoked the Farewell Address to justify doing nothing. Making the common mistake of confusing Jefferson's warning against "entangling alliances" in his first inaugural address with Washington's against "permanent alliances" in the Farewell Address four years earlier, Bocock promised to resist "entangling alliances" with European powers. Indeed, Bocock asserted that the United States should avoid interfering with European matters unless the rights of American citizens or the safety of the American republic were at stake.[35]

Just as the Farewell Address reached the zenith of its influence, Alexander Hamilton's widow and one of his sons pressed the New Yorker's claim to be the primary author of that iconic text, precipitating a historical controversy that remains unsettled. In his *Life of Alexander Hamilton* (1840), John C. Hamilton made his father's case in print much to the irritation of many Washingtonphiles. Confident that "controversy winnows truth" from falsehood, George Bancroft, the leading American historian, tried to convince the Hamiltons of the weakness of their position, but to no avail. Privately, Bancroft dismissed the quarrelsome scion as a "monomania[c] on the subject" and rejected his assertions as "foolish." Indeed, Bancroft believed that John Hamilton's ambition was to elevate his father above all the other Founders—to make him the "greatest man of his day"—by degrading Washington as well John Adams, Jefferson, and James Madison. In the final analysis, Bancroft concluded that the first president "tower[ed] majestically above all around him"—including his treasury secretary. Certainly Washington's descendants were not amused by John Hamilton's attempt to add to the aide-de-camp's luster by taking it from the general. George Custis Parke Washington privately claimed to have documents in his possession, including a draft from 1792, which clearly established his step-grandfather's authorship of the Farewell Address. He was confident that "all the thought and sentiments" of the address were the president's. At the same time, the step-grandson generously allowed, "it is probable that the phraseology may have been improved at the suggestion of Genl. H." He also believed that Hamilton himself never made or would have sanctioned such extravagant claims. His generosity was exceptional. All of the other concerned parties regarded the matter as a zero-sum game.[36]

Certainly Southerners were not willing to even share credit for the Farewell Address with a grasping Northerner who had helped to found the New York Manumission Society. The *Southern Quarterly Review* dismissed John Hamilton's claims as "mere impertinence." The *New Orleans Picayune* agreed that it was outrageous to maintain that an antislavery New Yorker actually wrote the slaveholding Virginia's Farewell Address. The *Memphis Appeal* had only contempt for this "absurd pretension." William Gilmore Simms, the leading antebellum Southern writer, fumed that the younger Hamilton's "monstrous" assertion amounted to the proposition that Washington "whittles down" to Hamilton. Although Simms thought the claim of a "secretary, who writes under direction, to be the real author of the letter," was absurd on its face, the South Carolinian worried that his fellow Americans might prize Hamilton's "*smartness*" over Washington's "*wisdom.*" After all, Hamilton knew "what was in books," Simms concluded, but Washington knew "what America needed at the time."[37]

In 1859, Horace Binney, a Philadelphia lawyer, tried to resolve the dispute. In *An Inquiry into the Formation of Washington's Farewell Address*, Binney painstakingly reviewed the correspondence and compared the drafts exchanged between Hamilton and Washington. After this exegesis, the Pennsylvania Whig concluded that it was a joint effort: Washington was the "original designer" of the Farewell Address, while Hamilton was its "composer and writer." While this dispute may seem a bit quixotic to modern Americans who accept as a matter of course that presidents (and virtually all other politicians) employ speechwriters and read words that they did not themselves compose, this was not the case in the nineteenth century. Today the dispute over the authorship of the Farewell Address continues apace.[38]

Mount Vernon was a stately and scenic reminder of Washington that many Americans found more appealing than the dry and dire Farewell Address. The river voyage to the District of Columbia passed by Washington's plantation, making it a sort of tourist attraction from afar. Passengers routinely commented on viewing the "seat of General Washington." As they passed by Mount Vernon, steamboats customarily tolled a bell to honor Washington and to remind their patrons that they were approaching Mount Vernon. *Emerson's Magazine* argued that this "simple, yet beautiful custom" was better than a monument erected in Washington's honor. Putting a positive spin on the embarrassing fact that the Washington Monument in the District remained less than half finished in 1858, the New York periodical reasoned that the musical tribute proved that it was upon the "*American heart,* rather than on marble, that the name of Washington has been inscribed." Many found it to be a moving experience in more ways than one. Just viewing the "most sacred spot in all America" reduced Samuel T. Jones, a South Carolina schoolteacher, to tears. The fact that the steamer's bell tolled the "solemn death-note" indicated to him that Americans "still mourn[ed] for Washington." Steamboat captains who did not honor the tradition faced disgruntled passengers. Julia Lord Noyes, a Connecticut woman, remonstrated that her steamboat's "bell did not toll" as it passed Mount Vernon for reasons that remain unclear to her and to history. Others could only curse the weather, the season, or the time of day for obscuring the view. Samuel Wells Leland, a South Carolina physician, could not cure the disappointment that he and his fellow travelers felt when they realized that it was too dark to see Washington's estate when their steamboat passed.[39]

Antebellum Americans visited Mount Vernon to pay their respects to the "Father of His Country." ("Mount Vernon, the Birthplace and Residence of George Washington." *Gleason's Pictorial Drawing-Room Companion,* Oct. 29, 1853.)

Not content to merely steam past, many Americans made a special trip to Mount Vernon. "In these days of steamboats and rail roads every body visits Mount Vernon," the *Southern Literary Messenger* noted, adding "and they—see everything." Even in the cold and gloom of winter, Mount Vernon charmed Thomas Hickling Jr., an elderly Massachusetts man. In fact, Washington's mansion became a standard stop on the itinerary of many visitors to the federal metropolis, including conventioneers from the American Association for the Advancement of Science. This "pilgrimage"—as Kentuckian Sallie Bullitt put it—excited ecstasy in some. George W. Patton, a Pennsylvania merchant, flushed with excitement when he first set foot on that "sacred spot." So overcome by emotion at the sight of Washington's abode was John Wheeler, a Yankee schoolteacher, that his heart pounded and his legs buckled.[40]

Not all were impressed with Mount Vernon. The mansion's seemingly modern appearance disappointed Mary Robertson, a Kentucky woman. Nonetheless, Robertson took "pieces of wood said to be some of one of the enclosure coffins of Washington." Others were not keen to visit. Despite having served the bulk of two terms, David Outlaw, a North Carolina congressman, had finally decided to go to Mount Vernon only after the fare of the omnibus and steamboat had dropped.[41]

On their visits to Mount Vernon, thoughtful antebellum Americans felt an ambivalence that is familiar to their modern compatriots. The awkward juxtaposition of liberty and slavery that characterized the United States for its first eight decades was put in bold relief at Mount Vernon even decades after Washington had manumitted his chattels. Edith Lukens, an antislavery Pennsylvania woman, regarded Washington as a "great man" and enjoyed seeing his effects. At the same time, however, a visit to Mount Vernon's "negro quarters" tempered her patriotism. Henry Ashworth, a British tourist, who passed by Washington's stately manor, could not help but note that soon afterward he saw fifty slaves "fastened together by Hand Cuffs" en route to New Orleans. A correspondent for *Frederick Douglass's Paper* enjoyed her excursion there until she met a young slave owned by Mount Vernon's owner, John Augustine Washington Jr., a great-grandnephew of the General. The very fact that a man named Washington held slaves on that sacred ground elicited howls of indignation from her. Another correspondent was also shocked to find that Mount Vernon still had a slave population despite Washington's emancipation. His dismay was aggravated by his suspicion that Washington's great-grandnephew had transformed Mount Vernon into a *"slave-breeding pen."* Scarcely a worse charge could have been raised against the memory of Washington than that his estate was part of the domestic slave trade. The entrepreneurs who practiced this commerce, transporting slaves from the Upper South to the Cotton Kingdom, were regarded by most Northerners and many Southerners as morally bankrupt because of that odious traffic's routine separation of children from their parents and husbands from their wives. The indignation of the two correspondents implicitly exonerated Washington's slaveholding, demonstrating how many abolitionists counted the Virginia slavemaster as one of their own. In fact, the distinction between slave owner and slave trader was arbitrary because almost every slaveholder by necessity also traded slaves.[42]

While the presence of slaves at Mount Vernon dismayed only sensitive abolitionists, many visitors were distressed by the fact that the mansion and the grounds had fallen into disrepair. As early as 1828, Leonidas Polk, a North Carolina planter and Episcopal priest, deplored the poor condition of Washington's tomb. By the 1850s, the decrepitude routinely outraged visitors. W. T. Allen, a New Englander, was shocked to see the disrepair into which Washington's tomb had fallen. The shabbiness offended his Yankee sense of order and the indifference his American sense of pride. A Philadelphia woman complained to her merchant husband that Washington's final resting place was "chocked [*sic*] with rubbish." Such criticism fell on Washington's great-grandnephew, though it did so obliquely as no one called him to account by name. Vandals aggravated Mount Vernon's dilapidation. "Unless immediate measures are taken to preserve the mansion," *Frank Leslie's Illustrated Newspaper* editorialized, "it will soon be irretrievably beyond repair."[43]

The taking of "relics" from Washington's estate was commonplace even by those who fretted about the "dilapidated" condition of the house and tomb. The reverence for Washington's tomb expressed by the Yankee schoolteacher John Wheeler did not prevent him from desecrating Mount Vernon. Although he criticized those who had vandalized Plymouth Rock and he had resisted the temptation to take a souvenir from Monticello, the schoolteacher picked up a small rock from the ground near Washington's tomb, rationalizing his actions by saying the pebble was "rendered sacred by its proximity to his tomb."[44]

For reasons that are not clear, in the spring of 1848, the concerns about the declension of Mount Vernon found expression in a seemingly coordinated national petition campaign. Between March and June of that year, dozens of petitions were submitted by congressmen and senators from the North and the South on behalf of their constituents urging the federal purchase of Washington's historic estate. Despite attracting positive newspaper comment, they were generally submitted with only a bland statement of their goal. An exception that proves the rule was the petition presented by Rep. Robert M. McLane, a Democrat from Maryland, which called for the federal government to buy Mount Vernon in order to properly preserve Washington's tomb from the vagaries of private ownership. The House and the Senate referred these petitions to their respective military affairs committees—after all Washington was a veteran—where they died. Due to concerns that such an action, if done solely for the purpose of historic preservation, would exceed the limited powers delegated to Congress by the Constitution, advocates proposed making Mount Vernon into a presidential cemetery or summer residence. (It is worth noting that these two functions are not mutually exclusive, though no antebellum American combined them in an extant proposal.) Predictably, the fire-eating *Charleston Mercury* opposed the centralizing tendencies of putting that "cherished spot" under federal control. As an appropriate state's rights solution, it proposed that Virginia, rather than the federal government, should buy the property. Many distraught visitors wondered why the Old Dominion suffered Mount Vernon to slowly fall into ruin. Virginia, however, could not be shamed into purchasing the property.[45]

As proposals for state or federal intervention were unavailing, a private organization stepped into the breach. In 1853, Ann Pamela Cunningham, a South Carolina woman, organized what became the Mount Vernon Ladies' Association (MVLA) to rescue Washington's estate. Writing as a "Southern Matron" in the *Mercury* and playing on sectional stereotypes of Yankees as moneygrubbers, Cunningham urged the "Ladies of the South" to prevent Mount Vernon from being sold to grasping "Northern capital[ists]" for "money-making purposes." Invoking women's duty to the domestic sphere, Cunningham demanded that they save that Southern idyllic mansion and tomb from becoming surrounded by factories with deafening machinery and obscuring smoke, "where money, money, and only money enters the thought." Despite her initial sectional appeal, Cunningham soon realized that the task was too large—the expense of purchasing Mount Vernon too great—for the women of the South to accomplish alone. So she made the

MVLA a national organization. Rather than aggravating sectional tensions, the MVLA played the role of "sectional mediator," appealing to Washington's love of country in both the South and the North. Predicated on the idea of a distinct female patriotism that was more selfless than the masculine variety, the MVLA was the most famous antebellum women's association.[46]

After an extensive lobbying effort by prominent Virginia women, including the wives of leading politicians led by former First Lady Julia Gardiner Tyler, John A. Washington Jr. allowed the MVLA to purchase the two-hundred-acre estate for $200,000 in several installments. Despite its Southern origins and slaveholder-venerating goal, the MLVA employed many of the same fund-raising techniques as female abolitionists. Both groups organized auxiliaries that operated at the state level. They held fairs, where they sold arts, crafts, and foodstuffs. They sponsored door-to-door solicitation campaigns. They sold tickets to orations. They held benefit theatrical performances. However, the MVLA utilized methods unavailable to their abolitionist sisters due to their superior wealth, connections, and public image. Their activities in this regard ranged from Ellen Key Blunt's dramatic reading of her father's "Star Spangled Banner" to publicly shaming the dilatory members of the Tennessee legislature to make good on their pledge to contribute$100, and from charity balls to auctions of "autograph letters" of Washington donated by a supporter.[47]

The MVLA's greatest fund-raiser was Edward Everett, a scholar and statesman from Massachusetts, who donated the proceeds from a four-year national speaking tour. A former congressman, president of Harvard College, diplomat, and senator, Everett hoped the effort to save Washington's plantation would bridge the sectional divide. Everett, a conservative Whig, had resigned from the Senate under heavy criticism for missing the vote on the Kansas-Nebraska bill because of an illness. Many of his constituents believed that he had feigned illness to avoid voting on that controversial piece of legislation. Symbolizing the increasing radicalization of the Bay State, the legislature appointed Henry Wilson, an antislavery shoemaker, in place of Everett, the pro-South professor. Mindful of the sectional rancor that colored almost every public act, Everett's "Character of Washington" oration extolled Washington's greatest virtue—devotion to the Union. Avoiding reference to Washington's slaveholding—a sensitive topic for both Southern and Northern audiences—Everett focused on Washington as a symbol of national unity. He asserted that the "star of Washington" eclipsed all others, shining the brightest in a time of great men. It shone brighter than those of Frederick the Great, Peter the Great, and Napoleon Bonaparte, Everett reasoned, because they mingled their great achievements with despotism, while Washington returned to Mount Vernon.[48]

Although Everett had drafted the oration for the Boston Mercantile Library Association to commemorate the 124th anniversary of Washington's birthday in 1856, it became wildly popular. In the following years, Everett was inundated with requests for his oration, forcing him to juggle his schedule to accommodate some, while disappointing many others. So hard-pressed was Everett that he decided to give just one address at the University of Virginia in response to separate invitations from Charlottesvillians, the citizens of Albemarle County, and the literary societies of the university. "Almost every part of the country," he privately complained, had sent requests that forced him to make a "*very* extended tour." In fact, he made several.[49]

During these tours, Everett burnished his reputation as the leading American orator. Newspaper correspondents and everyday Americans showered his speech with the same lofty praise he poured on Washington. "Nothing could exceed in force and propriety the material of the address," the correspondent of the *National Intelligencer* reported. Americans both in the South and the North praised it with identical superlatives, regarding it as the best speech that they had "*ever*" heard. At a time when members of Congress literally engaged in fistfights over sectional issues, moderate Americans, including Eliza Gilpin, a Kentucky Whig, found solace in Everett's "true patriotism"—a patriotism that knew no party or section and a patriotism that acknowledged slaveholding but did not glory in it. In Gilpin's eyes, Everett's decorum was underlined by the unseemly brawl in the House that involved some thirty congressmen, which gave added punch to the debates over the Lecompton Constitution.[50]

While pleased that Virginians applauded his speech as warmly as New Yorkers, Everett did not go further south than the Old Dominion until 1858 because of the additional sectional antipathies generated by Rep. Preston Brooks's caning of Sen. Charles Sumner and the Supreme Court's issuance of the *Dred Scott* decision. Despite requests from leading Southerners, including the Alabama fire-eater Yancey, and leading Southern newspapers, including the *Mercury,* Everett went with trepidation, observing, "it is rather a bold adventure for a Northern man . . . to traverse [that far] South." Despite

Everett's concerns, he spoke before rapt and crowded lecture halls, even in South Carolina. Most Southerners saw his campaign as a goodwill gesture on the part of the North for the sake of the Union. Many prominent Southerners sought his presence and those lucky enough to hear him, almost to a person, enjoyed the experience. The climax of his Southern tour was the stop in Charleston on April 13, 1858, which served as a sort of antithesis to the Brooks-Sumner Affair. Instead of a South Carolinian flogging a Massachusetts man, a Massachusetts man lionized a Virginian (and wooed South Carolinians). Everett's appearance in Charleston before two thousand of the state's worthies netted the greatest sum of any of his speeches, a telling indication of Everett's talent for speaking and Cunningham's for organizing, as well as Washington's appeal to Southern slaveholders.[51]

In contrast to Everett's general reception in the South, a few fire-eaters pilloried him as a crypto-abolitionist and a couple dismissed the MVLA as dupes or pyramid schemers. Before Everett courted the Deep South, the *Mercury* instructed South Carolinians to focus on raising funds for a Calhoun monument rather than Mount Vernon. It softened its stance after Everett spoke at Charleston and Columbia. Oscar Lieber, a young hotspur, brushed aside the effect of Everett's lectures in the Deep South with the boast that Southerners' valued their "rights as freemen" more highly than the Union itself. Even in Washington's natal state, Everett and the MVLA came under attack from hotspurs. Roger Pryor's fire-eating newspaper, the *South,* denounced the scheme to have the MVLA repay the Old Dominion for buying Washington's home for $200,000 as the "Mount Vernon humbug." Pryor charged that the MVLA and John Washington were interested in profiting from the state's gullible patriotism. Pryor singled out Everett for special criticism, claiming he was really an opponent of slavery who desecrated Washington's good name. Edmund Ruffin, Virginia's leading fire-eater, joined the fray. Ruffin denounced the project as a "great fraud" and worried that it would set a dangerous precedent that would allow a centralizing state government to purchase the homes of all its illustrious statesmen—an odd concern for an advocate of state's rights. Many Southern critics claimed that Everett had publicly expressed sympathies for Sumner after Brooks's attack when in fact the hapless Everett had been publicly denounced by opponents of slavery for not doing so.[52]

A few abolitionists also objected to Everett's speeches and the MVLA's project. Many opponents of slavery regarded Everett as a "doughface," i.e., a Northerner who did the South's bidding. The *Liberator* was amused by the hotspurs' attacks on Everett for being an abolitionist and a sympathizer of Sumner while he was feted by leading South Carolinians. It believed that his tour on behalf of the MVLA exposed the depths of his servility to the Slave Power. The *National Anti-Slavery Standard* ridiculed Everett's speech for its neglect of the fact that Washington, the "hero of the war for liberty, was supported all the time he was fighting its battles by the forced labor of slaves." Theodore Parker, the Boston abolitionist, faulted Everett for neglecting Washington's "noblest [*sic*] act"—the passage of a gradual emancipation law for Virginia—as well as the liberation of his own slaves. In his haste to make Washington an abolitionist, Parker exaggerated the General's antislavery accomplishments: while the Virginian planter did the latter discreetly, neither he nor his state did anything like the former. At any rate, Everett ignored even Washington's modest antislavery actions because to do otherwise would have required him to acknowledge that the General was indeed a slavemaster. On balance, Everett believed that the abolitionists' attacks "only add[ed] to the enthusiasm" with which he was received in the South. Just as Everett reached out to fire-eaters, he also enlisted some abolitionists in his cause. As events in Kansas Territory began to boil, he spoke at Rev. Henry Ward Beecher's Plymouth Congregational Church in Brooklyn, a notorious abolitionist pulpit and the scene for that pastor's call for Sharps Rifles over Bibles to aid the Free-Soil settlers in that territory. Indeed, Everett spoke shortly after Beecher made his famous appeal for what came to be known as "Beecher's Bibles."[53]

Anticipating modern concerns about the commercialization and exploitation of historic sites, John Washington received much criticism for the high price he put on Mount Vernon. Reversing sectional stereotypes by denouncing a Southerner for being greedy, *Ballou's Pictorial Drawing-Room Companion* accused Washington's great-grandnephew of behavior equal to that of any "nutmeg peddler" by cashing in on the fame of his distinguished ancestor and demanding four times the "intrinsic value" of the estate. The Boston periodical hoped that if the MVLA succeeded, it would then erect a tablet that indicated the "fact of the purchase, the name of the vender, and the price paid." Having greater concerns about Washington's slaveholding, the *National Anti-Slavery Standard* naturally inflated the asking price of the current slaveholder for Mount Vernon. It scoffed at the MVLA's efforts to "buy out" John Washington at "precisely forty times the value" of the plantation. Even before the MVLA was formed the *Mercury* worried about Washington's great-grandnephew's willingness to cash in on his family name and sell Mount Vernon to speculators. The *Picayune* decried John Washington for "extort[ing]" money from the MVLA by artificially inflating the price of the estate. Nonetheless, the complaints came largely from the North. Daniel R. Hundley, a sympathetic Alabamian who met John Washington in the hopes of securing some of his investment capital, complained about the abuse he received from the Northern press for valuing his ancestor's estate at market rates.[54]

The MVLA was largely immune to the sectional conflict that had divided many national institutions, including the leading Protestant denominations, in the antebellum era. Indeed, the leaders of the MVLA took pride in their ability to overcome sectional tensions; they believed the preservation of Mount Vernon was an act to maintain the Union as much as to honor Washington. It was largely the work of moderates in both sections, who eschewed extreme positions on political matters in general and sectional disputes in particular. Samuel B. Ruggles, a New York businessman, assured a Virginia woman that the "friends of the Union" would raise funds for the MVLA "under any circumstances." *Frank Leslie's Illustrated Newspaper* praised the MVLA as a modern analogue to the "patriotic zeal" shown by the female Founders. *Ballou's Pictorial Drawing-Room Companion* lauded the MVLA for having members in twenty-six of the Union's thirty-three states and urged every American to contribute to the fund to save Washington's home and grave from "venal speculation and criminal neglect." Americans from all walks of life answered the call. In 1859, the *Mercury* reported that a Georgia slave, named Maria, donated $1 to the MVLA after overhearing her mistress discuss the matter. The bondswoman declared that the United States was "her country as well as the [free] white people's and that her mother was raised in the vicinity of Mount Vernon, and had witnessed the burial of General Washington." Her mistress noted that "this servant's [sic] one dollar was as much in her station as one thousand would be to those who count their thousands by the score." In that same year, forty-two ordinary Cincinnatians, almost half of them women, sent fifty cents each to the MVLA via Everett.[55]

Ultimately, the MVLA realized its goal. On December 9, 1859, it successfully raised the $200,000 necessary to purchase Mount Vernon. Nonetheless, it continued to raise funds to establish monies to defray the operating expenses of Mount Vernon. Between 1856 and 1860, Everett spoke129 times on the MVLA's behalf and raised, by himself, one-third of the monies. Indeed, Everett considered rejecting his nomination as the Constitutional Union Party's vice-presidential candidate in the Election of 1860 for fear it would undercut or divert his efforts on behalf of the MVLA. Even without his exertions, Massachusetts placed second among the states, behind only New York, in its contributions. In fact, the South lagged behind the North in this effort to venerate a slaveholding Southerner. Only Alabama and North Carolina placed in the top six.[56]

In addition to Mount Vernon, antebellum Americans visited other sites graced by Washington. "Everything relating to Washington," the *North American Review* observed, had "historical interest." In 1850, the State of New York purchased the Hasbrouck House in Newburgh, making it into a sort of Northern Mount Vernon. Just sixty miles from New York City, it became a tourist attraction in the 1850s. The house had served as Washington's headquarters in that area. It was also the site of the famous "Newburgh Conspiracy" (March 15, 1783) where Washington scotched efforts to raise a military coup against the Confederation Congress because of dilatory payments to the soldiers and officers of the Continental Army. For these reasons, Americans who shuddered at the thought of the United States turning into a military dictatorship regarded Newburgh as a "hallowed place" and lauded Washington for "nobly quell[ing]" the proposed mutiny. Moreover, it was the site where the triumphant Continental Army disbanded—just a few weeks after the conspiracy came to naught—thus preserving the American republic and setting the stage for Washington's retirement to Mount Vernon.[57]

Even natural features became sacred because of an association with Washington. Again, most of these were in the North because Washington played little role in the Southern campaigns of the Revolutionary War and because the South had Mount Vernon. Antebellum Americans visited "Washington's Rock," a boulder perched atop a rocky outcropping in Somerset County, New Jersey, which the General in 1777 had "habitually frequented . . . to study out the probable movements of the foe." They visited "Washington's Elm" in Cambridge, Massachusetts, which marked the spot where Washington assumed command of the Continental Army on July 3, 1775. The story of the Washington Elm is apocryphal. There is no documentary or dendrochronological evidence linking man and tree.

The Hasbrouck House in Newburg, New York, became a Northern
Mount Vernon in the 1850s. ("Gen. Washington's Head Quarters at Newburg, N. Y." *Gleason's Pictorial Drawing-Room Companion,* June 5, 1852.)

At any rate, the Washington Elm became a regular stop for tourists to the
Boston area. One South Carolinian visitor proudly reported that he "stood
under the Tree where Gen. Washington first took command of the Army."
Another noted in her diary that she enjoyed the shade of the "first [tree]
under which Washington drew his sword &c."[58]

Americans also thronged the Patent Office to view Washington's personal
effects. The Washington correspondent of the *Louisville Courier* provided
vicarious thrills for those unable to travel to the reliquary. At the top of the
list of "curiosities" was a lock of Washington's hair, followed closely by
his cooking utensils. The *United States Magazine* noted that the "relics" of
Washington, such as his "camp-equipage," were "simple like the man—for
use, not for show." Some who came in person found that it lived up to its
advance billing. Dennis Cooley, a Michigander, reported that the items were

Even natural features, like this New Jersey boulder, became sites of patriotic veneration if they had even a small association with George Washington. ("Washington's Rock, Somerset County, New Jersey." *Ballou's Pictorial Drawing-Room Companion*, Sept. 24, 1859.)

"all cheap, common, and unattractive to most," but dear to him because of their connection to Washington. Others found it a bit underwhelming. Samuel T. Jones, the South Carolina schoolteacher, ticked off the relics of Washington he saw and then concluded that he had left the Patent Office with "about as much satisfaction as most visitors do," i.e., of being able to say that he "had seen it." *Frank Leslie's Illustrated Newspaper* agreed. The New York newspaper believed that the "almost superstitious veneration" Americans paid to Washington's mundane possessions amounted to "relic worship." None of Washington's slaveholding effects—whips, clubs, manacles—were put on display, showing that antebellum Americans were happy to forget this part of his legacy when remembering his greatness.[59]

. . .

In their disputed remembrances of George Washington, antebellum Americans revealed how they saw themselves as much as how they saw the Father of Their Country. The dispute revolved around slavery. Opponents of slavery tried either to make Washington into a proto-abolitionist or to indict him as *the* American slaveholder. In 1854, the *National Era* regretted that the "largest slaveholder" in the South would face a "coat of tar and feathers" for just the mild opposition to slavery made by Washington and the other slaveholding Founders. Of course, most Southerners claimed Washington as a fellow Southerner and some as a fellow slave owner. Many white Southerners believed that slavery had the sanction of Washington as much as it did that of God. The *Southern Quarterly Review* noted that the *"thirteen free and independent* SLAVEHOLDING *States"* had chosen as a matter of course the slaveholding Washington to lead their armies during the Revolution and to lead the federal government after it. The *Richmond Whig* scorned the notion that any American—Northerner or Southerner—in the Revolutionary era would have objected to Washington owning chattels. A Tennessean reasoned that the fact that Washington, the "great spirit of the Revolution," was a slavemaster ipso facto made the United States a pro-slavery nation.[60]

While moderates prized the Union above all else, sectional extremists in both the North and the South quarreled over the extent to which the United States practiced slavery. Moderates ignored Washington's slaveholding just as they ignored the fact that each of the original thirteen states held slaves as well. Instead, they lauded Washington's lack of ambition, military prowess, and political virtue. Distraught by sectional passions and lackluster enthusiasm that bedeviled the commemoration of Independence Day in the 1850s, the *North American Review* suggested an antidote to rally flagging American patriotism: Washington's birthday. Noting the slowly rising Washington Monument in the federal metropolis, several projected statues of the great Virginian in the North and the South, and the national effort to preserve Mount Vernon, the Boston periodical believed that Washington's example was "a bond of union, a conciliating memory, and a glorious watchword." The *Review* recommended making the birthday of Washington a "solemn national festival."[61]

# 4

# Antebellum History Wars over
# the American Revolution

While the Mount Vernon Ladies' Association rushed to preserve George Washington's mansion and plantation, other antebellum Americans erected monuments on the battlefields that marked the progress of the American Revolution: completing them at Groton Heights (1830), Concord (1836), Bunker Hill (1843), and Wyoming (1843), and beginning them at Savannah (1852), Saratoga (1856), Stony Point (1857), Cowpens (1857), Eutaw Springs (1858), and Lexington (1860). They made pilgrimages to the battle sites. They thronged the shrines that held the relics of the Revolution. They honored the aging Revolutionaries and mourned the passing of the great and the rank-and-file. While the Revolution brought Americans together, it also divided them. At the same time Americans shared a common reverence for the Revolution, they quarreled over exactly what it meant. By the mid-1840s, this dispute intensified and became sectional. This struggle over the meaning and legacy of the Revolution was both a flashpoint in the sectional conflict and an earnest exercise in the construction (and deconstruction) of national identity. In the midst of the mania of monument making of the 1830s, 1840s, and 1850s, the North and the South waged a historical war over the battles of the Revolutionary War. Some radical Northerners claimed that the war was fought for natural rights for all, including women, free blacks, and slaves as well as white men. Most Northerners and many Southerners believed that the sacrifices borne by the Revolutionaries in both sections laid a foundation upon which the United States had become the freest nation on earth. Some

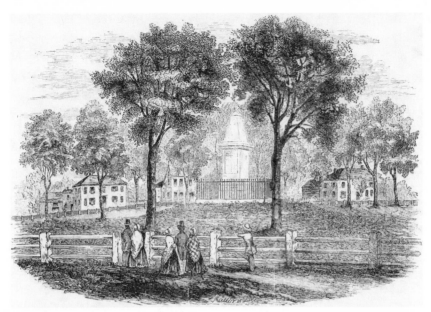

Antebellum Americans erected monuments to many Revolutionary battles, such as this one at Lexington, Massachusetts. ("View of the Monument and Battle-Ground at Lexington, Mass." *Gleason's Pictorial Drawing-Room Companion,* May 8, 1852.)

radical Southerners, however, argued that the Revolution was fought by white male property owners to protect minority rights to property from an overweening majority.

These conflicting understandings of the American Revolution underlay the political strife of the antebellum era. They also made seemingly innocuous events, such as celebrating anniversaries of battles, erecting monuments to the heroes of the Revolution, and writing histories of those events, exercises fraught with controversy. In particular, Southerners resented the fact that most of the historians who wrote about the Revolution were from the North, in particular New England. The *Southern Quarterly Review* chided "New-England historians" who claimed the "whole revolution to have been the work of 'the Saints' of Yankeedom purely." At the same time, Northerners took umbrage at Southern attempts to twist the Founders' antislavery impulses—as modest as they were—into pro-slavery apologetics. The problem, as Preston King, an aggrieved New York Free-Soiler, noted, was that the South had contorted "freedom as the fathers of the Republic understood it [in]to slavery as the modern Slave propagandist proclaimed it."[1]

As Americans had won their independence by force of arms, they could not help seeing the battlefields of their war of national liberation as prelapsarian oases of patriotism and shared sacrifice, even if many of them had rushed past the quaint notions of an agrarian republic based on a white yeomanry. At the same time that Northerners and Southerners argued over whether the United States should be an industrial democracy or a slaveholding republic, they agreed on the salutary effects of viewing "Revolutionary Relics" in situ. Just weeks after John Brown's raid on the federal arsenal at Harpers Ferry, the *Mobile Register* recommended a visit to the recently discovered campsite used by the Continental Army in the Princeton campaign. The holy detritus of George Washington and his soldiers was a calming reminder of the shared "privations and triumphs" of their Revolution. Battlefields then (and now), as historian Edward Linenthal observes, function as "ceremonial centers where various forms of veneration reflect the belief that the contemporary power and relevance of the 'lessons' of the battle are crucial for the continued life of the nation" while at the same time they are "civil spaces where Americans of various ideological persuasions come, not always reverently, to compete for ownership of powerful national stories."[2]

For antebellum Americans, the Revolution was not a distant historical event. It was immediate, intimate, and enduring. Even in the late 1850s, there were a few surviving members of the Sons of Liberty and veterans of the Revolutionary War who gave the struggle against the British a flesh-and-blood presence. Or at least they claimed to be veterans of that conflict. By this time, they commanded attention wherever they were found. Indeed, just greeting a ninety-one-year-old "revolutionary soldier" made a lasting impression on two Massachusetts women on a train bound for Aiken, South Carolina. Communities revered their veterans, no matter how humble their service may have been, as palpable links to the Spirit of '76 and the worthies who declared, fought for, and won American independence. Reporting the death of an eighty-nine-year-old veteran, the *Charleston Mercury* noted that he had been his town's "sole representative of the heroic struggles of the Revolutionary war, and appeared as one of another age and distinct generation." Due to the lapsed time and minimum age requirement for military service, even the youngest of the extant Revolutionaries were octogenarians in the 1850s. A few—a 111-year-old veteran of the battle of Yorkville in Cincinnati in 1847, a 104-year-old veteran of the Mid-Atlantic campaigns in New York City in 1860, a 101-year-old veteran of Bunker Hill in Boston in 1857, and so on—had passed the century mark, attracting national admiration for their longevity as well as their service.[3]

By the 1850s, the Revolutionaries were fighting a relentless foe that took no prisoners, so reports of their deaths outnumbered those of their vitality. Antebellum newspapers peppered their columns with such notices. In summing up the events of 1855, *Ballou's Pictorial Drawing-Room Companion* reported that "73 soldiers of the Revolution have died." In the late 1850s, almost every number of the weekly *Frank Leslie's Illustrated Newspaper* recounted the passing of at least one of these venerable veterans. Almost without exception, it found that they had lived exemplary lives after their service and had "voted in every presidential election" thereafter. These reports reflected the widespread American belief that service in the War for Independence, i.e., expressing the willingness to be killed (and to kill) to secure individual natural rights, ennobled ordinary Americans, transforming them into exemplars for others to emulate.[4]

Of course not all veterans of the Revolutionary War conformed to this ideal. Some experienced the difficulties familiar to veterans of more recent wars: homelessness, substance abuse, and posttraumatic stress syndrome. In 1853, Detroit authorities arrested a 105-year-old veteran, charging him with "vagrancy and drunkenness." Others fought for the wrong side. For the most part, antebellum Americans did not remember, and certainly did not honor, the Loyalists—those Americans who remained loyal to Britain and, in some instances, who even took up arms against their fellow Americans—even though they had comprised a significant fraction of the American population. The exception that proves the rule was the melancholy reflection of Jon Zug, a visitor to the unfinished monument to the dead of the battle of Wyoming (July 3, 1778) in eastern Pennsylvania, a notorious example of Loyalists aiding Amerindians in the massacre of some forty Patriots. The site of the incomplete obelisk over their remains prompted the agent of the Pennsylvania Colonization Society to observe that "there were those who considered the Friends of Liberty 'rebels to their King.' Families were often divided brother against brother & father against son." Nor did antebellum Americans honor the Germans who fought on the British side for money or the former slaves who did so for freedom. Enslaved people who fought for the Patriots, especially those who fought alongside their masters and remained slaves, were another matter. In 1858, white Southerners honored Jerry, supposedly Gen. George Washington's "body servant," who was then 107 years old and resided in Alabama. It was said that Jerry served with Washington in the war and took an "active part in all the battles in which Washington was engaged." As we have seen in Chapter 3, Washington tried to discourage both slave and free black soldiers from serving in the Continental Army and only grudgingly accepted them. There is no evidence to suggest that any of his slaves accompanied him on campaign.[5] That white Southerners tried to rewrite history to make one of Washington's chattels a brother-in-arms shows how important slavery was to their understanding of American nationality.

While they mourned the death of every Patriot, antebellum Americans reserved special grief for the passing of the last participant of any great Revolutionary event. Indeed, as the survivors fell to the side, Americans looked forward with an almost macabre anticipation to the expiration of the last. Perhaps the most eagerly awaited death was that of Charles Carroll, who, after the demise of Thomas Jefferson and John Adams in 1826, became the ultimate signer of the Declaration of Independence. As such, he became the embodiment of that document. Americans honored him in a flurry of eponyms, naming their sons, towns, and counties after him. In 1830, the embattled American Colonization Society, which advocated transporting ex-slaves and free blacks to Africa, sought protection from pro-slavery critics in the South and antislavery critics in the North by making him, at the age of ninety-three, its president. His position was clearly symbolic. Despite his advocacy of colonization, Carroll manumitted only one of his over three hundred chattels (and did not colonize him). In this way, Carroll joined other revered Southerners who occupied that post and remained slaveholders, including James Monroe. Two years later, Carroll died, his apotheosis complete. To commemorate his life, President Andrew Jackson closed the federal government—an honor previously accorded only to Washington, the victorious general and first president. Even the dimming of lesser lights of the Revolution generated similar feelings. In 1852, Americans eulogized David Kennison, a man who had claimed for four years to be the only remaining celebrant of the Boston Tea Party (December 16, 1773). Careful research by modern historians shows that Kennison was a veteran of the War of 1812 rather than the Revolutionary War, and that he was really eighty-eight years of age rather than 115.

Americans were so desperate for Revolutionaries to venerate that they made this down-and-out octogenarian who claimed to have tossed tea in Boston harbor and then fought in the Continental Army in every battle from Lexington to Yorktown into a national celebrity.[6]

After running through the Revolutionaries, antebellum Americans transferred their reverence to their surviving spouses. They lauded the widows of veterans, albeit to a lesser extent than their husbands. In 1857, New Englanders mourned the death of a ninety-nine-year-old widow of a veteran of Bunker Hill. Like modern-day Americans, they preferred to honor veterans (and their families) in parades rather than to provide the far more expensive practice of postbellum support. Despite laborious lobbying, Anne Newport Royall, a widow of an officer in the Continental Army, was repeatedly denied a pension on the grounds that she was married to William Royall in 1797, three years after the cutoff established by Congress. As she made her requests during the depths of the Panic of 1837, her failure hurt all the more. With "the high price of provi[sions,] the scarcity of money, high rents, &c.," she wondered how she would subsist until the next session of Congress. Five years later, Congress awarded her a half pension for ten years. There were literally thousands of women in similar straits. The hope of desperate descendants to receive some sort of financial assistance for their family members' service extended well beyond widows. On the eve of the Civil War, an Indianan wrote his congressman to see whether the fact that his grandfather had been wounded at the battle of Guilford Court House (March 15, 1781) would qualify him to receive a pension. The descendants of famous Revolutionaries tried to cash in on their forebears' celebrity. Over a half century after his death, the "heirs of John Paul Jones" tried to get Congress to pass a special bill for their relief, but, as their lobbyist reported, the bill was *"lost on the floor."*[7]

Of course, the widows of leading Revolutionaries received greater acclaim than did those of mundane Patriots. The widows of Elbridge Gerry, a signer of the Declaration (but remembered today for "Gerrymandering" an electoral district in Massachusetts in 1812 as that state's governor), James Madison, a drafter of Virginia's Statute for Religious Freedom during the Revolution (but remembered today as the principal author of the Constitution and Bill of Rights), and Alexander Hamilton, an aide-de-camp to Washington in the Revolutionary War (but remembered today as the first treasury secretary) were so honored. Ann Gerry, who died in 1849 at the age of ninety-six, was remembered as the last widow of a signer of the Declaration. In this way, antebellum Americans were able to extend their vicarious connection to that sacred document seventeen years past Carroll's death. Dolley Madison had earned lasting fame for her grace, wit, and savvy as First Lady and afterward. In particular, Americans lauded her bravery during the British occupation of Washington, D.C. (August 25, 1814), during the War of 1812. After her husband died in 1836, she moved to the federal metropolis and, despite suffering financial difficulties, entertained many prominent visitors. She was widely regarded as the last link to the Founders. Virginians mourned her death in 1849 and countless dignitaries attended her funeral in the federal capital. Just as Madison's widow had achieved almost celebrity status in the South, so "Old Mrs. Hamilton" had done so in the North. Indeed, Elizabeth Hamilton was "universal[ly] admir[ed]." In 1848, a twenty-eight-year-old Gothamite described the nonagenarian woman as an unprecedented "specimen of juvenile antediluvianism"—and she would live six more years! American periodicals followed her movements and issued breathless reports, describing her as a "relict of the Revolution" and a "model woman." When she died, she had survived her husband—who had been killed by Aaron Burr in a duel on July 12, 1804, at the age of forty-seven—by fifty years.[8]

This transfer of Revolutionary glory was not reserved exclusively to wives. It extended to sons, grandsons, and even granddaughters. Implicit in this process was the notion that the descendant, like the spouse, possessed at least a fraction of the virtue, love of country, and courage of their Patriotic forbear. When antebellum Americans mourned the death of George Washington Lafayette in 1850, in essence, they resumed mourning his father, the Marquis de Lafayette, who fought with the Patriots in the Revolutionary War and had died sixteen years earlier. When the *Charleston Courier* remarked that Charles Carroll was "third in descent from CHARLES CARROLL, signer of the Declaration of Independence," it was explicitly making him a personification of that historic document. When Hughes Hillard, a Virginia congressman, in a letter of recommendation, noted that the young man in question was a "grandson of Patrick Henry," he was explaining the source of the prospective cadet's "fine promise, and moral habits," which suited him for appointment to the U.S. Military Academy at West Point. So great was this desire to experience a vicarious Revolutionary thrill that it trumped vivacious current ones. In 1849, Martha Stanard, a Virginia woman, chose to visit the "Misses Hamilton, the granddaughters of Genl. Hamilton" rather than attend President Zachary Taylor's inauguration—unintentionally slighting the son of a veteran who had served with Washington for the granddaughters of another.[9]

Of course, having a glorious forbear had its drawbacks. For one thing it often required descendants to attend events where their chief function was to sit, smile, and bring to mind their ancestor. In 1859, Josiah Quincy, the son of the distinguished Patriot of the same name who had defended the British soldiers involved in the "Boston Massacre," declined an invitation to a celebration of a Revolutionary event. As an eighty-six-year-old man with poor hearing, he was not enticed by the "prospect of sitting, three or four hours, in the open air at this season of the year." Having an eminent forebear also tended to raise expectations beyond—often far beyond—the reach of most descendants. (Social scientists call this phenomenon regression to the mean.) It provided a convenient and exacting ruler against which to measure the living, pitting marble and bronze against flesh and bones. Nathaniel Henry, Patrick's youngest son, died, as the *Baltimore Sun* put it, destitute "without money, friends, or resources of any kind." Such a comparison was particularly easy and invidious when both descendant and forebear were dead and unable to defend themselves. A year and half after John Quincy Adams died on the floor of the House of Representatives, a Southerner denounced him for "sell[ing] his birthright and bring[ing] reproach upon the memory of his honored father" by making common cause with abolitionists. This critic believed that Adams the younger had failed in his efforts to attack the slave system because his constituents in Massachusetts, "the land that was moistened with the first blood of the Revolution," remained true to the slaveholding republic that they had helped to found. Admonishing the dead and ignoring his antislavery accomplishments, such as ending the notorious Gag Rule in 1844, he said that Congressman Adams should have been satisfied with the "observance—in spirit and letter—of the Constitution" rather than consorting with its enemies.[10]

It was not just descendants who lived (and died) in the reflected glory of the martyrs and saints of the American Revolution; their friends did so as well. When John Mason, a Georgetown merchant, died in 1849, the *New Orleans Picayune* eulogized him largely because he had been a "personal and intimate" friend of Jefferson, Madison, and Monroe. When George Coryell, a New Jersey veteran of Monmouth, died at the age of ninety-four in 1850, he was lauded as much for being a "confidential friend of Washington" as for his military service.[11]

So prevalent was this notion of inherited patriotism that antebellum Americans trumpeted their distinguished genealogies and pressed historians to do so as well. Samuel Breck, a prominent Philadelphia merchant, was so proud that his father played a (minor) role in the Revolutionary War that he boasted of his father's extant correspondence with "*John Adams, Benjamin Franklin* and many others." One American, distressed by previous scholars' failure to give his grandfather his historic due for being the first American to haul down the Union Jack in the early days of the Revolution, beseeched George Bancroft, the leading American historian of the United States, to remedy this mistake. To his credit, the grandson admitted he wrote to "gratify the natural pride" of his grandfather's descendants as much as to correct the historical record. Like many priority claims in history, it is unclear exactly how such an assertion could be proven. Indeed, the issue seems to be what a later historian of the British colonies identified as the "*fallacy of absolute priority.*" At any rate, Bancroft continued the slight in his *History of the United States.* In much the same vein, the town of Acton, Massachusetts, claimed the first three men "who fell by British Bullets in the Revolutionary War." Since they did fight at Lexington, it is possible that Acton does have this distinction.[12]

Not all of the interested genealogists were historical dilatants. William H. Prescott, one of the leading historians in the United States, repeatedly dunned Bancroft about who had commanded the Patriots at Bunker Hill. The great historian of Spain hoped to secure support for his contention that his grandfather, Col. William Prescott, was the "true commander at the Battle of Bunker Hill" or the "actual commander in the redoubt." Despite his anxiety, Prescott waited—not always patiently—eight years for the disappointing answer that his grandfather had to share credit with Israel Putnam and Joseph Warren. Prescott took the news gracefully, thanking Bancroft for doing "entire justice to my grandfather" while at the same time "giving due praise to Putnam & Warren." In a pique of penitence, Prescott confessed that "it was a difficult story to tell, considering how much it has been disfigured by feelings & personal rivalry & foolish pretension. . . . For the last 30 years or more the friends & kinsmen of the prominent chiefs of the action have been hunting up old revolutionary survivors . . . extorting from them such views as could carry no conviction to a candid mind."[13]

.   .   .

While many Americans claimed every battle of the Revolution as part of their shared legacy, locals held proximate ones, even if they were modest affairs, most dear. In 1857, Gothomites formed the Stony Point Association to erect a monument on that battlefield, commemorating Anthony Wayne's surprise attack on a British garrison on the night of July 15-16, 1779. Despite the ballyhoo, the battle was of little import. Although Wayne's initial audacity at Stony Point earned him the sobriquet "Mad," even he was not so foolhardy as to hold on to the position in the face of overwhelming British numbers. So the Americans abandoned the fort just a couple of days after taking it. Nonetheless, antebellum New Yorkers made the most of it. On the battle's seventy-eighth anniversary, they laid the cornerstone for the monument with fanfare and pomp. In the following year, in much the same way, South Carolinians commemorated the battle of Eutaw Springs, a desultory skirmish famous chiefly for being the last battle of the war fought on the Palmetto State's soil. On the battle's seventy-seventh anniversary, Charleston's Washington Light Infantry erected a monument in honor of William A. Washington, who was captured after leading an unsuccessful but daring cavalry charge against the Redcoats, to show appreciation for the "simple virtues and heroic courage of those who illustrated Southern manhood & secured Southern liberty."[14] In truth, the monument in South Carolina, like the one in New York, honored futility as much as bravery.

Revolutionary battlefields fascinated antebellum Americans much as Civil War battlefields do modern Americans. On a trip to his native New England, a federal officeholder left Washington City to retrace the route of the British troops retreating from Lexington and Concord eighty years earlier. Upon visiting the King's Mountain battlefield in that same year, emotion overwhelmed a South Carolina woman who considered the privations her "forefathers" endured to obtain independence. The battlefields had special resonance for veterans of subsequent American wars. In 1849, Capt. John W. Phelps, who saw action against the Seminoles and the Mexicans, revered Bunker Hill as a sacred spot where liberty nobly fought oppression. It was not necessary to visit the battlefields to be susceptible to these impulses. In 1850, Frederick H. Wolcott, a dry goods merchant, privately observed the anniversary of the battle of Bunker Hill at his home in New York City.[15]

Of course, not all were moved. Many antebellum tourists put the Bunker Hill Monument on their itinerary, but few spent much time reflecting on the bravery of the soldiers, the carnage of the battle, or its place in the war. Most enjoyed the superb view of Boston it afforded. Some were disappointed to find that there was no "conveyance" to its top. In 1850, a group of Pennsylvanians gamely made the ascent, though they feared they "would give out twenty times" before reaching the top.[16]

A few visitors to the Bunker Hill Monument were underwhelmed. In 1842, Charles Lyell, the British geologist, surveyed the monument. Not inspired by the Pyrrhic victory of his red-coated forebears seven decades earlier or the igneous rocks that comprised the monument, Lyell thought the unfinished obelisk looked like a factory chimney. Five years later—after the monument's eighteen-year construction was over—*Yankee Doodle,* a satirical New York periodical, ran a cartoon that echoed the Briton's assessment. Mocking both immigrants and Gotham's rival city of Boston, *Yankee Doodle* depicted a German who mistook a factory chimney for the Bunker Hill Monument. In that same year, a correspondent for the *National Anti-Slavery Standard* chided "this funniest of all possible nations" for "glorify[ing] the time and the place of a *licking* they once caught."[17] This was American exceptionalism of a different kind.

Several Revolutionary battles had a regional, and a few even a national, appeal: Lexington and Concord as the first; Bunker Hill as the North's Thermopylae; King's Mountain and Cowpens as the South's decisive victories over the British and the Loyalists; and Yorktown as the last. While Massachutians, South Carolinians, and Virginians generously shared the battles with their respective sections, they retained special claim to them. This smug sense of entitlement grated on others. As one Georgian complained in 1846: "a man from Massachusetts is prouder than one from Connecticut. And a South Carolinian is haughtier than a Georgian, because there have been more battles fought in the former than in the latter. A Massachusetts man, see him where you will, looks and feels like he was a cap stone of the Bunker Hill monument. And a S. Carolinian supposes that when you see him it naturally reminds you of [King's Mountain,] Eutaw, and the Cowpens."[18]

While Massachutians took pride that Lexington and Concord were the "soil that drank the very first blood of the martyrs of liberty," they were not alone. Even the South celebrated Northern battles, at least initially. In 1841, a Charleston militia company celebrated the anniversary of the battle of Lexington—"when the sons of New England first watered with patriot blood the young tree of liberty." But the *Charleston Courier* noted the South's role, observing that the tree "bloomed in glory and clustered with the fruits of final victory on the field at Yorktown."[19]

While Lexington and Concord were first, Bunker Hill was the iconic Revolutionary battle of the North. It was not immediately obvious that this American defeat would be so well regarded in subsequent decades, but both Northerners and Southerners claimed it. In fact, Bunker Hill was the archetype battle of American history—what historian Tom Engelhart calls the "mobilizing" defeats that serve as "preludes to victory." Before the sectional conflict polarized the antebellum remembrance of the American Revolution, many Southerners lauded Bunker Hill. In 1850, the *Baltimore Sun* observed that the anniversary of Bunker Hill was a "National festival." Just a visit to the obelisk rekindled the patriotism of John B. Minor, a Virginia college professor. In 1852, the *New Orleans Picayune,* noting the near coincidence of the anniversaries of the battles of Bunker Hill and Waterloo (June 16 and 18 respectively), asserted that the American defeat was more important than the British victory. Attempting to justify this absurd solipsism, the *Picayune* reasoned the "skirmish on Bunker Hill" made the grand Napoleonic defeat possible because the Americans demonstrated it was possible to resist tyrants.[20]

Even incomplete, the Bunker Hill Monument served as powerful symbol of national unity. During the run-up to the Election of 1840, Hugh Swinton Legaré, a South Carolina Whig, accepted the invitation made by his Massachusetts partisans to attend a rally beneath the growing obelisk. Legaré took delight in pilgrimaging to the "*Mecca* of our Independence." In 1849—before the sectional controversy passed the point of no return, but after the monument had been completed—even the *Charleston Mercury* could link Joseph Warren, the martyred hero of Bunker Hill, with George Washington, joining a Northerner with a Southerner in the common effort of winning American independence.[21]

Although these patriotic rites were largely the preserve of men, women played an important role. Just as they had done in the effort to preserve Mount Vernon, American women took the lead in fund-raising for the Bunker Hill obelisk as well as other monuments. Just as women played the key role in raising funds for worthy causes of various sorts—ranging from abolition lecturers' traveling expenses to clothes for the indigent—their efforts were crucial for the eighteen-year ordeal necessary to crown the obelisk. In doing so, they were able to stay largely within the domestic sphere. While selling homemade crafts and foodstuffs, local women raised money to finish the Bunker Hill Monument. One admitted that she felt "somewhat out of [her] *sphere perched* up behind the table selling articles to the highest *bidder*"—and entering the public sphere of commerce—but she decided that she could "do almost anything in a *good* cause." At the "great fair" she and her petticoat patriots across Massachusetts raised some $30,000—an incredible sum, especially considering the nation was mired in the Panic of 1837—exceeding their goal by 10 percent. At another Bunker Hill fair, a Southern observer was astonished at the diligence of "those delicate [middle-class] women . . . toil[ing] from morning to night, and from Monday to Saturday, with a constancy and effort of shop women." Two years *before* the monument was completed, he believed that they were Bunker Hill's new heroes.²²

In place of the North's Bunker Hill, Southerners celebrated the battle of King's Mountain (October 8, 1780), a conflict along the South Carolina-North Carolina border between Patriots and Loyalists. The former won a resounding victory, making it what the *Mercury* called the "Mecca of our liberties." Reverent South Carolinians by the thousands made the hajj to the upcountry every October. In 1855, David Wyatt Aiken, a Palmetto planter, who lived along the route from Charleston to the battlefield, marveled at the "large crowds of soldiers & citizens" who passed through. As South Carolina's iconic battle, it was thought improper to defile its anniversary with partisan harangues. When ambitious "demagogues" broke this unwritten rule and used the battlefield as a backdrop for a political campaign, they received a just rebuke from outraged public opinion.²³

As the last major battle of the Revolutionary War and the occasion of a humiliating surrender of a large British force to American forces, the battle of Yorktown (October 19, 1781) was an unequivocal Patriot victory. Certainly, it was regarded as such by subsequent generations of Americans. Nonetheless, the pivotal role played by French forces on land and at sea in cornering Gen. Charles Cornwallis on the York peninsula and laying a three-week siege, as well as the fact that two more years of negotiating in Paris would be necessary before the war ended and the Americans won their independence, stripped some of the élan from this battle. While Yorktown was not forgotten, it was not universally celebrated either. Indeed, by the mid-1850s it had been relegated to being essentially a Southern battle.

To combat this distressing trend, the *Picayune* recommended in 1854 that the anniversary of the battle become a national day of commemoration. Nonetheless, six years later, *Frank Leslie's Illustrated Newspaper* pointedly observed that white Southerners exclusively mourned the death of a ninety-seven-year-old veteran of Yorktown.[24]

Some Americans, especially Westerners, remembered that Amerindians played an important role in the Revolutionary War. Some Native Americans fought with the Patriots, but most fought against them. On an 1843 trip from New York City to Pennsylvania, a traveler stopped by the nearly completed monument to the "Wyoming Massacre" (July 3, 1778). The battle, which took place near Wilkes-Barre, pitted Patriots against Loyalists and their Iroquois allies. Construction of the monument began in 1833, when a cornerstone was laid over the remains of the Patriot dead, but did not conclude until 1843. The westward traveler was irritated when his companions did not show sufficient patriotism when passing by that sacred spot.[25]

Because of the paucity of battles fought in the West, many Westerners offered battles from the French and Indian War, the Northwestern Indian Wars, or the War of 1812, as substitutes. They celebrated their ancestors' participation in the battle of Monongahela (July 9, 1755), where Amerindians and a smattering of Frenchmen routed Anglo-American forces, killing 430 and wounding 550. Although "Braddock's Defeat" was the greatest Amerindian victory over an Anglo-American army, Americans took pride in it, if for no other reason than Washington was one of the American militiamen who fought and suffered defeat there. Indeed, one old man took vicarious credit for the service of his grandfather with the "great and good Washington" there. In 1858, Pittsburghers celebrated the "first *centennial anniversary*" of the Anglo-American victory over the French three years later, which resulted in the construction of Fort Pitt, and the de facto beginning of their city. In doing so, they spared no expense, importing historian George Bancroft from the East to speak. At the same time, Americans visited battle sites of conflicts that pitted white Americans against the British and their Native American allies, like the battle of Tippecanoe (November 7, 1811). They were right in doing so. In effect, this battle was part of an ongoing war between the United States and Northwestern Amerindians that raged from 1776 to 1815.[26]

Unlike modern Americans who have largely forgotten the War of 1812 or dismissed it as a "failure," antebellum Americans, especially those in the

West, remembered it as the Second War for Independence. Westerners erected statues and monuments to its heroes just as Easterners did to the First War for Independence's. Clevelanders celebrated the anniversary of the battle of Lake Erie (September 10, 1813) with cannonade, picnics, and orations. Although involving only a modest number of vessels—just fifteen in all—the battle was significant as it allowed the United States to control the strategically important Great Lakes. Both sides took heavy casualties, but Commodore Oliver H. Perry's men defeated the entire British squadron, prompting him to famously report: "we have met the enemy; and they are ours—two ships, two brigs, one schooner, and one sloop." On September 10, 1860, Westerners erected a statue to Perry with the requisite fanfare, including a battle reenactment. Like Pittsburgh, Cleveland summoned Bancroft for the occasion. The Clevelanders spoke for their section, but made a national appeal to the Eastern historian: the "people of the West claim you as national property." Indeed, the mayor of the city keenly wanted the American historian to speak at the inauguration of the statue because "everybody in the West wants to see him." Bancroft did not disappoint. An Easterner who made a trans-Appalachian journey to see the statue inaugurated was impressed by the historian's eloquence and the crowd's size. Five weeks later, one of the surviving veterans of the battle wrote Bancroft thanking him for the oration and offering firsthand corrections to the historian's account of the battle.[27]

The battle of Lake Erie was not the only War of 1812 clash commemorated by antebellum Americans. New Orleanians celebrated the Eighth of January like all Americans did the Fourth of July. In 1859, a Yankee architect working in New Orleans noted in his diary: the "day was ushered in by the booming of cannon as usual." Moreover, veterans of the battle marched and militia of the city paraded. In fact, the *Picayune* self-consciously admitted that Louisianans held the "glorious Eighth" more dear than "even our birth-day as a Republic." Like all Americans in the 1810s, they believed the fact that Andrew Jackson's ragtag force of five thousand defeated the cream of the British Army almost twice their number in stunning fashion on January 8, 1815, proved that a large standing army was unnecessary in a republic because a free people "will rise to crush an invader." So great was the enthusiasm of New Orleanians that the Crescent City carried on with the celebrations despite occasional epidemics of cholera and yellow fever.

Though the Eighth of January was celebrated by all in New Orleans, it had partisan overtones elsewhere—as Democrats lustily celebrated it in honor of Jackson—and was only sporadically honored beyond Lake Pontchartrain. The occasional New England village celebrated it. So did New York City.[28]

During the monument mania of the 1850s, New Orleanians erected an equestrian statue to Jackson in what became Jackson Square. They had planned, of course, to inaugurate the monument on the anniversary of Jackson's improbable victory, but shipping delays led to a postponement until February 9. Nonetheless, an immense crowd, including a "great number of ladies," turned out to enjoy the ceremonies. The crowd, estimated to be in excess of twenty thousand, was so large that only a small fraction could hear the orator. At any rate, the day was bright and sunny and the festivities were capped with a one-hundred-gun salute (which was presumably audible to all). The appeal of Jackson's victory was felt not just by Louisianans. En route to the Crescent City in 1857, A. H. Kingman, a New England sailor, marveled as he sailed past the battlefield. In addition to being a symbol of American independence, Jackson was an antidote to sectionalism, especially that of the Southern variety. After all, he was a Southern slaveholder who had resisted South Carolina's attempts to nullify the federal tariff in 1832-33 with the threat of military force.[29]

Some Easterners visited War of 1812 battlefields and honored that conflict's commanders as well. In 1859, Julia Marsh Patterson, the Georgia teenager, visited the site of the battle of Lundy's Lane (July 25, 1814) with her parents and shuddered at the thought of the fierce contest. As it is near Niagara Falls, countless tourists viewed it each year. Americans also journeyed to Fort McHenry in Baltimore, which was, as *Ballou's Pictorial Drawing-Room Companion* observed, a "spot dear to every American" for resisting British efforts to bombard it into submission. Antebellum Americans used the bravery of its garrison as their descendants have done, i.e., to exonerate the American forces who allowed the federal metropolis to be occupied and the government's buildings razed. In 1853, Newport, Rhode Island, held a "grand celebration of the birthday of Commodore Perry," its native son. By the 1850s, all American communities honored War of 1812 veterans on July 4 and February 22, if not on any other day. A few began to mourn the passing of veterans of the War of 1812 as they had done for two decades for those of the Revolutionary War.[30]

. . .

As sectional tensions grew more intense in the 1850s, Northerners and Southerners clung more tightly to the Revolutionary icons from their respective sections. As Massachusetts had played a key role in the struggle against British tyranny and was taking a similar role in the struggle against the Slave Power, abolitionists likened their battle against slavery to the Sons of Liberty's defiance at the Boston Tea Party, the minutemen's bravery at Lexington and Concord, and the Patriots' determination at Bunker Hill. For their part, fire-eaters likened their efforts against the opponents of slavery to their forebears' against George III. For example, one Southerner compared the Wilmot Proviso to the "tax on tea." Moderates repeatedly reminded extremists of the shared sacrifices that were necessary to achieve independence. During the Crisis of 1850, the *Cincinnati Commercial,* which traded across the Ohio River to slaveholding Kentucky and much of the South, chided Americans to disregard Northern and Southern fanatics and remember that Northerners and Southerners were a "band of brothers" during the Revolution. In 1851, the *Louisville Democrat,* which from a downriver vantage looked back across the river to free Ohio, made the same appeal because the American republic was the "hope of every true friend of liberty throughout the world." As late as 1858, the *Memphis Appeal* reminded fire-eaters that American independence could only have been achieved by the "common efforts and united energies of all the colonies." In the Patriots' struggle for Liberty, the *Appeal* claimed, "Southern men fought on Northern soil, Northern men fought on Southern soil." Accordingly, the *Appeal* urged patriotic Southerners to "fight for our rights *in* the Union and not *out* of it."[31] Even though the *Appeal* made the common mistake of calling the newly independent states "colonies," its historical analysis was spot-on.

Abolitionists likened their refusal to comply with the Fugitive Slave Act of 1850 to that of the colonists in the Boston Tea Party or the Patriots in the battles of Lexington, Concord, and Bunker Hill. Theodore Parker, a Boston abolitionist, called the rescue of Shadrach Minkins on February 18, 1851, the "noblest deed done in Boston since the destruction of the tea in 1773." Henry David Thoreau, abandoning his nonviolent stance, determined that an armed mob's attempted rescue of Anthony Burns on May 26, 1854, which resulted in the death of a guard, was bloodier and more heroic than the Boston Tea Party. As the latter was a symbolic act of property destruction, while the former was a haphazard act of violence, the comparison was ill conceived. While Burns was not liberated, both the United States and Massachusetts were forced to muster soldiers to escort him to a steamboat in Boston harbor, which returned him to bondage in Virginia. Eight thousand Bostonians lined the streets in protest. Proud of this achievement, Melissa Bryant, a Bay State abolitionist, boasted that it took two thousand soldiers to enforce that odious law in Boston. Bryant attributed the state's abolitionist activities to the fact that Massachusetts's soil was "hardly dry with the blood-stained struggles of the Revolution." Consequently, "the time will come," she predicted, "when Massachusetts citizens will stand between the fugitive and United States [soldiers'] sabers."[32]

Staking an African American claim to the first battles in the struggle for American independence, abolitionists noted that American blacks, enslaved and free, fought at Lexington, Concord, and Bunker Hill, and were victims of the Boston Massacre. The *Liberator* was delighted to learn that Crispus Attucks, the "first martyr," was likely a fugitive slave. That a runaway slave helped strike the "*first* blow for liberty" revealed to abolitionists just how un-American the Fugitive Slave Act was. Indeed, as early as 1851, opponents of slavery attempted (and failed) to get state funding for a monument to Attucks on Boston's State Street.[33]

Theodore Parker, the abolitionist minister, repeatedly wrote to George Bancroft correcting the historian's account of Lexington and Bunker Hill in his *History of the United States.* The minister—who practiced what he preached by violating the Fugitive Slave Act—thought that the historian should note that one of the Americans killed at Lexington in defiance of British tyranny was a "*Negro*" and two other "*Africans*" were "*fighting in*" the battle. Surprisingly, Bancroft did. The historian reminded his readers—most of whom would have blanched at the thought of African Americans bearing firearms—that "free negroes of the colony" fought at Bunker Hill and in other battles. Moreover, Bancroft noted they fought in fully integrated units—a feat that the United States would not manage again until the Vietnam War nearly two hundred years later. Nonetheless, Bancroft did commit a sin of omission. Not all of the black soldiers who fought were freemen. Some were enslaved. "On the subject of bondage," even his sympathetic biographer Lilian Handlin acknowledged, "Bancroft said little," and, it might be added, he wrote even less.[34]

Bancroft also omitted the fact that Washington prohibited the enlistment of black soldiers a few months after Bunker Hill. When reminded of this fact by a rhetorical question posed by the dogged Parker, the historian curtly replied, "Washington did not forbid the enlistment of negroes, on the contrary he sanctioned it, subject to the approbation of Congress." At best, this was an incomplete answer. In fact, the historical reality is complicated: on November 12, 1775, Washington purged his army of black soldiers—five days after Lord Dunmore's proclamation promised freedom to bondsmen who took up British arms against their rebellious Virginian masters—to placate anxious Southern slavemasters. However, by 1778, with the recruitment of white soldiers lagging, Washington accepted black soldiers who had been mustered by the states. This was an episode that many antebellum Americans were happy to forget. Most Northerners shuddered at the notion of blacks bearing arms even in the militia, while most Southerners regarded their exclusive right to bear arms as a necessary precondition for slave patrols. Many states had explicitly disarmed both slaves and free blacks. By mid-century, a few radical abolitionists advocated that slaves use firearms to resist slavery, striking a nerve. In the eighth volume of *The History of the United States,* which was published just one year before the Civil War began, Bancroft avoided the topic. In just a few years' time both the United States and the Confederacy would arm former slaves—just as virtually all slaveholding regimes have done during wartime.[35]

Apparently unaware that African Americans—freemen and slaves—fought in the early battles, fugitive slave turned abolitionist editor Frederick Douglass likened the three fugitive slaves who precipitated the Christiana Riot (September 11, 1851) to the minutemen at Lexington solely on the grounds of their willingness to shed blood in defense of liberty. It was a fair point. At Christiana, Pennsylvania, blacks, free and fugitive, killed one Marylander and wounded another who had tried to render their three wayward chattels under the auspices of the Fugitive Slave Act across the Mason and Dixon Line. Even moderate opponents of slavery adverted to the minutemen to justify their resistance to slavery. On June 22, 1854, Free-Soilers in Concord mustered their forebears to join in their opposition to the Kansas-Nebraska Act. "The citizens of Concord, whose fathers were among the first to resist the tyranny of 1775," they promised, "will not be the last to resist that of 1854."[36]

Abolitionists also used the early battles of the Revolutionary War, especially Bunker Hill, as markers for freedom's halting progress, noting that slavery's oppressive reach, especially the odious Fugitive Slave Act, encompassed even the battle's monument. Promoting his plan for African Americans, free and enslaved, to move to Canada to escape the pervasive racial discrimination in the United States, Henry Bibb, a Kentucky fugitive slave who had found liberty in Canada, observed that Georgia fugitives Ellen and William Craft were not safe from their master beneath the "shadow of Bunker Hill monument (which was consecrated to Liberty!)." Instead the famous fugitive couple was forced to "flee Boston to England for liberty"—inverting the traditional American narrative of the geography of freedom. A Mainer visiting Boston was outraged by the recent arrest of the fugitive Thomas Sims on April 4, 1851, and his rapid rendition to bondage in Georgia. Those who defied the law felt fear as well as outrage. Melissa Bryant, the Bay State abolitionist, took a special interest in both the legal niceties and the moral implications of that notorious statute. Bryant harbored a nine-year-old fugitive from South Carolina, remonstrating that the girl "could not be protected near Bunker Hill." Freedom did not always stumble. Encouraged by a petition sent to the Massachusetts legislature advocating the repeal of the Fugitive Slave Act, a Massachusetts abolitionist wanted to use the obelisk as a symbol of a state's defiance of federal law. Weary of hiding fugitives, he looked forward to a time when a self-emancipated slave could stand atop the Bunker Hill Monument to proclaim to the world that he was a *"freeman."*[37]

As the sectional storm intensified, it lashed Bunker Hill. Beginning in the late 1840s, abolitionists held up that battle as a symbol of resistance to tyranny comparable to the efforts of abolitionists and slaves against the Slave Power. Some invoked Bunker Hill privately, taking solace in the fight against oppression. While traveling in rural Arkansas, Corydon E. Fuller, a Hoosier peddler, privately fumed about the fulminations of some of his slave-driving customers. Although not an abolitionist before going to the South to sell atlases door-to-door, Fuller became one in short order after meeting numerous masters, who were confident that their slaves were the "happiest creatures . . . on earth." After one of his patrons indulged in an anti-Yankee (and pro-slavery) harangue, the successful but nonetheless frustrated salesman muttered to himself that if civil war came, Southern slavemasters would find "another Bunker Hill" when fighting free Northerners. Fuller's mistaken impression that the Patriots won that battle was common then and now. Well aware that the Patriots lost the battle, abolitionist Theodore Parker nevertheless lauded Sen. John P. Hale, a Free-Soiler from New Hampshire, for attempting to present a petition for the abolition of slavery in the District of Columbia on December 22, 1847. Hale had unsuccessfully challenged the Senate's decision to automatically table such petitions—a kind of mini-Gag Rule—prompting Parker to compare Hale's lone defense of the constitutional right to petition the government as exceeding the bravery of those who fought at Bunker Hill. Although Parker's praise was hyperbole, Hale had struck a telling blow. Northerners and Southerners attached great "symbolic importance" to the presence of slavery in the nation's capital. It drove home the undeniable but often forgotten fact that the United States was a slaveholding republic.[38]

Others invoked Bunker Hill publicly. In 1856, Republicans scheduled their first national convention to meet in Philadelphia on the anniversary of the battle. In that same year, Lucy Stone, an abolitionist and women's rights advocate, compared Margaret Garner, a fugitive who tried to kill her children and herself rather than return to slavery under the auspices of the Fugitive Slave Act, to the Patriots who defended Bunker Hill. It was an apt comparison. Just as the Patriots ultimately ceded Bunker Hill to George III's minions after suffering heavy losses, so Garner managed to kill only one child, her two-year-old daughter, before she and the remainder of her family were consigned to servitude in Kentucky. Three years later, the *Liberator* used similar rhetoric to describe John Brown's quixotic attack on a federal arsenal in Virginia. Despite the fact that its pacifist editor opposed the Harpers Ferry Raid, the Boston newspaper lauded Brown as a "second Warren" and the ragtag rebellion as the "Bunker Hill of our second Revolution." With the advantage of hindsight, it was a fair analogy: both conflicts were initial defeats for an ultimately triumphant liberty and both leaders were martyred for the "glorious" cause.[39]

Not all opponents of slavery were prepared to make as heroic a resistance as Garner or Brown. So abolitionists also used Bunker Hill to inspire the timid. In 1855, the fugitive-turned-abolitionist Frederick Douglass believed that someday the people of Massachusetts would be as proud of their ancestors who participated in the rescue of the fugitive Jerry McHenry in 1851 as they were of those who had fought at Bunker Hill in 1775. During the skirmishing between Free-Soil and pro-slavery settlers in Kansas Territory in 1856, Boston abolitionist J. H. Webb longed for a contingent of Kansas emigrants imbued with the "true Bunker Hill spirit" to keep slavery from expanding westward.[40]

The symbolism of Bunker Hill, however, cut both ways. After all, most Northerners neither opposed slavery nor respected African American rights. These conservative Northerners held up Bunker Hill as an icon of a herrenvolk democracy and slaveholding republic. After a racist mob razed Prudence Crandall's integrated school in New Hampshire in 1834, a local newspaper regarded the smoldering heap as a "monument of the folly of those living spirits, who are struggling to destroy what our fathers have gained"—i.e., a white man's democracy. It argued that the school was the obverse of the Bunker Hill Monument, which had been "erected in memory of those departed spirits, which fought and fell, struggling for Liberty." Boston abolitionist Theodore Parker's claim that he was motivated by the ideals of those who had fought at Bunker Hill dumbfounded the *Boston Herald* because his abolitionism would tear apart the Union, which the Patriots had sacrificed everything to cement.[41]

Even secession-minded Southerners took inspiration from Bunker Hill. Speaking at the 1860 Democratic National Convention in Charleston, William Lowndes Yancey, the "prince of the Fire-Eaters" from Alabama, called for the "Cotton States" to secede and fight a "Bunker's hill, to drive the foe from the city." Like Corydon E. Fuller, the Indiana peddler, Yancey forgot that the Patriots lost that battle and only drove the British from Boston by adroit placement of artillery on Dorchester Heights nine months later. Yancey would also have to wait. Although he would lead the withdrawal of Deep South Democrats from the convention in a few days' time, another seven months passed before the formation of the Confederacy.[42]

Because of Bunker Hill's location in Massachusetts—considered the storm center of antislavery fanaticism—and its appropriation by abolitionists, some Southern defenders of slavery belittled the battle and mocked the monument. In 1852, Josiah Stoddard Johnston, a Kentucky teenager, visited the battlefield. Johnston left unimpressed, reducing the monument to a "tall pile of rocks." In a public but no less juvenile assessment, the *Southern Quarterly Review* dismissed New England's initial struggles against British tyranny as evidence of their devotion to self-interest rather than liberty. Trafficking in the regional stereotype of the grasping Yankee, the *Review* claimed that the New England Patriots were not courageous but "selfish." Showing a poor grasp of military and economic history, the *Review* wrongly asserted that they fought at Bunker Hill because New England had become Britain's rival in manufacturing.[43]

Rejecting the notion that the obelisk was a pole on the sectional spectrum, most antebellum Americans regarded it as a symbol of pan-sectional unity. During the furor over the status of slavery in the Mexican Cession, the *Louisville Courier* assured its readers that the overwhelming majority of New Englanders were not abolitionists and predicted that the "land of Old Bunker Hill" would allow the Southern institution into at least a part of the land taken from Mexico. During the ensuing Crisis of 1850, Sen. Daniel Webster, a Massachusetts Whig, used the monument as the backdrop for his exhortation for patriotic Northerners to support the Fugitive Slave Act. Webster's endorsement of this law—the North's key concession to the South in the Compromise of 1850—transformed him from a sectional irritant to a national statesman in the eyes of many white Southerners. On the seventy-fifth anniversary of the battle, Webster urged "every true American" to join him in "stand[ing] between the assaults of extreme factions and the Constitution" and to "uphold the CONSTITUTION as it is, and the UNION as it is."[44] Of course, Webster meant to maintain the United States as a slaveholding republic.

Seven years later, moderates again used the monument to quell sectional antagonisms in a way that favored the slaveholding status quo by erecting a statue of Gen. Joseph Warren, a Boston physician who died defending Bunker Hill, next to the obelisk. Rather than making Warren a hero of Massachusetts, New England, or the North, the speakers, headlined by Edward Everett (who interrupted his speaking tour on behalf of the Mount Vernon Ladies' Association for the occasion), explicitly cast him as a national figure. Among the dignitaries invited to inaugurate the statue was President James Buchanan of Pennsylvania, the quintessential "Northern man with Southern principles." Buchanan was derided by many abolitionists as a "doughface"—a Northerner who did the South's bidding. The president, who had just months before endorsed the notorious *Dred Scott* decision, was thought to be just the man to bridge sectional strife by appealing to conservatives in the North and the South. "Warren no more belongs to Massachusetts," the president declared, "than the Father of his Country belongs to Virginia." Both were Americans, Buchanan intoned, who knew no section while fighting the British.[45]

Joining Buchanan and Everett on the dais were Southerners and other Northern doughfaces, including Rep. Robert Winthrop of Massachusetts and Sen. James M. Mason of Virginia. These two legislators had played nearly opposite roles in the sectional crisis that culminated in the Compromise of 1850. The attempt by the Northern majority to make the nominally Free-Soil Winthrop Speaker paralyzed the House for three weeks in December 1849, which served as the opening salvo in the nine-month effort to pass the compromise; for his part, Mason authored the infamous Fugitive Slave Act, the compromise's most controversial provision. If these two could put aside their differences and appear arm in arm, moderates reasoned, surely all well-intentioned Americans could do so as well.[46]

Many did. Having passed under a banner that read "Our Whole Union" on his way to the statue's inauguration, Eliab P. Mackintire, a Massachusetts Free-Soiler, enjoyed listening to the "union-saving" orations with several thousand others. The *Boston Herald* approved. Forget sectional disputes, the *Herald* instructed all patriots, and "go back to the fountain head of our civil and religious liberty, and be baptized anew." Certainly Everett did his best. Even in private correspondence to his friend South Carolina historian William H. Trescot, Everett ducked the issue of slavery. In response to Trescot's question about *Scott v. Sandford,* Everett confessed that not only had he not read the decision, but also that he shrank from the "subject in all its bearings" because of its disunion potential. Others accepted the terms of this arrangement with as much ease and thought as breathing. Caught up in the patriotic waves, A. H. Kingman, a New Hampshire sailor looking for work, serenely observed that the inauguration of the Warren statue was a "great day in Boston." Mason charmed the pro-South *Boston Post,* which declared his speech to be "appropriate, eloquent, and national," notwithstanding the wretched excess of the sectional legislation he authored. Southerners also enjoyed the ceremony. Gov. Henry A. Wise of Virginia assured Everett that Virginians savored his address.[47]

Such pro-slavery moderation left abolitionists nonplussed. When local authorities prevented the descendants of black veterans who had fought at Bunker Hill as well as an abolitionist descendant of Warren from joining the procession, the *Liberator* cried foul. If the exclusion of descendants who did not fit the white pro-slavery profile outraged the *Liberator,* then the presence of the "author of the Fugitive Slave Law" disgusted Garrison's newspaper. Thomas B. Drew, an antislavery dentist from Massachusetts, believed that it was ridiculous to hear Mason speak of "American Freedom, &c., knowing what and who he is, and how little he has ever done for Freedom." Abolitionists did not spare the Northern doughfaces either. The *Liberator* denounced Everett as the "man ready to buckle on his knapsack and shoulder his musket to shoot down the slaves of the South, whenever they shall venture to imitate the example of Warren!" It indicted Winthrop in similar terms.[48]

As the sectional crisis deepened, some white Southerners began to celebrate a parallel list of battles and heroes. Just as they held up the North Carolina's Mecklenburg Declaration—an act of filiopietistic forgery as we shall soon see—as trumping the Declaration of Independence, so they replaced Lexington and Concord with Fort Moultrie (June 28, 1776) and Bunker Hill with King's Mountain and Cowpens (June 17, 1781). Eventually, they purged Northern battles and generals from the Southern pantheon of Revolutionary fame. At the 1854 anniversary of the South's "Lexington," one South Carolinian toasted that battle as the "bright spot in the expanse of our country's history," putting it above mere Northern battles. In truth, the battle of Fort Moultrie was more important than the battles of Lexington and Concord. When the militiamen at Fort Moultrie fired on nine British ships on June 28, 1776, they repelled an invasion of Charleston and perhaps much of the South (while the militiamen at Lexington and Concord did not save Boston from British occupation). The fort had been hastily constructed of green Palmetto logs and sand, which repelled British cannonballs. In honor of this resistance, South Carolina adopted the Palmetto as its symbol and celebrated June 28 as "Palmetto Day." While King's Mountain could not lay claim to Bunker Hill's mantle, South Carolinians still held it most dear. Just as Southerners lauded Washington as a Southerner, so they elevated Francis Marion, the South Carolinian "Swamp Fox," above his Northern counterparts. William Gilmore Simms, a South Carolina writer, disappointed a compatriot seeking a relic of the Swamp Fox by informing him that even Marion's autograph was impossible to obtain. Georgian William K. Pillsbury had to solace himself with the memory that one of his forebears "fought with Marion" at Eutaw Springs.[49]

Many Southerners excised Northern battles and heroes with reluctance. At the 1859 celebration of Forefathers' Day at the New England Society of Charleston, one speaker acknowledged there was a "romantic chain around Bunker Hill, Fort Moultrie, Lexington, Camden, Princeton, Savannah, Monmouth, King's Mountain, Brandywine, [and] Yorktown," but insisted that those "hallowed associations" should not blind Southerners to the menace posed by their erstwhile allies against Britain. He asserted that most Northerners opposed slavery and many were "out-and-out John Brown and Garrett [*sic*] Smith abolitionists," alluding to the Harpers Ferry raider and one of his financiers.[50]

In the 1850s, there was a flurry of monument erection, or at least the laying of cornerstones, on Southern battlefields. In 1852, one was placed at Savannah in honor of Casmir Pulaski; in 1857, another at Cowpens; and, in 1858, still another at Eutaw Springs in honor of William Washington. This was due as much to shame as pride. Observing that "other states" had built "worthy monuments" to their Patriot forebears, the *Mercury* called for a monument at King's Mountain. That a Boston periodical and a New York newspaper agreed only added to Palmetto shame. At the same time that they removed Northerners from their battles, white Southerners removed the United States from their collective memory. Instead of a union of thirteen states bravely resisting Britain, they fancied it was an alliance of convenience of the states, or at least, the sections. They used anniversaries of Revolutionary battles to drive their revisionist history home. At Charleston's 1854 celebration of the battle of Fort Moultrie, one fire-eater toasted: "The Southern Confederacy: The only union to which the sons of the Palmetto will owe allegiance." In preparation for the 1859 commemoration of the battle of Eutaw Springs, a group of Charlestonians lauded the courage of those who "secured Southern liberty," making it clear that it was Southern rather than American liberty that was at stake.[51]

Because Massachusetts boasted of Lexington and Concord and abolitionists made the Declaration of Independence unappealing, Southerners gave their section priority in the American Revolution by dating its beginning *before* July 4, 1776, if not April 19, 1775. At the meeting of the '76 Association during the 1850 Independence Day celebration in Charleston, James Gadsden—three years before negotiating his eponymous land purchase from Mexico—toasted the fact that South Carolina "struck the first blow for independence" at Fort Moultrie. Not content with claiming the Declaration's author as a native son, Virginia was keen to honor its own contribution to American independence. In the early 1850s, professors at the College of William and Mary underlined the fact that Virginia had declared its independence on June 29, 1776—"*five days in advance*" of the national Declaration. Thus their commonwealth antedated the American Union. A clear implication of Old Dominion's priority in declaring independence was that the simple act of secession would restore Virginia to its natural state.[52]

Not all Southern claims for Revolutionary priority were valid. In their haste to claim an important role in beginning the Revolution for the Tar Heel State, many North Carolinians adverted to the "Mecklenburg Declaration of Independence," which purportedly declared American independence over a year before Jefferson's. Towns across North Carolina read the Mecklenburg Declaration as well as or in lieu of the Philadelphia Declaration as part of their Independence Day celebrations. Nonetheless, the evidence for the Tar Heel State's claim is threadbare. The Mecklenburg Declaration was first published in the *Raleigh Register* on April 30, 1819, within an article written by Joseph McKnit Alexander. Alexander claimed that representatives of militia companies in Mecklenburg County were so inspired by word of the battles of Lexington and Concord that on May 20, 1775, they passed a set of resolutions that asserted their independence from George III. The North Carolina militiamen were alleged to have used language in several places that was amazingly similar to Jefferson's Declaration. Moreover, the document itself is not extant. Alexander's father had been the clerk at the meeting and so it had fallen to him to keep the Mecklenburg Declaration. The original had been destroyed by fire in 1800, but Alexander claimed to have memorized it verbatim.[53]

At its publication in 1819, Jefferson immediately pronounced the Mecklenburg Declaration a Federalist fraud designed to deny him priority for penning the first American declaration of independence. Most modern historians agree, though they believe that Alexander himself was well intentioned. They suspect that Alexander attempted to summarize from memory resolutions passed on May 31, 1775, that anticipated a reconciliation between Britain and the colonies, and that along the way, he had inadvertently incorporated language from Jefferson's Declaration into the Mecklenburg Declaration. Although evidence of the May 31 resolutions had been found in 1838, antebellum North Carolinians refused to concede the error and steadfastly maintained that their state was first in declaring American independence. Indeed, their devotion to the spurious declaration only intensified as the sectional conflict worsened. After reading the Mecklenburg Declaration at an 1857 Independence Day celebration in New Bern, a local dignitary defended it from Northern "traducers." He asserted that the Mecklenburg Declaration had awakened the colonies from their "dreamy slumbers of thralldom," making the Tar Heel State the "birthplace" of the United States. He noted that Virginia, South Carolina, and Massachusetts had also covered themselves in glory during the Revolution, but insisted that North Carolina would not be denied its rightful place alongside them.[54]

Unsurprisingly, George Bancroft, the leading antebellum historian of the American Revolution, and Henry S. Randall, the biographer of Jefferson, were drawn into the dispute. Although Bancroft apparently had intended to expose the Mecklenburg document as a fraud, the historian had a change of heart. In his magisterial *History of the United States,* Bancroft devoted a paragraph to the matter, concluding, "thus was Mecklenburg county, in North Carolina, separated from the British empire." At least one of his correspondents—Virginia historian Hugh B. Grigsby—could not believe Bancroft's conversion from a skeptic of the Mecklenburg Declaration into a defender, concluding that the newspaper report was erroneous. Unfortunately for both, it was Bancroft who had succumbed to falsehood, not the newspaper. Randall, a New Yorker who had only recently renounced Free-Soilism, faced a dilemma: he worried about offending Southern readers by dismissing the North Carolina document, but at the same time, he wanted to refute the charges bruited by fire-eaters that Jefferson was "guilty of plagiarisms." Randall discreetly asked for Bancroft's assistance on this sensitive subject. Upon learning of Bancroft's decision to affirm the authenticity of the dubious document but to minimize its importance, Randall complimented his discretion. With the confidence that he was not going to be out of step with Bancroft, Randall included the "Mecklenburg Declaration of Independence" in an appendix at the end of the last volume of the biography, commenting that "there is nothing at all noticeable" in the similarities between the two declarations. "Any man might use as his own such collocations of words as 'free and independent,' 'all political connection,' etc., in 1776, or at any time before or since," Randall asserted, "without the imputation of plagiarism."[55]

Perhaps inevitably, the sectional struggle over the meaning of the American Revolution led to a historical controversy over the roles of the two sections played in the Revolutionary War. While this dispute has been covered by professional historians, its significance has not been fully appreciated.[56] Although there had been intermittent sparring over the matter for decades—including an exchange on the issue in the famous Webster-Hayne debates of 1830—the controversy began in earnest in the late 1840s, when several Northern historians, especially Lorenzo Sabine in *The American Loyalists* (1847) and Richard Hildreth in *History of the United States* (1851), cast doubt on Southern military prowess during the conflict. Adding insult to injury, Sabine attributed the South's laggard behavior to the natural conservatism of slavemasters. This tendency, Sabine claimed, was aggravated by Lord Dunmore's proclamation, which offered liberty to slaves who resisted rebel masters in Virginia. Sabine had the facts on his side: uncounted thousands accepted Dunmore's offer and a similar offer made by Sir Henry Clinton in 1779 before invading Georgia and South Carolina. Indeed, far more African Americans fought *for* the British than fought against them and many other black slaves from the West Indies joined the fight against the Patriots as well. Facts be damned, white Southerners regarded Sabine's assertions as a thinly veiled attack on American slavery and Southern honor.[57]

Moreover, Free-Soilers and abolitionists applied the same arguments to the second War of Independence as well as the first. As early as 1841, the Free-Soil *New York Tribune* noted that Massachusetts alone supplied more soldiers to the Continental Army than all the Southern states combined (67,907 vis-à-vis 59,335). Citing this historical fact fifteen years on, the *Liberator* taunted, "South Carolina, with a Northern army to assist her, could not even preserve her own capital from falling into the hands of the British." In a speech against the annexation of Texas, Byron Paine, a Wisconsin Free-Soiler, reasoned that slavery made the South the Achilles' heel of the United States. Paine pointed to Southern weakness in both the Revolutionary War and the War of 1812. In the former, Paine claimed that Massachusetts was forced to "rescue" South Carolina from "the British and negroes and tories" who had "overrun" the state. In the latter, Paine observed, "our [national] capital was laid in ashes because slaveholders could not defend themselves at the same time from their slaves and the British."[58]

As white Southerners began to read the histories of the Revolution written by Northerners, they detected a distinct anti-Southern (and pro–New England) bias. They found that some Northern historians diminished or even ignored the role played by the South in winning American independence. During the wrangling over the Compromise of 1850, a South Carolinian complained that when Northern historians deigned to notice the South's contributions in the Revolutionary War, they gave it in the "briefest and driest possible details." Sensitive Southerners believed that the problems with

Northern histories went beyond omission. The *Southern Quarterly Review* complained that "our histories are slurred over by Yankee historians, the most important truths suppressed; our heroes receive but cold applauses, and our relative claim to rank with sister States is constantly disparaged by false glosses and misrepresentations." Three years later, the *Mercury* denounced those Northerners who had "belitt[ed]" Southern sacrifices to the Revolutionary cause. Comparing two iconic battles of Massachusetts and South Carolina, the *Mercury* noted that while Bunker Hill was a signal defeat for the Patriots and Fort Moultrie a great victory, Northern historians depicted the former as a "grand era" and the latter a "successful skirmish." These concerns were largely confined to intellectuals. Everyday Southerners snapped up Northern accounts of the Revolution as quickly as steam-presses printed and steamboats carried them. Because a "plantation is a monotonous place," a Southern woman was grateful that Robert Sears's *Pictorial History of the American Revolution* (1846) "will occupy some time." For exactly the same reason, another Southern woman "prise[d]" another Northern book on the Revolution "very much indeed."[59]

More worrisome still to white Southern intellectuals was the way the Revolution was portrayed by Northern history textbooks. While Northern historians besieged historical truth and wounded sectional pride, Southern intellectuals fretted that Northern textbooks imperiled young Southerners. For several decades they had rued the fact that the "school-books of the South *originate* in the North." Muscoe Garnett, a Virginia fire-eater, declared, "the Southern mind will remain in bondage so long as Southern children are supplied with Yankee school books." Anticipating modern battles over textbooks, the *Mercury* called for Southern history textbooks to remedy the slurs, falsifications, and perversions of Northern productions. The *Mercury* decried the fact that Southern schools and libraries were filled with "the fabrications of Northern writers, in which Bunker's Hill is held up as the greatest achievement of the Revolution—nay [as] the Revolution itself—while [Fort] Moultrie, and King's Mountain, and Cowpens, and a score of other Southern battles, are almost ignored, or perhaps treated as instances of 'shameful imbecility.'"[60]

Southern concerns about the pernicious effects of Northern textbooks extended far beyond history to *mathematics*. The *Southern Literary Messenger* feared that a "large collection of abolition cosines and antislavery hypothenuses [*sic*]" were gathering for a frontal assault on Southern math. In response to these concerns, Daniel Harvey Hill, an Alabama mathematician, wrote an algebra textbook for exclusive use in Southern colleges because it suited the "wants of our Southern institutions." It is unclear whether Hill meant the South's institutions of higher education or its peculiar labor system. The proud author boasted that his *Elements of Algebra* was "southern in its character [and] southern in its problems," making no mention of the fact it was published in Philadelphia![61]

Just as some Southern intellectuals defended bond labor as superior to free labor, so others claimed the South won independence for all of the United States with little assistance from the North. Just as the conceit that slavery was a positive good returned the moral attack on slavery made by abolitionists, so the notion that the South won the war returned the charge of cowardice back to the North. Some Southerners argued that the South had led resistance to British tyranny from the Stamp Act to Yorktown. Rather than the North coming to the aid of the South, the *Southern Quarterly Review* argued, it was exactly the other way around. Massachusetts was "outlawed and her port of Boston was shut" by the Intolerable Acts, the *Review* observed, while the South suffered little from British tyranny in the 1770s. Nonetheless, "*we* took up arms, in *her* quarrel." While acknowledging that Northern generals aided the South in repelling the British invaders, the *Review* claimed that the only battles the South lost occurred when Southern forces were led by "Northern Generals," such as Benjamin Lincoln of Massachusetts at Charleston. In contrast, the *Mercury* confidently asserted, "Virginians and [South] Carolinians" were invariably the generals at glorious Patriot victories.[62]

In the 1850s, Southern efforts to portray the American Revolution as a conservative pro-slavery movement increased in volume and intensity. Indeed, Southerners asserted that the United States had been founded as a slaveholding republic and that by maintaining slavery, they were being true to the Spirit of '76. *De Bow's Review* repeatedly sounded this theme. James D. B. De Bow stated, "negroes constituted an article of traffic in *all* the colonies" and that at the time independence was declared, there were some 500,000 slaves in the thirteen new states. To his credit, De Bow acknowledged that the new states varied considerably in their slaveholding, from 620 slaves in New Hampshire to 165,000 in Virginia. In similar fashion, a Georgian declared that all thirteen states practiced "domestic slavery." He dismissed the processes of immediate abolition and gradual emancipation that rid the North of slavery as naked self-interest masquer-ading as principled self-denial. If the Northern climate had permitted the cultivation of staple crops, he argued, the North would still be exploiting "slave labor." Matthew Fontaine Maury went further. Northerners did not emancipate their slaves, the Virginia oceanographer asserted, "they banished them." Instead of liberating their bondsmen, Maury claimed, most Northern masters sold their chattels to Southerners. Citing the ten thousand or so slaves manumitted in late-eighteenth-century Virginia, he triumphantly concluded, the South was the "principal scene of emancipa-tion." Maury was wrong. In fact, the overwhelming majority of manumis-sions in the Chesapeake during the late eighteenth and early nineteenth centuries were the result of masters granting slaves freedom as a reward for loyal behavior or hard work so that manumission reinforced the slave system rather than challenged it.[63]

Taking inspiration from Jefferson's draft of the Declaration of Indepen-dence, which blamed the international slave trade (and implicitly slavery) on George III, some Southern intellectuals argued that slavery had been "forced upon" the South, first by the British and then by the North. In 1853, a Southern reviewer of Harriet Beecher Stowe's *Key to Uncle Tom's Cabin* blamed Britain and, to a lesser extent, the North for shackling the South to slavery! Completely ignoring the fact that Southerners chose to purchase slaves, he remonstrated against the British and Northerners for complaining when Southerners kept the slaves the former's grandfathers had sold to the latter's grandfathers.[64]

Southerners rejected the notion that black service in the Revolutionary War proved that African Americans enjoyed natural rights, much less that chattels who took up arms wanted their freedom or that their armed par-ticipation transformed that conflict into an abolitionist struggle. William J. Rivers, a Georgia historian researching the battle of Fort Moultrie, informed a South Carolina historian that bondsmen had largely constructed the fort, thus linking the South's Lexington with its peculiar institution. The Geor-gian thought this was entirely appropriate as slaves "assist[ed] in military operations" in King George's War (1745-48) with "compensation being given the master for his slave if killed." Indeed, Rivers noted that the Southern colonies had raised black troops on several occasions. Writing in the *South-ern Quarterly Review,* Samuel A. Cartwright, the Mississippi physician who diagnosed the desire of fugitive slaves for freedom as mental illness, claimed that "negro slave labor in war" was superior to free labor. Cartwright asserted that while the first indication of British invasion prompted Northern farmers to flee, Southern bondsmen "continued to labor patiently in the fields." Rather than flocking to the British standard, Cartwright maintained that Southern slaves hid from the red-coated invaders despite blandishments of "liberty, land, money, and equality." Once the British had departed, the slave psychologist argued, Southern slaves calmly returned to their "daily labor." As we have seen earlier in this chapter, Cartwright's history was no better than his psychology. The *New Orleans Picayune* adverted to the fact that a few slaves fought side by side with their masters—body servants who went on campaign—as evidence of slavery's benevolence, if not its military efficacy. When abolitionists held up rebellious chattels—whether fugitives or insurrectionists—as the moral equivalent of the minutemen at Lexington, most Southerners dismissed this as ludicrous on its face. "Has it come to this?" asked an indignant Virginian. "The hellish plots and massacres of [Jean-Jacques] Dessalines, Gabriel [Prosser], and Nat Turner, are to be compared to the noble deeds and devoted patriotism of [Marquis de] Lafayette [and Tadeusz] Kosciusko?" He neglected to include Toussaint Louverture in his list of slave rebels due to the ironic fact that white Southerners regarded the Father of the Haitian Revolution as a symbol for maintaining slavery in the New World because he forced Haiti's freedmen to work in the black republic's sugar plantations.[65]

This dispute went beyond books and periodicals as well as historians and reviewers. It also went well beyond the Revolutionary War. In 1848, the *Richmond Whig* complained that the North was happy to have Southern assistance against the British in 1776 without any scruple about slavery, but after the Mexican-American War, the North objected to having slavemaster Zachary Taylor elected president. *De Bow's Review* pushed the Richmond newspaper's logic further still. The New Orleans periodical claimed that the South actually supplied "about *one-third* of the whole number of enlistments" when the Revolutionary War was fought in the North from 1775 to 1779 and "*more than one-half of all the enlistments*" when the war was fought in the South from 1780 to 1783. With equal vehemence, the *Review* adduced the South's disproportionate contribution to the ranks for the "late war with Mexico." As the South supplied "twice as many effective" soldiers for the Mexican-American War, the *Review* was particularly galled by the prospect that the Wilmot Proviso would exclude slavery (and, it reasoned, all Southerners) from the Mexican Cession. While Southerners' claims about their disproportionate service in the Revolutionary War were based on cherry-picking the enlistment records, they were spot-on regarding Southern commitment to the Mexican-American War. Southerners failed to note that Western states, even those north of the Ohio River, sent far more soldiers to fight south of the Rio Grande than did the Eastern states. This fact was due, in part, to the proximity of the West to Mexico.[66]

This gendered dispute over sectional cowardice during wartime helped to fuel the periodic violent outbursts between Northerners and Southerners in Congress. During the Crisis of 1850, Northern charges about Southern cowardice allowing the British to occupy Washington City during the War of 1812 almost led to a duel between congressmen Jefferson Davis of Mississippi and William H. Bissell of Illinois. While Rep. David Outlaw, a moderate North Carolina Whig, saw no "ground for any personal difficulty" between the two Democrats, he joined Davis in thinking Bissell's "allusion to the battle of Bladensburg and the burning of the Capitol in connection with Southern courage" was "offensive" to their section's honor. Five years later, R. L. Scott, a Southern observer of Congress, fumed that a land bounty bill would reward the "New England militia man that refused in the last war to fight the battles of the country [and] the old and faithful solider, who served through the War of 1811 [*sic*]." As the New England militia did shirk its responsibility to join the regular army and other state militias in the 1813 offensive against Canada, the aggrieved Southerner had a point. At any rate, as members of both houses of Congress began taking bowie knives, pistols, and even *rifles* to the debates, it is fortunate that the warm words did not lead to even warmer blood flowing and spilling.[67]

In the following year, to be sure, Rep. Preston Brooks did spill some of Sen. Charles Sumner's blood. Although it is not well known, this North-South (and Massachusetts-South Carolina) dispute over their respective roles of the sections (and the states) in the Revolutionary War was an underlying issue in Brooks's famous assault on Sumner. On May 22, 1856, Brooks, a state's rights Democrat from the Palmetto State, found Sumner, a Republican from the Bay State, at his desk and pummeled him with a cane while his fellow South Carolina congressman, Laurence M. Keitt, kept observers from interfering by brandishing a pistol. Most, but not all, of the scholarly accounts of this event properly credit Sumner's indecent attack on Sen. Andrew P. Butler in his "The Crime against Kansas" speech

(May 19–20, 1856) as the immediate spur to Brooks's resort to the cane, but they neglect the context of the long-simmering sectional dispute over the Revolutionary War. In fact, most historians have *missed* the crux of the dispute between Brooks and Sumner.[68]

In addition to being related to Brooks, Butler was one of the leading defenders of Southern military service in the Revolutionary War. Certainly, this subtext was not lost on the sectional analysts in 1856. The *Mercury* lauded Brooks's assault as a "complete vindication of the Revolutionary fame and history of South Carolina." The *Mercury* hoped that "every calumniator" of South Carolina would be similarly punished. However, the fire-eating newspaper did not explain how Brooks's ad hominem "discussion" clinched the argument. Not surprisingly, Northerners were not convinced. Making an ad rem rejoinder, the *National Anti-Slavery Standard* denied that Sumner had libeled the Palmetto State's military service. "Slavery weakened South Carolina," the *Standard* explained, "so that she was a drag upon the fight not only, but [also] a perpetual point of danger to the common cause." The *Standard* argued that South Carolina was hardly unique in this regard. The South's "incapacity" due to slavery made it an "open avenue of danger to the Americans struggling with Great Britain for their freedom." Facing expulsion from Congress for his role in the assault, Keitt resigned. In his resignation speech, Keitt made it clear that it was Sumner's "attacks on the revolutionary history of South Carolina" that prompted Brooks's attack and his assistance. The two congressmen meant to vindicate the honor of South Carolinians, living and dead, and the Palmetto State itself. They wanted to rewrite history with the cane and the gun. Using standard sectional shorthand in the historical controversy, Keitt explained that the South Carolinians were enraged by Massachutians' claim that "Bunker Hill [w]as the whole of the revolutionary war."[69]

In December 1856—when Northern outrage over the Brooks-Sumner Affair was still boiling—William Gilmore Simms, the leading Southern man of letters, embarked on a speaking tour of the North to defend the South's role in the American Revolution. The *Mercury* lauded Simms for giving a "complete reply to SUMNER'S ignorant tirade against the revolutionary fame of our state." Although it was complete, it was not long. After just three speeches, Simms quit and returned to South Carolina because tickets could not be sold or even given away. While Simms professed to be astonished by the "public hostility" he faced, his private correspondence suggests that the North's apathy stung more than its antipathy. Simms complained that the "game of the Black Republicans was to identify me with Brooks," but he made that association come easily to his auditors. In the course of his remarks, Simms vilified the convalescing Sumner for provoking the attack. Even the *New York Express*—a Northern newspaper that generally sympathized with the South—faulted Simms for blaming the victim, noting that if a Northerner went to Charleston and lectured upon the intellectual preeminence of Massachusetts, he would fear for his life. For his part, Simms believed the fact that he had not explicitly endorsed Brooks during the tour was evidence of his good faith. Perhaps it was. Many Southerners regarded Sumner's submission to Brooks's blows as unmanly and Northern rejection of Simms's words as ungrateful. The *Mercury* explained the North's rejection of Simms's tour to "vindicate the truth of History" on the grounds that it was an "offence against Northern pride."[70]

The Northern ill will Simms experienced was reciprocated by Southerners to George Bancroft. The year before the Brooks-Sumner Affair, South Carolinians had welcomed Bancroft, whom the *Mercury* lionized as the "historian of the country," to the seventy-fifth anniversary of the battle of King's Mountain. But the year after, the *Mercury* rejected history as practiced by Northerners as a caustic compound of the "ashes of Pilgrim Fathers, BANCROFT putty, and the bone dust of Massachusetts martyrs, gathered on Revolutionary battle grounds in [South] Carolina—all worked up with Abolition yeast." The *Southern Literary Messenger* warned that Bancroft was a "New England author" who made repeated attacks on slavery throughout his work.[71]

Of course, Bancroft was not an abolitionist. In fact, Bancroft had tried not to take sides in the sectional conflict. In the end, the historian had to stake out a position. In the mid-1850s, Bancroft had quietly opposed Southern efforts to make Kansas a slave state on the grounds that the Lecompton Constitution violated the settlers' Free-Soil preference. To counter charges of sectional bias, Bancroft sought the suggestions from the "adepts in [South] Carolina history" for his account of the Southern theatre of the Revolutionary War. He wooed Southern authors by lining up distinguished Northerners to buy their books. He lent historical manuscripts to Southern historians. Most important, he downplayed unflattering events and played up flattering ones. In the former category, Bancroft hurried past the successful effort of British commanders to liberate the bondsmen of rebellious masters and the unsuccessful effort of enslaved people themselves to turn the Revolutionary War into an attack on slavery itself. In much the same way that Bancroft neglected Washington's purge of black soldiers shortly after Dunmore's proclamation, he mentioned the proclamation itself only to discount its efficacy. Indeed, Bancroft claimed that no slave joined Dunmore's forces from a "longing for an improved condition or even from ill will to their masters." Despite fears of a slave insurrection, Bancroft contended, the Virginians reacted to Dunmore's proclamation with "moderation and tenderness," taking care "lest the attempt to raise bondsmen against their masters in Virginia should be followed by severity against the negro." In fact, as many twenty thousand slaves, including seventeen chattels owned by Washington and eleven by Jefferson, answered the call of Dunmore and the other British commanders who tried the same tactic. While some of these slaves continued to harass planters in South Carolina and Georgia long after the war ended and others were freed and sent to Nova Scotia or Sierra Leon, most were re-enslaved by the British and sent to labor on sugar plantations in the Caribbean.[72]

At any rate, a few Southern intellectuals questioned Bancroft's motives and some dismissed his efforts. In 1858, William C. Preston, a proud former resident of South Carolina, was suspicious. "Why does Bancroft write to me about the negro laws of South Carolina?" Preston asked Francis Lieber, a fellow former South Carolinian. "What is he at?" Two years later, George Fitzhugh, the Virginia pro-slavery advocate and self-styled "sociologist," answered that question simply: "socialism." The sociologist believed that the historian's celebration of the everyday democracy of the Patriots during the Revolution had elided into "socialism." Fitzhugh charged that Bancroft's citations of "Utopian and infidel philosophers of every age and clime and country" revealed that the historian had become an atheist and an advocate of unrestrained "Jeffersonian democra[cy]."[73]

Moderates in the North and the South tried to calm the waters by offering hyperbolic praise to Southern triumphs, especially those made by South Carolinians, in the Revolutionary War. In 1850, the editors of the *Cincinnati Commercial* observed that "every schoolboy" knew of South Carolina's glorious victory at the Cowpens. In 1856, *Ballou's Pictorial Drawing-Room Companion* lauded that obscure battle as "one of the most brilliant exploits of the Revolutionary war." Two years later, Lewis Cass, a Michigan Democrat and doughface in good standing, unable to attend the inauguration of the statue at Eutaw Springs, expressed the "great interest" all Americans had in South Carolina's commendable service during the Revolutionary War. James Dixon, a Connecticut Republican, also unable to attend, assured the South Carolinians that New Englanders "never tire[d] of the recital of revolutionary scenes" from the South.[74]

Even some sectional extremists tried to defuse the tensions created by this historical controversy. They reminded Americans in both sections that all had marched in the same army against the British. During the hubbub over the annexation of Texas as a slave state in 1845, Isaac E. Morse, a Louisiana Democrat, thanked a Massachusetts Whig for his public admonition of abolitionists as the only way to preserve the Union made by our ancestors fighting "shoulder to shoulder" during the Revolutionary War. Even as dogged a defender of slavery as Samuel Cartwright pleaded for calm. The truth of the matter was, the slave psychologist asserted, South Carolina and Massachusetts fought "shoulder to shoulder in the cause of American liberty, power, and progress." Cartwright and Morse alluded to Daniel Webster's "Second Reply to Hayne," where the Massachusetts senator had recalled that those two states went through the Revolution "shoulder to shoulder." Ignoring the crucial military support of France, Joseph Johnston, a Southern historian, confided to Bancroft that the South was "recovered from the British unaided by the arms of our foreign Allies, & with no other support than our Sister States in Congress. The Union preserved us from being a British Colony." Even *De Bow's Review*—rarely the voice of moderation in sectional disputes—chided the disputants to be "mindful of the glorious old time of the republic, when our fathers at Bunker Hill, York Town, or New Orleans, or in all of the perilous periods of our history, stood shoulder to shoulder." But, reverting to type, *De Bow's Review* then made the point with a sectional twist aimed at Northerners: "with such a concord of heart and purpose, what a nation WE have made of this, and what madmen are YOU to urge its *inevitable destruction!*"[75]

While the Brooks-Sumner Affair was the climax of the dispute, it was not the conclusion. Rejecting South Carolina's claim to have done the heavy lifting in the Revolutionary War, the *North American Review* observed that the "manufacturing colonies" rallied to preserve their "chartered rights" by asserting their independence, while the "planting colonies" sought "reconciliation" with Britain. The *North American Review* observed acidly that Southern accusations of Northern laxity "fall strangely enough from

Loyalist lips." In truth, there were far more Loyalists in the South than in the North, a fact that made the Revolutionary War in South Carolina a civil war as much as a conflict between Americans and Britons. Reacting to the *Boston Traveller*'s observation that Patriot forces at Eutaw Springs were led by a Rhode Islander and that South Carolina could not defend its capital city from the Red Coats, the *Mercury* countered that neither Pennsylvania nor New York could defend their seaboard capitals against the powerful British Navy. (Of course, the *Mercury* ignored Massachusetts's success in liberating Boston.) The *Mercury*'s readers took offense as well. A correspondent who took the name ""EUTAW" acknowledged that Yankees did much of the fighting at Eutaw, snidely noting that in those days "Rhode Islanders were our friends." In addition to sending soldiers to aid the Palmetto State, he noted that Rhode Island also provided South Carolina planters with "cheap slaves, by means of their fast clipper ships [*sic*] from Newport."[76]

In their battles over the Revolutionary War, antebellum Americans revealed how they saw themselves and each other as much as how they saw their revolution. Northerners and Southerners alike agreed that nothing less than the fate of the United States was at stake in this historical dispute. This urgency helps to explain the fierceness of the antebellum history wars over what would have been merely academic matters of how many Southerners fought in the Northern campaigns and vice versa. Perhaps no one felt these pressures more acutely than George Bancroft. As the leading historian of the American Revolution, Bancroft tried to rise above the fray. He labored to include the experiences of all Americans, Northerners and Southerners, as well as Westerners. He tried to write a social history of the war *avant la letter,* by including the contributions of Americans from all walks of life. He made repeated overtures to the South. And he softened or ignored controversial matters like the role of black soldiers in the early battles and the tendency of many American slaves to seek freedom across British lines. Nonetheless, he bore the brunt of criticism from all sides. Even New Englanders believed that their states' service was, as one Connecticutian put it, "generally overlooked." At the same time, the fire-eater campaign to protect the South's military reputation was insufficient. In a school essay that would have surely infuriated Southern ideologues, John Steele Henderson, a young North Carolinian, described Lexington and

Bunker Hill in glowing terms and then observed in passing that "there was [*sic*] a great many [other] battles fought in the revolution."[77]

While most Americans grappled with what historian George Fredrickson called "America's Original Sin," not all did. Northern opponents of slavery made the American Revolution into a struggle for natural rights for *all* Americans or a cynical exercise in protecting that institution. They either blamed the serpent for tempting them or justified eating the apple so that they would realize their nakedness and find clothes. In 1847, the *National Era* mocked South Carolinians for claiming that the British could not entice their bondsmen with promises of freedom. Noting that even David Ramsay's *History of South Carolina* (1809) recorded that thousands of slaves sought refuge with the British and that the Palmetto Patriots worried about British incitement of a slave insurrection, the *Era* concluded that contemporary South Carolinians had made a "willful sacrifice of truth to the cause of human bondage."[78]

Southern nationalists argued that the United States had been founded as a slaveholding Eden and that it was the North that had disobeyed God by first liberating its own slaves and then trying to liberate the South's. A correspondent to the *Memphis Appeal* proudly observed that not only did the author of the Declaration of Independence and the commander of the Continental Army rule a "number of happy and contented slaves," but so did a majority of those who "maintained [American Independence] with their blood."[79]

Moderates tried to ignore the fact that each of the original thirteen states drove slaves. Instead, they lauded the bravery and valor of the American soldiers and the exceptional quality of the freedom they obtained. In a diatribe against the new Republican Party, which appealed only to the North, Robert J. Walker, who was born in Pennsylvania, but became a Mississippi planter, invoked the "memory of the commingled blood of the North and the South poured out on the battlefields of the Revolution" to urge Americans to support the pan-sectional Democratic Party in the Election of 1856.[80] Most Americans did not participate in the history wars. Instead they visited battle sites, erected monuments, and read thrilling accounts of the various battles of the American Revolution.

# 5

# Finishing What the Founders Started

Antebellum Americans were devoted to the Revolution. They mourned the passing of rank-and-file Revolutionaries. They apotheosized the leading Revolutionaries. They revered the leading Revolutionaries' descendants (and even their friends). They made pilgrimages to Revolutionary battlefields. They erected monuments to the men, battles, documents, and ideas that marked the progress of the Revolution. They thronged the shrines that held the relics of the Revolution. While the Revolution brought Americans together, it also divided them. At the same time Americans shared a common reverence for the Revolution, they quarreled over exactly what it was. By the mid-1840s, this quarrel intensified and became sectional. As historian Michael Morrison observes: "increasingly the nation was unable either to recapture the spirit or to agree on the essence of their Revolution." Indeed, this struggle over the meaning and legacy of the Revolution was both a controversy in the sectional conflict and an exercise in national myth-making. While Southern hotspurs emphasized the Revolutionary legacy of self-determination and resistance to encroachment on individual rights, slaves, abolitionists, and some Free-Soilers looked to the Revolutionary legacy of natural rights for all, and sectional moderates in the North and the South took pride in the notion that the common sacrifice of the Patriots in the North and the South had bestowed a Revolutionary legacy of individual liberty that made the slaveholding United States the most free nation on earth. By the 1850s, fire-eaters and fugitive slaves invoked the right to rebellion—to different ends—while at the same time moderates tried to keep the fire of the old Revolution alight while smothering that of the new. As historians Elizabeth Fox-Genovese and Eugene Genovese noted, the "more pronounced the quarrel over slavery, the more important the interpretation of the Revolution became" to Americans in the North and the South.[1]

Perhaps no legacy of the Revolution put the issue of slavery in American nationality in bolder relief than Northern emancipation. If slavery was an essential component of American nationalism, if all original thirteen states had once been *"Slave States,"* then how to explain the decision by the worthies of the Revolution to abolish it, in some cases even before independence itself was won? At the same time, the persistence of slavery in the Southern half of the new nation raised its own questions. All antebellum Americans acknowledged that the Founders had established a union of thirteen slave states in 1776. As the *Anti-Slavery Bugle* observed, when the original thirteen had declared independence, "slaves were held, to a greater or lesser extent, *in every one of them."* Making the same point from the other side of the slavery divide, the *Delaware State Reporter* cautioned Northerners to remember that slavery "existed originally in all the States, and not just the South only." But their agreement on that historical fact only served to focus their conflict on what came next. Seven of the original thirteen slave states freed their chattels, while nine more slave states joined the remaining six original slave states in the Union.[2]

Just as antebellum Americans took pride in the service of their fathers and grandfathers in the various battles of the Revolutionary War, so they basked in the inherited glory of their forebears' emancipatory actions. Charles Lowell, pastor at Boston's West Church, demanded that historian George Bancroft give his father, John, proper credit for introducing the "clause into the Bill [*sic*] of Rights of Massachusetts, which exterminated slavery from our state." Like most proud descendants of a historic forebear, the son exaggerated his father's contributions. In *Commonwealth v. Jennison* (1783)—the famous Quock Walker case—Chief Justice William Cushing ruled that slavery was unconstitutional as it violated Article I of Massachusetts's Declaration of Rights (1780), which asserted that "all men are born free and equal." Despite this ruling, slaves continued to be bought and sold in the Bay State for several years longer. Nonetheless, the example of Walker proved inspirational: some Massachusetts enslaved people brought suit against their masters, while others simply voted with their feet. So widespread was this sentiment that the first federal census found that there were no slaves in the state in 1790. In short, slaves affected the abolition of slavery in Massachusetts far more than Lowell's father or any other free person. In the same way, George J. Bryan, a South Carolina historian, took pride in his grandfather's "connexion" in the passage of Pennsylvania's gradual emancipation act in 1780. Bryan's family history was more accurate than Lowell's. In fact, George Bryan, an Irish immigrant and Philadelphia merchant, did play the leading role in drafting and passing Pennsylvania's gradual emancipation act. The proud grandson observed that the Keystone State's antislavery legislation permitted Southern masters to "sojourn" in Pennsylvania with their slaves for as long as six months at a time in direct contrast to the efforts of second-wave abolitionists who tried to lure slaves away from their visiting masters. Due to the moderation of the first-wave abolitionists, Bryan claimed their efforts enjoyed the "best wishes of all the Southern members of Congress." Of course, he overstated Southern support for or even tolerance of the first-wave abolitionists. If Southerners did not worry about the actions of the Pennsylvania Abolition Society in ending slavery in a single Northern state, then they took great umbrage at efforts by first-wave abolitionists to lobby the national legislature to pass bills that would prohibit the domestic slave trade and the westward expansion of slavery. Indeed, petitions to those ends prompted Southern threats of secession and civil war in the very first session of Congress.[3]

Just as antebellum Americans honored the last living veterans of the American Revolution, so opponents of slavery hailed the sole surviving Northern ex-slaves. Even Southern newspapers mourned the passing of Bristol Underwood, the last former slave of Rhode Island. However, it was opponents of slavery who took special delight in mourning the last freedmen and women of the North. In the *Voice of the Fugitive,* Henry Bibb, himself a self-liberated Kentucky slave residing in Canada, hailed an unnamed 111-year-old woman who had the "honor of having been the last slave in Connecticut." In the same way, the *Anti-Slavery Bugle* noted the passing of the last surviving former enslaved person in Pennsylvania. The *Bugle* described the 103-year-old Abram Kirck as the "last relic of the 'civilized barbarism' of our fathers." Linking Kirck not just to Northern emancipation but also to the Revolutionary War, the *Bugle* reported that the Pennsylvania slave had assisted both the Marquis de Lafayette and George Washington, helping to transport Franco-Americans forces across the Susquehanna River en route to the siege of the British at Yorktown.[4]

Antebellum Americans interpreted the historical fact that the founding thirteen states were originally all slave states in different and sometimes disparate ways. Just as they differed in their remembrances of the slavehold-ing of Thomas Jefferson and George Washington, the response of Southern slaves to British offers of freedom, and so on, so mid-nineteenth-century Americans took inspiration, solace, or comfort from the fact that the North-ern states used to practice slavery. Antislavery Northerners hoped that just as the North rid itself of slavery, so would the South. James G. Birney, a reformed slaveholder and the Liberty Party's two-time presidential candi-date, believed that slavery was a regrettable colonial legacy imposed on the United States by the British. The Founders, Birney argued, allowed slavery only a "temporary existence" and planned for its "gradual extinction" in the North and the South. Moderates in both sections likewise believed that Northern emancipation showed that it was possible in the South as well, if only holier-than-thou Northern fanatics would let them find the path to abo-lition in their own way and time. The *Providence Post* blamed the presence of slavery in the colonies and hence the early United States on the British. Indeed, the *Post* claimed that the mother country had foisted slavery upon the colonies against the colonists' "repeated and earnest remonstrances." Fire-eaters believed that the North had fallen away from the Founders' true path right from the beginning. In 1776, slavery was "a fact and a fact recog-nized by law" in each of the original thirteen states, Sen. Robert Toombs, the Georgia Whig of Bunker Hill Monument fame, boldly reminded Bos-tonians. Indeed, the Georgian noted the Declaration of Independence was "drafted by a slaveholder, adopted by the representatives of slaveholders, and did not emancipate a single African slave; but on the contrary, one of the charges which it submitted to the civilized world against King George was, that he had attempted to excite domestic insurrection among us."[5]

The triumph of freedom over slavery in the Northern states during the two decades after Independence was won struck anti-slavery Northern-ers as a logical consequence of the Spirit of '76, an unmitigated good deed performed by the worthies of the Revolution. Ranging from Free-Soilers to Garrisonian abolitionists, opponents of bond labor counted Northern emancipation as one of the enduring triumphs of the American Revolution.

The *Anti-Slavery Bugle* heralded the fact that a majority of the original thirteen states had "effected the abolition of slavery in their borders" by the end of the eighteenth century. To be sure it was a majority, but a slight one. If seven of the original thirteen had ended, or, in the case of most, begun to end slavery, then six had not. In fact, the highest antislavery honors went to the fourteenth state—Vermont. Antislavery advocates gloried in the fact that in 1777 the Green Mountain State, then an independent republic, became the first polity in the New World to abolish slavery. In a poetic turn of phrase, the *New York Tribune* declaimed that Vermont's "pure breezes never fanned the cheek of a slave."[6]

Most antislavery Northerners believed that the Founders were personally opposed to bond labor and had taken concrete steps to lay the groundwork for its gradual abolition in the South as well as in the North. Rejoicing that the leading lights of the Revolution had succeeded in the North, Massachusetts abolitionist V. Wright Kingsley predicted that they would have triumphed in the South as well were it not for the cotton gin. That diabolical device had thwarted their "plans." Despite Kingsley's praise of the Founders' antislavery "forethought," in fact, they had only expectations (and no plans) for the end of slave labor in the South. C. H. Winslow, a Free-Soiler, acknowledged that his native New York State, like all thirteen original states, was once a slave state, but he boasted that the Empire State had gradually emancipated its slaves just as the leading Revolutionaries had hoped. Cherry-picking the antislavery Founders—John Jay, Robert R. Livingston, and Benjamin Franklin—from the pro-slavery bunch, Winslow claimed that the first rank of American statesmen had thought it "best to be rid of slaves." Winslow maintained that all Americans—including Southern slaveholders—had agreed with them until cotton, tobacco, rice, and sugar had "revolutionized the Southern mind." Salmon P. Chase went several steps further. The Ohio Republican contrasted the slaveholding of the leading Revolutionaries with that of the leading fire-eaters, arguing that late eighteenth-century slavery was a milder and more humane alternative to that of the mid-nineteenth century. In effect, Chase exonerated Thomas Jefferson's slave-driving while at the same time he indicted Jefferson Davis's.[7]

The fact that all of the original Northern states were once slave states gave moderate Northerners hope that abolition was possible. Doughfaces had faith that the South would ultimately end slavery if given the time and the space to do so. The *Scioto Gazette* chided Northern extremists for pressuring Southerners to do the right thing too rapidly. After all, the *Gazette* inaccurately observed, "all the States but one were Slave States" a decade after independence had been declared. Rather than castigate the South for still driving slaves, the *Gazette* believed that Northerners should be grateful to be rid of the "irksome institution" and have compassion rather than scorn for their "less fortunate neighbors" to the south. The *Providence Post* agreed. Northern opponents of slavery had undercut the natural disposition among Southern slaveholders to free their slaves, the *Post* averred, by agitating the issue. If radical abolitionists would suffer white Southerners to work out their own solution to slavery in their own time, they would revert to the "strong anti-slavery feeling" of Jefferson and the other slaveholding Founders.[8]

Moderate Southerners echoed the doughfaces' claims that abolitionist agitation was self-defeating—i.e., that Southern slaveholders had not manumitted their chattels because opponents of slavery had hurt their feelings. Jim M. Douglas, a Vermonter who had moved to Kentucky, remembered that "not very long [ago]" Massachusetts and New York had liberated their slaves. Douglas asserted that the Southern states would have "followed their example . . . had it not been for the Abolitionists." In the same way, George J. Bryan, the South Carolina historian, contrasted the moderation and manners of first-wave abolitionists with the "blind zeal and indomitable temper" of the second wave. James Manney, a North Carolina Whig and son of New York slaveholder, believed that each Southern state would end slavery in "such manner and [at] such time" as it deemed best. Efforts by "fanatical" Northerners to pressure Southerners into expediting the process would only delay it. Manney argued that New York slaveholders, his father among them, would have surely resented efforts by out-of-state fanatics to incite their chattels to "cut our throats and burn our houses" in the 1780s and 1790s just as antebellum Southerners objected to Northern abolitionists' appeals to their bondsmen in the 1840s and 1850s.[9]

The *New York Tribune* dismissed Southern claims that the excesses of second-wave abolitionists forced proud Southerners to defend slavery despite their economic incentive and moral imperative to end it. The *Tribune* observed that during the half century between the winning of independence and the rise of Garrison and his ilk, white Southerners had done nothing to stop the rise of slavery. Indeed, the Southern statesmen expanded the empire of slavery westward, encouraged their slaves to reproduce, and sought additional legal protections for slave property.[10]

Of course, the practice of Northern emancipation lost much of its luster, once you looked at the details. In every state, except Vermont, Massachusetts, and New Hampshire, slavery was ended gradually, delaying freedom to the slaves and cushioning the economic blow of manumission to the slaveholders. Moreover, the process of gradual emancipation neglected slaves born before the date the law went into effect, consigning them to perpetual bondage unless their masters voluntarily manumitted them or the state legislature later passed a general abolition act. For example, New York's gradual emancipation law applied to enslaved people born on July 4, 1799, and afterward. The rest of the Empire State's chattels remained in bondage until the legislature passed a general abolition act effective July 4, 1827. For Connecticut bondspeople the relevant dates were 1784 and 1848. The *Delaware State Reporter* observed in 1855 that several Northern states held slaves "until a very recent period." Although Quakers had helped George Bryan make Pennsylvania the first state to pass a gradual emancipation bill, the Keystone State never did get around to liberating slaves born before July 4, 1780. For this reason, the dough-faced *Pennsylvanian* observed that the Keystone State still had seven elderly slaves on the eve of the 1850 federal census. Rather than worry about slaves in the South, the *Pennsylvanian* chided Northern do-gooders to purchase the freedom of the remaining Northern slaves. Likewise, the Census of 1860 counted eighteen black indentured servants serving lifelong apprenticeships in the "free state" of New Jersey.[11]

Moreover, many Northern slavemasters sold their chattels to another slave state before they reached their emancipatory birthdays. Indeed, some Southerners claimed that Northerners had cynically ridded their states of bond labor by selling their slaves to the South, ending slavery in the North while at the same time guaranteeing its presence in the South. Ruth Hastings, a Massachusetts woman who worked as a tutor on the plantation of a great South Carolina cotton baron, reported that her mistress said that the "Northern people brought the slaves here [to the South], not the Southerners, and that when they were freed by law there, they *sold* them to the South & lost nothing, [where]as *they* [Southerners] would lose *all* to give them up." The *Pennsylvania Freeman* scoffed at the claim of some Southerners that the North ended slavery by selling its slaves to the South. The *Freeman* cited the fact that New York's emancipation law prohibited selling slaves before their emancipatory birthdays. Indeed, New York and New Jersey prohibited this practice, but the legislation allowed the sale to continue if the chattels "consented."[12] Of course, consent from a coerced person was easy to obtain.

Antebellum critics of Northern emancipation took special care to criticize Massachusetts, considered to be the leading abolition state. *De Bow's Review* erroneously claimed that the Bay State was the "first state" to ply the international slave trade. With more historical accuracy, the *New York Day Book,* the most stridently pro-slavery newspaper in the North, observed that slavery was abolished in Massachusetts by activist judges rather than by the people's representatives. After all, it was the Massachusetts Supreme Court that ruled that the state's bill of rights applied to African Americans, thus invalidating slavery. The *Day Book* triumphantly concluded that Massachusetts had "never abolished slavery." Rather slavery ended in the Bay State due to the "perverse doggedness of a judge, who insisted upon construing a clause, which evidently only referred to white men, to have reference to negroes."[13]

Americans across the political spectrum of slavery argued that the North would have practiced slavery in the mid-nineteenth century had the climate and soil been congenial to the production of the staple crops. Stephen F. Miller, a Georgia lawyer, indicted the North for ending slavery for economic reasons and then, long after the fact, hypocritically claiming to have done so for moral ones instead. "African slavery would have existed to this day in the Northern States, had it been sufficiently profitable; but as the climate was too cold for cotton, rice, and sugar, slave labor was discarded," Miller charged. "It did not pay." For this reason, Missouri slaveholder William B. Napton refused to give Northerners any credit for abolishing slavery. They were merely doing what came naturally—following the money. Even the *Anti-Slavery Bugle* generously conceded that it was "very questionable" whether the North would have abolished slavery if bond labor were as profitable there as it was in the South. Likewise, a letter writer to the *National Era* observed that it was easy to summon the courage to end bond labor in the Northern states where slaveholders wielded little political power and slaves yielded even less profit.[14]

·   ·   ·

During the buildup to and the fallout from the Secession Crisis, Americans across the political spectrum reacted to events in light of their understandings of the role slavery played in American nationality. Moderates in the North and the South despaired for their beloved Union. They expected the appropriate compromises to be made to preserve the Union of free and slave states just as the Founders had done time and time again since "76." Thomas B. Lincoln, an Iowa Democrat, was incredulous that a "great nation [was] to be broken up [and] thirty millions white people to be made miserable for a few Negroes." Lincoln regretted that sectional demagogues threatened to explode the Union established by the worthies of that annus mirabilis. In a series of rhetorical questions tinged with nostalgia, John Minor Botts, a Virginia moderate, adumbrated the way the United States used to function. "Why," Botts wondered, "shouldn't the South be content with her institutions unmolested & undisturbed as they are and have been for the last two hundred years without attempting to force it where it does not naturally or rightfully belong?" At the same time, he asked, "Why should not the North condemn, rebuke, & punish if necessary, all attempts on the part of her citizens to disturb our peace, our happiness, & our safety?" Lastly, he inquired, "Why should we not all dwell together as our fathers did in peace, harmony, & brotherhood under that glorious 'Star Spangled Banner?'"[15] Indeed, why not? The United States had been a slaveholding republic since 1776.

While abolitionists and fire-eaters disagreed about the essence of the United States, they agreed that the moderates had gotten it wrong. In 1862, John Lothrop Motley, the American minister to Austria—his patriotism amplified by war and distance—believed that the North's victory would be proof positive that the United States was a "free, not a slaveholding commonwealth." Before the "accursed rebellion," Motley, a Massachusetts Republican, had been willing to countenance bond labor in the fifteen Southern states, content to let slavery die a slow and natural death. After slavemasters rebelled and attacked the United State government, he believed the only recourse was to "smash" the South's peculiar institution. "But for slavery," Motley reasoned with typical American certainty, the United States would be the "greatest, strongest, & best government on earth." Southern ideologues valued what Virginian Frank V. Winston called their natural right to hold slaves in the states and to carry slaves to the territories. After all, Winston observed, slavery was the "basis of society, prosperity, and wealth in fifteen of the States of this Union." The Virginian neglected to note that it had been a part, significant if not integral, of all the states in 1776. When Winston and other Southerners doubted that the Union established by their fathers and grandfathers could ensure those rights they seceded. Democracy had nothing to do with it. After Abraham Lincoln's inauguration, Winston declared his "infinite" preference for the rule of a "Southern King to that of Northern Mobocracy."[16]

After these seven states in the Deep South had seceded between December 1860 and February 1861, moderates despaired for the Union, fire-eaters gloried in their new revolution, and abolitionists shrugged. William S. Pettigrew, a North Carolina cotton planter, lamented the "timeserving politicians" in the North and the South who were threatening the ruin of the American Republic by cynically exploiting the political issue of slavery. Pettigrew longed for the "expansive patriotism" of the Founders, which would surely stem the disunion tide. Jacob Brown, a Philadelphian with nativist tendencies, deplored the Republicans' strategy of alienating moderate Southerners by making common cause with abolitionists and boldly declaring their opposition to the westward expansion of slavery. Brown believed that slavery was already fading away and that "if only let alone," it would fall victim to its own contradictions. Although a "strenuous" opponent of slavery, Brown asserted the Republicans' "agitation of the question" provoked an "opposite Spirit in the South" precisely because it was a violation of the founding principles of the United States.[17]

To rally support for secession, fire-eaters of 1861 used the Lockean rhetoric of the American Revolution. John H. Graham, the scion of a Mississippi cotton plantation, organized a militia company composed of his fellow students at the University of Mississippi. They drilled daily during the Secession Winter and boldly spoke of making the ultimate sacrifice to protect their natural rights to deny chattels of theirs. "Southern boys," Graham proclaimed, would gladly die rather than "be deprived by of our rights guaranteed by our heritage." Although Graham did not make good on that threat, it was not for want of trying. As a part of the 11th Mississippi, Graham fought at First Bull Run, the Seven Days battles, Second Bull Run, and Antietam.[18]

In addition to blustering about natural rights, secessionists adopted the symbols and the methods of the Patriots of 1776. They erected liberty poles. They flew their own idiosyncratic flags. They formed companies of

"Minutemen." They harassed Unionists as "Tories," complete with torch-light parades and effigy-burnings. Several states celebrated the passage of ordinances of secession with patriotic displays usually reserved for the Fourth of July. After the unanimous vote for secession made South Carolina a "free and independent Commonwealth," white South Carolinians exploded "[fire]crackers, guns, and rockets" through the night. Thomas Kelah Wharton, a Yankee architect working on the New Orleans Customs House, claimed that news of South Carolina's secession aroused as much celebratory gunfire in the Crescent City as was fired in anger against the British in the battle of New Orleans. A month later, Wharton reported slightly more subdued celebrations when the Pelican State finally seceded.[19]

Moderates worried about and abolitionists dismissed the parallels between the early 1860s and the mid-1770s. "The South are arming and preparing for the struggle," the *New York Herald* observed. "Committees of safety and bands of Minute Men, after the fashion of the Revolution of 1776, are being organized in Virginia and South Carolina." Abolitionists found the comparison risible. The *National Anti-Slavery Standard* wondered at the spectacle of a "Revolution for the greater security of Injustice and the firmer establishment of Tyranny!" The *Standard* believed that the slaveholder's rebellion was the American Revolution in reverse.[20]

At the same time and with equal cause, opponents of slavery and secession also wrapped themselves in the mantle of the Patriots. John Bigelow, a Republican pleased by Lincoln's election, boasted to an English friend that the progress of liberty in the United States during the 1850s was a "bloodless revolution" greater than "our rebellion and revolution in '76."[21] Of course, Bigelow's expectation of the latter revolution being "bloodless" was horribly wrong,[22] and his premise that it had already been achieved sanguine.

Moderate Southerners regarded secession (and not Lincoln's election) as a "revolution" and they did not mean that to be a compliment. William Davidson Harris, a Marylander living in Philadelphia, rejected secession as "premature, uncalled for, & unjustifiable." Although Harris conceded that revolution was a "right which justly belongs to all oppressed people," he argued that the South's grievances did not "justify this last resort." Alexander H. Stephens, a Georgia Whig who would soon be the Confederate vice-president, fretted that "revolutions are much easier started than controlled, and the men who begin them, even for the best purposes and objects, seldom end them." Stephens feared the South's revolution might resemble France's in 1789 (or perhaps Saint-Domingue's in 1791) rather than the America's in 1776. With 40 percent of its population enslaved, the Confederacy would have to fight a two-front war for independence—one against the United States and the other against its 3.5 million slaves. Jason O. Harrison, a New Orleanian involved in trade with the North, felt helpless as a revolutionary tide carried the Deep South of the Union into an unknown and quite possibly a dangerous future.[23]

Despite the bluster about abolition rule and threats of disunion in the presidential campaign of 1860 and the resultant Secession Crisis, most Americans went about their business more or less as usual. Americans made "pilgrimage[s]" to Mount Vernon. Ann Pamela Cunningham and Edward Everett continued their efforts to raise funds for the Mount Vernon Ladies' Association (MVLA). Although Everett suspended his speaking tour while seeking the vice-presidency on the Constitutional Union ticket so as not to entangle the MVLA in politics, he planned a trip to the Southwest in November. Ordinary Americans continued to send donations to the MVLA. In the interval between the two waves of secession, a North Carolina woman contributed $2 to the cause, all the while hoping that a permanent breach to the Union could be avoided.[24]

Most Americans celebrated Independence Day with unabated enthusiasm even as the sectional crisis approached the tipping point to Civil War. The celebration of July 4, 1860, in New York City embraced "every variety of amusement—excursions, theatricals, balloon ascensions, salutes, military parades, regattas, and fireworks." On that same day, George Bancroft, the leading American historian, rescued the Declaration of Independence from the critics of natural rights. As we have already seen, Bancroft was no abolitionist. Indeed, he had served in the cabinet of pro-slavery expansionist James K. Polk. Nonetheless, Bancroft announced that Thomas Jefferson's heart "beat for all of humanity" when he drafted the Declaration, i.e., that the Sage of Monticello believed that slaves had natural rights. Some abolitionists celebrated that day by gathering at the grave of violent abolitionist John Brown in North Elba, New York, and honoring the "Martyr of Virginia" and his family for acting on the principles of the Declaration. Abolitionists also commemorated the ninth anniversary of Jerry's Rescue as a sort of "shadow" holiday.[25]

Secession and war changed matters. July 4, 1861, was a new day on the civil calendar. The Civil War had made the Fourth of July into a different holiday. Rather than extolling the American Revolution for making the United States the freest nation on earth, Americans and Confederates argued that this new conflict would finish what the Founders started nearly nine decades ago. Rather than extolling the common sacrifices made by Patriots in the North and the South, Americans and Confederates committed themselves and the nation to burn off the imperfections that threatened the national alloy. Opponents of slavery believed the Civil War would finally end slavery—an awful anomaly on a republic consecrated in liberty. Thomas B. Drew, a Massachusetts dentist with abolitionist convictions, believed that the *fête nationale* was honored in a "different manner" in the United States because of the "open rebellion" of eleven slave states. Bradford hoped the war would continue "until Slavery, the root of the evil, is destroyed, root and branch." Moderates wanted to restore the delicate balance between the North and the South and between liberty and slavery, which the Founders had established in 1776. James H. Campbell, a Pennsylvania Republican, was pleased to see that despite the commencement of hostilities, Washingtonians celebrated the day in style with parades and flags flying. This time, Campbell exulted, "there will be no compromise" with the secessionists who would wreck the noble system of self-government established by the Revolutionaries. Confederates believed that by setting up an avowedly pro-slavery republic, they would realize the Founders' hopes and plans. While on campaign in Virginia, Thaddeus W. Swank, a twenty-one-year-old in Company A, 8th Regiment Georgia Volunteer Infantry, explicitly cast the Confederate cause with that of the Patriots: both groups were nobly fighting for the "right of self-government." Indeed, the young Georgian quoted the Declaration to argue that like the Patriots, the Confederates were pledging their "lives, the[ir] fortunes, [and] the[ir] sacred honor" to be "recognized among the nations of the earth as a 'free and independent people.'"[26] Of course, just like many of the Patriots, the Confederates were fighting to be free to own slaves.

Fire-eaters yearned to have a new Independence Day, a day when the South asserted its independence from the tyrannical North. They fell back upon the familiar tropes and themes of the Fourth of July and the Declaration of Independence in their efforts to make a clean cut of the frayed political bonds that connected the South to the North. Impatiently waiting for his Tar Heel State to dissolve its bonds to the Union, John Steele Henderson, a young secessionist at preparatory school, reported with satisfaction that the state's secession convention was held on May 20, 1861, the "anniversary of Mecklenburgh [*sic*] Independence." On that day North Carolina became the tenth state to secede and join the Confederate States of America. The fact that North Carolina seceded on the anniversary of the Mecklenburg Declaration was no coincidence.[27]

Abolitionists turned the tables, invoking the right of revolution to justify enslaved people's resistance to slavery rather than slavemasters' resistance to abolition. Comforting a mother who mourned the death of her son in the Harpers Ferry Raid, Theodore Parker, the Boston abolitionist and member of the Secret Six, who funded John Brown's aborted slave revolt in Virginia, likened him to her ancestors who had fought at Lexington. "Slaves have a *natural Right to destroy their oppressors,*" Parker asserted, and it was the duty of all free people to help them. The *Liberator* derided efforts by the seceding slaveholders to invoke the Declaration as justification for their "unprovoked rebellion." The *Liberator* unconvincingly added that Southern secession was in no way analogous to abolitionists' appeals to Northern secession from the pro-slavery federal government.[28]

Moderates were nonplussed. John T. Dye, an Indianapolis lawyer, despaired over seeing the greatest government in the world "broken up *without cause.*" William Bodley, a Kentucky colonizationist, wrote to a Mississippi planter, hoping that the prodigal example of South Carolina would not induce the other "Cotton States," especially Mississippi, to secede. To clinch the argument, Bodley invoked the Declaration's preamble. "We have now a government that has secured to us 'life, liberty, & the pursuit of happiness' better than any government has ever done for any other people on the face of the earth." With good cause, North Carolina cotton planter William S. Pettigrew argued, federal government was as much the South's as the North's. "Let us not abandon our rich inheritance," Pettigrew implored, "to our enemies."[29]

The wounds inflicted by sectional quarrel over the American Revolution were reopened by secession and civil war. In 1860, the eighth volume of Bancroft's *History of the United States* appeared. It covered the period between June 17, 1775, and July 4, 1776, between the battle of Bunker Hill and the Declaration, which seemed apropos to many Southerners. Having written the chapter on the British attack on Fort Moultrie with the assistance of several South Carolina correspondents, Bancroft craved their approval.

Sectional moderates emphasized the fact that the United States had been
founded as a union of slave states. ("The Columbian Artillery, Boston." *Gleason's
Pictorial Drawing-Room Companion,* July 10, 1852.)

Despite the tumultuous times, the Northern historian got it. Nonetheless,
William Porcher Miles, a South Carolina hotspur, also took inspiration from
Bancroft's account of the Patriots' "spirit of *home* patriotism and the desire
for *self-government* in preference to the dictation of *distant interests.*" Miles
hoped that other Southerners would do so as well. The *Southern Literary
Messenger* was not so forgiving. The Virginia periodical believed that the
Northern historian's "prejudices" remained. The *Messenger* was offended by
Bancroft's argument that the origin of the Revolution came from the bottom
up. "The Revolution in Virginia did *not* spring form the masses, pushing
onward the 'gentry'—but from the gentry, who led the masses," the *Messenger* indignantly declared. "The ball of revolution," it protested, "was set
in motion by the *Cavaliers of the Tide-Water.*" The *Messenger* protested too
much. In the minds of elite planters, the only thing worse than slaves not
knowing their place was poor whites stepping outside their lowly station.
Charles F. Mayer, a Unionist living in Maryland in between the two waves of

secession, was outraged that that state's chief justice, John Carroll Legrand, writing under "cotton state inspiration" had "disparage[d] the merit of Massachusetts in her first Revolutionary movement, and in her relations during the Revolutionary War to the Southern States" as the Bay State had sent soldiers to help the South win its independence. Indeed, Mayer sputtered, the "scope of the reproach takes in all the Northern States." He believed that New England's small population rather than "indifference to the perils of the South" accounted for the modest number of New Englanders serving in that theater. Mayer wrote to Bancroft asking for assistance in refuting Legrand's "defamation of Massachusetts" in hopes that the *"truth of history"* would serve the "cause of the Union" in the "Middle States" by allaying the "waywardness of *Secession.*" While there is no record of Bancroft replying to Mayer nor of Mayer correcting Legrand, Massachusetts soldiers returned to the South shortly after Mayer's request. Rather than defending the South from the British, these Massachusetts soldiers were defending the United States from the South. On April 19, 1861, pro-secession Baltimoreans attacked the 6th Massachusetts as they walked through Charm City en route to the federal metropolis. The rioters used bricks, paving stones, and pistols and several soldiers returned fire. In all, four soldiers and twelve civilians were killed and dozens more on both sides were wounded and injured in the Pratt Street Riot. While four more slave states did secede after hostilities commenced in April 1861 at the ramparts of Fort Sumter and on the streets of Baltimore, Maryland was not one of them.[30]

Once the Confederates made the abstraction of secession into the reality of rebellion by attacking the U.S. Army garrison at Fort Sumter, Northerners tended to laud the Patriots as opponents of slavery, who merely tolerated that doomed colonial vestige for the sake of the Union. Freed from the need to mollify sensitive Southerners, Bancroft boldly informed a Briton that the South's revolt was proof that slavery was an American "anomaly" that could not be reconciled with the "doctrine of liberty." Even moderates, like Edward Everett, who were turned off by the Republicans' antislavery rhetoric and sectional appeal, believed that if the "present struggle [must be] compared with the Revolution," the North had Patrick Henry and the other Founders on its side. That Everett's claim of the slaveholding Virginian for the United States was based on Henry's call for "our Fathers to throw off the Yoke of the Oppression" applied equally well to slaves, abolitionists, and Confederates was lost on him.[31]

It was not lost on the *Richmond Enquirer* nor on Confederate soldiers. The *Enquirer* boasted that "all the descendants of the old Revolutionary patriots in the South are warmly enlisted in the resistance of Yankee invasion," including the son of Light Horse Harry Lee and the grandsons of Jefferson and Henry. Confederates in the field and at home invoked the Patriots. Henry Calvin Conner, a South Carolina infantry man in camp near Fairfax County, Virginia, paraphrased Henry to indicate the Confederates' desire to make a "vigorous defence" and to "show the Yankees and the world that the Spirit that animated their ancestors in the days of Seventy-Six has not Lost that fixed determination to be freemen or die." John H. Graham, a member of the 11th Mississippi, bragged to his diary that Lincoln could not rule "this fair land where 'Liberty or death'" was the motto of every man and boy.[32]

It was not lost on the *Liberator* nor on Union soldiers. In its efforts to defend the right to freedom of speech for abolitionists in the North, the *Liberator* came close to spurning its pacifism. "We may live as vassals or die like freedmen," it thundered. "Whether we be *resistants or non-resistants,* we cannot debase our manhood, stultify our souls, and willingly wear the tyrant's chain. The word of Revolutionary times should echo from every true heart—'Give me liberty or death.'" Americans in the field and at home invoked the Patriots. Thomas B. Drew, the abolitionist dentist, thought it was no coincidence that the Pratt Street Riot took place on April 19, 1861. That day, of course, had been consecrated by the Massachusetts militiamen eighty-six years earlier in Lexington and Concord. It was Massachusetts who had shed the first blood of the Civil War in just the same way as the Bay State had done in the Revolutionary War. James H. Campbell, the Pennsylvania Republican, visited Yorktown during the Peninsular Campaign and reflected on the melancholy fact that Americans, white and black, North and South, were fighting on the same battlefield where their forebears, white and black, North and South, had won American independence from the British: "Flowers enclosed grave[s] on the battle field. Old lines of the revolution army. White stone to mark where Cornwallis surrendered and enclosed yard with two trees where an aid of Gen. Washington was killed. Then the new Rebel lines. The heavy guns left spiked and loaded with shell. The Rifle pits. Some misc. contrabands digging graves—a daily task—as the hospitals contain 1600 wounded and sick and many die daily."[33] For patriotic Americans in the North and the South, it was indeed a world turned upside down. Their one nation had been divided by slavery.

# Permissions Acknowledgments

The author and publisher wish to thank the following institutions for permission to reproduce the following material from their collections:

Albert and Shirley Small Special Collections Library, University of Virginia: Thomas S. Bocock Papers; Cabell Family Papers; Cocke Family Papers; Edward Everett Papers; Gordon Family Papers; Hunter-Garnett Family Collection; Robert M. T. Hunter Papers; Letters to Socrates Maupin; Minor and Wilson Family Papers; Louisa H. A. Minor Diary; Anna Cora Ogden Mowatt Ritchie Papers; Rives Family Papers; Alexander H. H. Stuart Papers

David M. Rubenstein Rare Book & Manuscript Library, Duke University: Letter from Dennis Cooley to [R. Shane], June 1, 1853 (Dennis Cooley Letters); Letter from Andrew W. Cartwright to James D. B. De Bow, June 5, 1860 (James D. B. De Bow Papers); February 23, 1856 Diary entry (Julia Lord Noyes Loveland Papers); Committee of Arrangements to Charles Wilkes, Aug. 31, 1853 (Charles Wilkes Papers); Feb. 22, 1853, entry, 1852–1853 Diary (Matthew Jouett Williams Papers)

Southern Historical Collection, Wilson Library, The University of North Carolina at Chapel Hill: Material from the Joseph Nathaniel Allen Papers; Bryan and Leventhorpe Family Papers; John Bowen Bynum Papers; Gale and Polk Family Papers; John S. Henderson Papers; William H. Holcombe Diary and Autobiography; Franklin A. Hudson Diaries; James Manney Papers; William Porcher Miles Papers; David Outlaw Papers; John Perkins Papers; Pettigrew Family Papers; Scott Family Papers; William Henry Tripp and Araminta Guilford Tripp Papers; Benjamin C. Yancey Papers

William L. Clements Library, The University of Michigan: Material from the African American History Collection; American Travel Collection; James Birney Papers; Boynton Family Papers; Burwell-Guy Family Papers; James Hepburn Campbell Papers;

Lewis Cass Papers; Lydia Maria Child Papers; Corydon E. Fuller Journals; John H. Graham Journals; Artemas Hale Papers; Ruth N. Hastings Letters; Daniel R. Hundley Diary; A. H. Kingman Diaries; Miscellaneous Collections; John Wheeler Diary

Wisconsin Historical Society: William Henry Brisbane Papers; James D. Davidson Papers, McCormick Collection; John Givan Davis Correspondence; James R. Doolittle Papers; Edward D. Holton Papers; Byron Paine Papers; John F. Potter Papers

# Notes

## INTRODUCTION

1. James Ward Hopkins, June 26, 1856, Diary, James Ward Hopkins Papers, USC; Augustus James Pleasonton, Oct. 23, 1838, Augustus James Pleasonton Diary, HSP; Julia Marsh Patterson, n.d. [Aug. 1850], Journal of Julia Marsh Patterson, Benjamin C. Yancey Papers, UNC.

2. Byron Paine, "Speech," n.d., [1850], Byron Paine Papers, WHS; Giles Richards to Amos Adams Lawrence, Dec. 23, 1855, Amos Adams Lawrence Papers, MaHS; *Boston Liberator,* Oct. 28, 1859.

3. Winthrop D. Jordan, *Tumult and Silence at Second Creek: An Inquiry into a Civil War Slave Conspiracy,* rev. ed. (Baton Rouge: Louisiana State Univ. Press, 1995), 40; *Providence Post,* June 17, 1853; William Morris Davis to Henry K. Brown, Aug. 21, 1855, William Morris Davis Correspondence, HSP; *New York Tribune,* Mar. 11, 1857. For more on the importance of roll call in plantation discipline, see Stephanie M. H. Camp's *Closer to Freedom: Enslaved Women & Everyday Resistance in the Plantation South* (Chapel Hill: Univ. of North Carolina Press, 2004), 20-22.

4. *Hartford Courant,* May 27, 1854; *Boston Liberator,* Aug. 3, 1855; *Washington (D.C.) National Era,* Aug. 23, 1855; Pillsbury quoted in *Salem (Ohio) Anti-Slavery Bugle,* Oct. 3, 1857; Schurz quoted in Kenneth M. Stampp, *America in 1857: A Nation on the Brink* (New York: Oxford Univ. Press, 1990), 105; (Rochester) *Frederick Douglass's Paper,* June 8, 1855; Leonard W. Levy, *The Law of the Commonwealth and Justice Shaw* (Cambridge, Mass.: Harvard Univ. Press, 1957), 62-68.

5. Ellen Grover to Theodore Parker, Nov. 5, 1857, Theodore Parker Papers, MaHS; Colby quoted in *Salem (Ohio) Anti-Slavery Bugle,* Feb. 6, 1858.

6. *Boston Liberator,* Aug. 28, 1857; Theodore Parker to William R. Alger, July 7, 1857, Theodore Parkers Papers, MaHS; *St. Louis Missouri Democrat,* June 26, 1857.

7. *Boston Post,* June 22, 1857; *Cincinnati Commercial,* July 10, 1857.

8. William Cabell Rives Jr. to Judith P. Rives, Dec. 16, 1856, Rives Family Papers, UVA; Georgian quoted in *Boston Post,* Sept. 11, 1856; James Hamilton Couper to Francis P. Corbin, July 17, 1854, Francis Porteous Corbin Papers, NYPL.

9. John Hope Franklin, *Southern Odyssey: Travelers in the Antebellum North* (Baton Rouge: Louisiana State Univ. Press, 1975), 224-28; *Boston Post,* Jan. 28, 1856; *Boston Herald,* Jan. 25, 1856; Ulrich Bonnell Phillips, *The Life of Robert Toombs* (New York: Macmillan, 1913), 184; Robert Toombs, "Relation of the States," Feb. 20, 1860, U.S. Congress, *Congressional Globe,* 36th Cong., 1st sess., 838.

10. "The South-Side View of Slavery," *New Englander and Yale Review* 13 (Feb. 1855): 89; Robert C. Winthrop Jr., ed., *A Memoir of Robert C. Winthrop,* 2d ed. (Boston: Little, Brown, and Company, 1897), 220n2; Richard Hofstadter, *The Paranoid Style in American Politics and Other Essays* (New York: Knopf, 1965), 4; Eric Foner, *Free Soil, Free Labor, Free Men: The Ideology of the Republican Party Before the Civil War,* rev. ed. (New York: Oxford Univ. Press, 1995), 97.

11. *Cincinnati Commercial,* Oct. 31, 1859; John P. Hale to Theodore Parker, Dec. 23, 1856, Theodore Parker Papers, MaHS; Pleasant A. Stovall, *Robert Toombs: Statesman, Speaker, Soldier, Sage* (New York: Cassell Publishing Co., 1892), 119; Toombs quoted in *New York Times,* July 8, 1879. The modern biographers of Hale and Toombs ignore the controversy entirely. See Richard H. Sewall, *John P. Hale and the Politics of Abolition* (Cambridge, Mass.: Harvard Univ. Press, 1965), and William Y. Thompson, *Robert Toombs of Georgia* (Baton Rouge: Louisiana State Univ. Press, 1966).

12. *New York Times,* Sept. 27, 1856; *Lawrence Republican,* Feb. 2, 1860.

13. William Frederick Keeler to Anna Keeler, Mar. 28, 1863, in Robert W. Daly, ed., *Aboard the USS Florida, 1863-65: The Letters of Paymaster William Frederick Keeler, U.S. Navy, to His Wife, Anna* (New York: Arno Press, 1980), 11; *New York Times,* Mar. 24, 1863; Charles Eliot Norton, ed., *Orations and Addresses of George William Curtis* (New York: Harper and Brothers, 1894), 2:148; Oliver P. Temple, *East Tennessee and the Civil War* (Cincinnati: R. Clarke Company, 1899), 336 (thanks to Bruce Levine for this reference); William J. Bennett, *America: The Last Best Hope,* vol. 1, *From the Age of Discovery to a World at War* (Nashville: Nelson Current, 2006), 294. For more references to Toombs's boast, see Parker Pillsbury, *Acts of the Anti-Slavery Apostles* (Concord, N.H.: Clague, Wegman, Schlicht, 1883), 463-64; John Minor Botts, *The Great Rebellion: Its Secret History, Rise, Progress, and Disastrous Failure* (New York: Harper & Brothers, 1866), 115; William A. Sinclair, *The Aftermath of Slavery: A Study of the Condition and Environment of the American Negro* (Boston: Small, Maynard, 1905), 18; George Spring Merriam, *The Negro and the Nation: A History of American Slavery and Enfranchisement* (New York: Henry Holt, 1906), 136-37.

14. William L. Andrews, ed., *From Fugitive Slave to Free Man: The Autobiographies of William Wells Brown* (Columbia: Univ. of Missouri Press, 1993), 77-78; *Sandwich (Canada West [Ont.]) Voice of the Fugitive,* Feb. 12, 1851. For more on William and Ellen Craft's improbable escape, see Richard J. M. Blacklett, *Running a Thousand Miles for Freedom* (Baton Rouge: Louisiana State Univ. Press, 1999).

15. Gary B. Nash, Charlotte Crabtree, and Ross E. Dunn, *History on Trial: Culture Wars and the Teaching of the Past* (New York: Alfred A. Knopf, 1997); Edward T.

Linenthal and Tom Engelhardt, eds., *History Wars: The* Enola Gay *and Other Battles for the American Past* (New York: Henry Holt, 1996).

16. Seymour Drescher, *Abolition: A History of Slavery and Antislavery* (Cambridge: Cambridge Univ. Press, 2009), 297.

17. Michael A. Morrison, *Slavery and the American West: The Eclipse of Manifest Destiny and the Coming of the Civil War* (Chapel Hill: Univ. of North Carolina Press, 1997), 95; Eric Foner, *Story of American Freedom* (New York: W. W. Norton, 1998), 90; David Goldfield, *Still Fighting the Civil War: The American South and Southern History* (Baton Rouge: Louisiana State Univ. Press, 2002), 17; Edward L. Ayers, *In the Presence of Mine Enemies: War in the Heart of America, 1859-1863* (New York: W. W. Norton, 2003), 417; Shearer Davis Bowman, *At the Precipice: Americans North and South during the Secession Crisis* (Chapel Hill: Univ. of North Carolina Press, 2010), 3.

18. Paul C. Nagel, *This Sacred Trust: American Nationality, 1798-1898* (New York: Oxford Univ. Press, 1971); Fred Somkin, *Unquiet Eagle: Memory and Desire in the Idea of American Freedom, 1815-1860* (Ithaca, N.Y.: Cornell Univ. Press, 1967); Major Wilson, *Space, Time, and Freedom: The Quest for Nationality and the Irrepressible Conflict, 1815-1861* (Westport, Conn.: Greenwood Press, 1974).

19. Carl N. Degler, "Thesis, Antithesis, Synthesis: The South, the North, and the Nation," *Journal of Southern History* 53 (Feb. 1987): 5-6.

20. Charles S. Sydnor, *The Development of Southern Sectionalism, 1819-1848* (Baton Rouge: Louisiana State Univ. Press, 1948); Avery O. Craven, *The Growth of Southern Nationalism, 1848-1861* (Baton Rouge: Louisiana State Univ. Press, 1953); John McCardell, *The Idea of a Southern Nation: Southern Nationalists and Southern Nationalism, 1830-1860* (New York: W. W. Norton, 1979).

21. Gary Gallagher, *The Confederate War: How Popular Will, Nationalism, and Military Strategy Could Not Stave Off Defeat* (Cambridge, Mass.: Harvard Univ. Press, 1997); Drew Gilpin Faust, *The Creation of Southern Nationalism: Ideology and Identity in the Civil War South* (Baton Rouge: Louisiana State Univ. Press, 1988).

22. Paul D. Escott, *After Secession: Jefferson Davis and the Failure of Confederate Nationalism* (Baton Rouge: Louisiana State Univ. Press, 1978); George C. Rable, *Civil Wars: Women and the Crisis of Southern Nationalism* (Urbana: Univ. of Illinois Press, 1989).

23. Susan-Mary Grant, *North over South: Northern Nationalism and American Identity in the Antebellum Era* (Lawrence: Univ. Press of Kansas, 2000).

24. Paul Quigley, *Shifting Grounds: Nationalism and the American South, 1848-1865* (New York: Oxford Univ. Press, 2012).

25. Andre M. Fleche, *The Revolution of 1861: The American Civil War in the Age of Nationalist Conflict* (Chapel Hill: Univ. of North Carolina Press, 2012).

26. Charles Grier Sellers Jr., "Introduction," in Charles Grier Sellers Jr., ed., *The Southerner as American* (Chapel Hill: Univ. of North Carolina Press, 1960), 2; Edward L. Ayers, "What We Talk about When We Talk about the South," in Edward L. Ayers and Peter S. Onuf, eds., *All over the Map: Rethinking American Regions* (Baltimore: Johns Hopkins Univ. Press, 1996), 65; Wilbur Zelinsky, *Nation into State: The Shifting Symbolic Foundations of American Nationalism* (Chapel Hill: Univ. of North Carolina Press, 1988), 231; Larry J. Griffin and Don H. Doyle, "Introduction," in Larry J. Griffin and Don H.

Doyle, eds., *The South as an American Problem* (Athens: Univ. of Georgia Press, 1995), 1; Grant, *North over South,* 9, 17; James C. Cobb, *Away Down South: A History of Southern Identity* (New York: Oxford Univ. Press, 2005), 2–3; Liah Greenfield, *Nationalism: Five Roads to Modernity* (Cambridge, Mass.: Harvard Univ. Press, 1992), 476.

27. Benedict Anderson, *Imagined Communities: Reflections on the Origin and Spread of Nationalism,* rev. ed. (New York: Verso, 1991), 6–7; Eric Hobsbawm, "Introduction: Inventing Traditions," in Eric Hobsbawm and Terrence Ranger, eds., *The Invention of Tradition* (Cambridge: Cambridge Univ. Press, 1992), 1–4.

28. Leonard L. Richards, *The Slave Power: The Free North and Southern Domination, 1780–1860* (Baton Rouge: Louisiana State Univ. Press, 2000), 113n7.

29. William C. Rives, *Letter from the Hon. William C. Rives to a Friend, on the Important Questions of the Day* (Richmond, Va.: Whig Book and Job Office, 1860), 8; *New York Herald,* Feb. 27, 1850; W. M. Corry to Lewis Sanders, Mar. 26, 1859, Sanders Family Papers, FHS; *Memphis Appeal,* July 25, 1854; Thomas Carlyle, "Occasional Discourse on the Nigger Question" (1853), in Oliver Cromwell and Thomas Carlyle, eds., *Complete Works of Thomas Carlyle,* vol. 4, *Critical and Miscellaneous Essays* (New York: P. F. Collier, 1901), 293–326. Randall Kennedy explains, "*nigger* is a key word in the lexicon of race relations"; Randall Kennedy, *Nigger: The Strange Career of a Troublesome Word* (New York: Pantheon, 2003), 4.

30. *New York National Anti-Slavery Standard,* Mar. 15, 1856.

31. *Richmond Whig,* Oct. 7, 1848.

32. Daniel Huger, Wade Hampton et al. to Peter Bryce, Aug. 2, 1847, Glass Family Papers, USC; Frank V. Winston to John B. Minor, Mar. 10, 1860, Minor and Wilson Family Papers, UVA; Glover Moore, *The Missouri Controversy, 1819–1821* (Lexington: Univ. of Kentucky Press, 1953), 103–4, 201–3, 209–10; John Russell Bartlett, *Dictionary of Americanisms: A Glossary of Words and Phrases Usually Regarded as Peculiar to the United States* (Boston: Little, Brown, 1860), 128; Michael F. Conlin, "The Dangerous *Isms* and the Fanatical *Ists:* Antebellum Conservatives in the South and the North Confront the Modernity Conspiracy," *Journal of the Civil War Era* 4 (June 2014): 221–25; David Outlaw to Emily B. Outlaw, May 20, 1850, David Outlaw Papers, UNC.

33. Abolitionist quoted in (Rochester) *Frederick Douglass's Paper,* Apr. 14, 1854; William Lloyd Garrison, "Preface," in Frederick Douglass, *Narrative of the Life of Frederick Douglass, an American Slave,* ed. Deborah E. McDowell (1845; New York: Oxford Univ. Press, 1999), 11; *Charleston Mercury,* Mar. 18, 1850; George M. Dallas to Muscoe R. H. Garnett, July 5, 1851, Hunter-Garnett Family Collection, UVA.

34. Len Travers, *Celebrating the Fourth: Independence Day and the Rites of Nationalism in the Early Republic* (Amherst: Univ. of Massachusetts Press, 1997) focuses on the Early Republic; Mitch Kachun, *Festivals of Freedom: Memory and Meaning in African American Emancipation Celebrations, 1808–1915* (Amherst: Univ. of Massachusetts Press, 2003), focuses on African Americans, especially those in the North; Paul Quigley, "Independence Day Dilemmas in the American South, 1848–1865," *Journal of Southern History* 75 (May 2009): 241–53, focuses on whites in the states that ultimately seceded; and Adam Criblez, *Parading Patriotism: Independence Day Celebrations in the Urban Midwest, 1826–1876* (New York: New York Univ. Press, 2014), focuses on the North.

35. Merrill D. Peterson, *The Jeffersonian Image in the American Mind* (New York: Oxford Univ. Press, 1960), 162-209.

36. Jeremy J. Tewell, "Assuring Freedom to the Free: Jefferson's Declaration and the Conflict over Slavery," *Civil War History* 58 (Mar. 2012): 75-96.

37. Michael F. Conlin, "'All Men Are *Born Free and* Equal': The Radicalization of the Declaration of Independence by Slaves, Abolitionists, Slavemasters, and Doughfaces, 1840-1861," in John R. Neff, ed., *"And the War Came": Essays on the Coming of the Civil War* (Jackson: Univ. of Mississippi Press, forthcoming).

38. Charlene Mires, *Independence Hall in American Memory* (Philadelphia: Univ. of Pennsylvania Press, 2002).

39. Gerald E. Kahler, *The Long Farewell: Americans Mourn the Death of George Washington* (Charlottesville: Univ. Press of Virginia, 2008); Barry Schwartz, *George Washington: The Making of an American Symbol* (New York: Free Press, 1987); François Furstenberg, *In the Name of the Father: Washington's Legacy, Slavery, and the Making of a Nation* (New York: Penguin, 2006).

40. Alfred E. Young, *The Shoemaker and the Tea Party: Memory and the American Revolution* (Boston: Beacon Press, 1999); Sarah J. Purcell, *Sealed with Blood: War, Sacrifice, and Memory in Revolutionary America* (Philadelphia: Univ. of Pennsylvania Press, 2002); Thomas A. Chambers, *Memories of War: Visiting Battlegrounds and Bonefields in the Early American Republic* (Ithaca, N.Y.: Cornell Univ. Press, 2012).

41. Jonathan B. Crider, "De Bow's Revolution: The Memory of the American Revolution in the Politics of the Sectional Crisis, 1850-1861," *American Nineteenth Century History* 10 (Sept. 2009): 317-32; Margot Minardi, *Making Slavery History: Abolitionism and the Politics of Memory in Massachusetts* (New York: Oxford Univ. Press, 2010); Chambers, *Memories of War*, 159-84; Robert E. Bonner, *Mastering America: Southern Slaveholders and the Crisis of American Nationhood* (New York: Cambridge Univ. Press, 2009).

## 1. THE FOURTH OF JULY

1. James R. Doolittle, "Remarks on the Declaration of Independence," July 4, 1835, James R. Doolittle Papers, WHS; *Richmond Whig*, July 4, 1849.

2. William C. Preston to Francis Lieber, July 3, 1858, Francis Lieber Papers, USC; Dennis F. Dealy, July 4, 1855, Diary, Dennis F. Dealy Papers, HSP. For more on the memory of Independence Hall, see Charlene Mires, *Independence Hall in American Memory* (Philadelphia: Univ. of Pennsylvania Press, 2002).

3. *Charleston Courier*, July 9, 1849.

4. Review of George Sumner's *An Oration Delivered before the Municipal Authorities of Boston, July 4, 1859, North American Review* 89 (Oct. 1859): 558; John C. Bullitt, Fourth of July Oration, n.d., [1842], Bullitt Family Papers—Oxmoor Collection, FHS.

5. *Charleston Courier*, July 10, 1850, and July 8, 1850; Thelma Jennings, *The Nashville Convention: Southern Movement for Unity, 1848-1851* (Memphis: Memphis State Univ. Press, 1980), 146-47; Ohio abolitionist quoted in *Boston Liberator*, July 25, 1851.

6. Paul Quigley, "Independence Day Dilemmas in the American South, 1848-1865," *Journal of Southern History* 75 (May 2009): 247; Paul Finkelman, *Slavery and the Founders: Race and Liberty in the Age of Jefferson,* 2nd ed. (Armonk, N.Y.: M. E. Sharpe, 2001), 6; Don E. Fehrenbacher, *The Slaveholding Republic: An Account of the United States Government's Relations to Slavery* (New York: Oxford Univ. Press, 2001), 306; William B. Napton, Aug. 10, 1856, Diary Typescripts, pp. 166-67, William B. Napton Papers, MHM; *Charleston Mercury,* July 9, 1852.

7. *Charleston Courier,* July 9, 1849; "The National Anniversary," *Southern Quarterly Review,* 2nd ser., 2 (Sept. 1850): 190-91; *Charleston Mercury,* July 9, 1851, and July 21, 1852.

8. *Charleston Mercury,* July 7, 1849; emphasis added. For more on how antebellum Americans reacted to the Revolutions of 1848, see Timothy Mason Roberts, *Distant Revolutions: 1848 and the Challenge to American Exceptionalism* (Charlottesville: Univ. of Virginia Press, 2009).

9. Corydon E. Fuller, July 4, 1857, Corydon E. Fuller Journals, vol. 1, Schoff Civil War Collection, Diaries and Journals, UMich; J. M. Wallace to B. T. Watts, July 6, 1844, Beauford Taylor Watts Papers, USC; *Charleston Mercury,* July 7, 1849; Avery O. Craven, *The Growth of Southern Nationalism, 1848-1861* (Baton Rouge: Louisiana State Univ. Press, 1953), 63; Carol K. Bleser, ed., *Secret and Sacred: The Diaries of James Henry Hammond, a Southern Slaveholder* (New York: Oxford Univ. Press, 1988), 151.

10. William Porcher Miles, *Oration Delivered before the Fourth of July Association* (Charleston, S.C.: James S. Burges, 1849), 13; *Charleston Courier,* July 9, 1849; Gilbert Lafayette Strait, W. A. Peden, and O. Barber to James Craig, June 1, 1859, Papers of the Gaston, Strait, Wylie, and Baskin Families, USC.

11. James C. Drew, Amos R. Strong, Joseph Spurlock et al. to John Perkins, June 5, 1855, John Perkins Papers, UNC; R. P. Starke to Benjamin C. Yancey, Feb. 3, 1850, Benjamin C. Yancey Papers, UNC; Kentuckian quoted in *Louisville Democrat,* July 7, 1851; *Charleston Mercury,* July 28, 1859.

12. William Henry Holcombe, Jan. 18, 1855, William Henry Holcombe Diary, UNC; Rogene A. Scott to Hannah Scott Warren, July 22, 1859, Scott Family Papers, UNC; *Memphis Appeal,* July 6, 1860; *Charleston Mercury,* July 17, 1852; Corydon E. Fuller, July 16, 1857, Corydon E. Fuller Journals, vol. 1, Schoff Civil War Collection, Diaries and Journals, UMich; Henry Mayer, *All on Fire: William Lloyd Garrison and the Abolition of Slavery* (New York: W. W. Norton, 1998), 226-28; Cassius M. Clay to the Republican Association of Washington, Feb. 8, 1856, Cassius M. Clay Papers, FHS.

13. Patience Essah, *A House Divided: Slavery and Emancipation in Delaware, 1638-1865* (Charlottesville: Univ. Press of Virginia, 1996), 86-87; Matthew Dennis, *Red, White, and Blue Letter Days: An American Calendar* (Ithaca, N.Y.: Cornell Univ. Press, 2002), 22-23; William H. Tripp, July 4, 1854, William H. Tripp Diary, William Henry and Araminta Guilford Tripp Papers, UNC; Curtis W. Jacobs, June 26-July 5, 1856, Curtis W. Jacobs Diary and Account Book, MdHS; Winthrop D. Jordan, *Tumult and Silence at Second Creek: An Inquiry into a Civil War Slave Conspiracy,* rev. ed. (Baton Rouge: Louisiana State Univ. Press, 1995), 134.

14. Eugene D. Genovese, *Roll, Jordan, Roll: The World the Slaves Made* (1972; New York: Vintage, 1976), 575, 577; William S. Pettigrew to Moses, July 6, 1857, in Robert

S. Starobin, ed., *Blacks in Bondage: Letters of American Slaves* (Princeton, N.J.: Markus Wiener, 1988), 22-23; Kenneth M. Stampp, *The Peculiar Institution: Slavery in the Ante-Bellum South* (1956; New York: Vintage Books, 1989), 169; David Wyatt Aiken, July 5, 1858, Diary, David Wyatt Aiken Papers, USC; *Charleston Mercury,* July 6, 1849; *New York National Anti-Slavery Standard,* Aug. 7, 1858.

15. Charlestonian quoted in William H. Freehling, *Prelude to Civil War: The Nullification Controversy in South Carolina, 1816-1836* (New York: Oxford Univ. Press, 1965), 52; *Richmond Whig,* July 6, 1850.

16. Frederick Douglass, "What to the Slave Is the Fourth of July?" in John W. Blassingame, ed., *Frederick Douglass Papers, Series One: Speeches, Debates, and Interviews,* vol. 2, *1847-54* (New Haven, Conn.: Yale Univ. Press, 1982), 360, 371; John Wheeler, Aug. 3, 1859, John Wheeler Diary, UMich; Turner quoted in Louis P. Masur, *1831: Year of Eclipse* (New York: Hill and Wang, 2001), 9; Freehling, *Prelude to Civil War,* 250. For a thoughtful analysis of Douglass's ambivalence toward the Fourth of July and the Constitution, see James A. Colaiaco, *Frederick Douglass and the Fourth of July* (New York: Palgrave Macmillan, 2007).

17. Eric Foner, *The Story of American Freedom* (New York: W. W. Norton, 1998), 89; Douglass, "What to the Slave Is the Fourth of July?" 2:361. Indeed, Douglass compared his own battle for freedom with that of Henry's; see Frederick Douglass, *Narrative of the Life of Frederick Douglass, An American Slave,* ed. Deborah E. McDowell (1845; New York: Oxford Univ. Press, 1999), 77-78.

18. Julie Roy Jeffrey, *The Great Silent Army of Abolitionism: Ordinary Women in the Antislavery Movement* (Chapel Hill: Univ. of North Carolina Press, 1999), 65; (Rochester) *Frederick Douglass's Paper,* June 10, 1853.

19. Brown quoted in *New York National Anti-Slavery Standard,* July 16, 1859. For more on the practice of hiring out slaves, see Jonathan D. Martin, *Divided Mastery: Slave Hiring in the American South* (Cambridge, Mass.: Harvard Univ. Press, 2004), and John J. Zaborney, *Slaves for Hire: Renting Enslaved Laborers in Antebellum Virginia* (Baton Rouge: Louisiana State Univ. Press, 2012).

20. William Henry Brisbane, July 4, 1845, Diary, William Henry Brisbane Papers, WHS; Ohioan quoted in *Salem (Ohio) Anti-Slavery Bugle,* July 30, 1853; *New York National Anti-Slavery Standard,* July 15, 1854; free blacks in New York quoted in Leon F. Litwack, *North of Slavery: The Negro in the Free States, 1790-1861* (Chicago: Univ. of Chicago Press, 1961), 235-36.

21. Foner, *Story of American Freedom,* 87; Ira Berlin, *Slaves without Masters: The Free Negro in the Antebellum South* (New York: Random House, 1974), 314-15; Laurent Dubois, *Avengers of the New World: The Story of the Haitian Revolution* (Cambridge, Mass.: Harvard Univ. Press, 2004), 1, 298-301; Edwin G. Burrows and Mike Wallace, *Gotham: A History of New York City to 1898* (New York: Oxford Univ. Press, 1999), 547; William Henry Brisbane, Aug. 1, 1849, and Aug.1, 1859, Diary, William Henry Brisbane Papers, WHS; Mitch Kachun, *Festivals of Freedom: Memory and Meaning in African American Emancipation Celebrations, 1808-1915* (Amherst: Univ. of Massachusetts Press, 2003), 55-56; *Philadelphia Pennsylvania Freeman,* July 10, 1852; (Rochester) *Frederick Douglass's Paper,* Sept. 22, 1854, and Sept. 24, 1852. For more

on the celebration of West India Day across the Atlantic, see J. R. Kerr-Ritchie, *Rites of August First: Emancipation Day in the Black Atlantic World* (Baton Rouge: Louisiana State Univ. Press, 2007).

22. Samuel J. May to Samuel E. Sewall, Sept. 23, 1853, Robie-Sewall Family Papers, MaHS; *Boston Liberator,* Apr. 2, 1852.

23. *New Orleans Picayune,* July 18, 1851; *Charleston Mercury,* July 12, 1851.

24. John Wolcott Phelps, July 4, 1851, Diary, John Wolcott Phelps Papers, NYPL; Cullen Bryant to Cyrus Bryant, July 5, 1860, Bryant Family Papers, NYPL; Theodore J. Crackel, *West Point: A Bicentennial History* (Lawrence: Univ. Press of Kansas, 2002), 123-31.

25. Abolitionist quoted in *Baltimore Sun,* July 17, 1856; Leonard L. Richards, *"Gentlemen of Property and Standing": Anti-Abolition Mobs in Jacksonian America* (New York: Oxford Univ. Press, 1970), 69; Nicholas B. Wainwright, "The Age of Nicholas Biddle, 1825-1841," in Russell F. Weigley et al., eds., *Philadelphia: A 300-Year History* (New York: W. W. Norton, 1982), 295; David Grimsted, *American Mobbing, 1828-1861: Toward Civil War* (New York: Oxford Univ. Press, 1998), 58-60.

26. Elliot Crisson to John H. Cocke, July 4, 1851, Cocke Family Papers, UVA; John Bowen Bynum, Fourth of July oration, 1849, John Bowen Bynum Papers, UNC; *Charleston Courier,* July 6, 1850.

27. Robert W. Johannsen, *Stephen A. Douglas* (1973; Urbana: Univ. of Illinois Press, 1997), 445-56; Dennis F. Dealy, July 4, 1854, Diary, Dennis F. Dealy Papers, HSP.

28. Albert J. Von Frank, *The Trials of Anthony Burns: Freedom and Slavery in Emerson's Boston* (Cambridge, Mass.: Harvard Univ. Press, 1998), 279; Michael Kammen, *A Machine That Would Go of Itself: The Constitution in American Culture* (New York: Alfred A. Knopf, 1986), 98.

29. *New Orleans Picayune,* July 13, 1854; *Charleston Mercury,* July 31, 1854.

30. *Boston Herald,* June 28, 1858; *New Orleans Picayune,* June 23, 1854; (New York) *Frank Leslie's Illustrated Newspaper,* July 12, 1856.

## 2. THOMAS JEFFERSON

1. W. M. Corry to Lewis Sanders, Dec. n.d., [1857], Sanders Family Papers, FHS; "Thomas Jefferson," *De Bow's Review* 24 (June 1858): 508-9; *Cincinnati Commercial,* Apr. 2, 1851.

2. Oscar J. C. Stuart to Alexander H. H. Stuart, Aug. 8, 1859, Alexander H. H. Stuart Papers, UVA; *New York Tribune,* Apr. 22, 1850.

3. Agnes Richardson, Aug. 31, 1859, Agnes Richardson Travel Journal, John Smythe Richardson Papers, USC; William C. Preston to Francis Lieber, July 3, 1858, Francis Lieber Papers, USC. In the twenty-first century, some 450,000 people visit Monticello each year. (Edward Rothstein, "Jefferson's Blind Spot and Ideals, in Brick and Mortar," *New York Times,* Apr. 10, 2009.)

4. Melvin I. Urofsky, *Levy Family and Monticello, 1834-1923: Saving Thomas Jefferson's House* (Charlottesville: Thomas Jefferson Foundation, 2002), 68-75; (New York) *Frank Leslie's Illustrated Newspaper,* Oct. 18, 1856; William S. Pettigrew to H. Hardi-

son, Oct. 15, 1857, Pettigrew Family Papers, UNC; Marc Leepson, *Saving Monticello: The Levy Family's Epic Quest to Rescue the House That Jefferson Built* (New York: Free Press, 2001), 71-75; John Wheeler, n.d. [Aug., 1859], John Wheeler Diary, UMich; Charles B. Sanford, *The Religious Life of Thomas Jefferson* (Charlottesville: Univ. Press of Virginia, 1984), 85-88. In 1923, the Levy family sold Monticello to the Thomas Jefferson Memorial Foundation, which maintains the estate today.

5. William Fitzhugh Gordon to Elizabeth Lindsay Gordon, Mar. 29, 1830, Gordon Family Papers, UVA; John B. Minor to Nancy C. Minor, Apr. 13, 1859, Minor and Wilson Family Papers, UVA; Louisa H. A. Minor, Apr. 18, 1857, Louisa H. A. Minor Diary, UVA.

6. Philip Alexander Bruce, *History of the University of Virginia, 1819-1919: The Lengthened Shadow of One Man* (New York: Macmillan, 1921), 2:355-59; Alison Good-year Freehling, *Drift toward Dissolution: The Virginia Slavery Debate of 1831-1832* (Baton Rouge: Louisiana State Univ. Press, 1982), 129.

7. George W. Randolph to John B. Minor, July 14 1851, Minor and Wilson Family Papers, UVA; Joseph C. Cabell to John H. Cocke, July 12, 1850, Cabell Family Papers, UVA. For the text of the offending oration, see Muscoe R. H. Garnett, *An Address Delivered before the Society of Alumni of the University of Virginia* (Charlottesville, Va.: O. S. Allen, 1850). The Dialectic Society at the U.S. Military Academy was disbanded after it broached sectional issues in 1843; Theodore J. Crackel, *West Point: A Bicentennial History* (Lawrence: Univ. Press of Kansas, 2002), 123.

8. John Bigelow, Apr. 13, 1851, 1843-1853 Diary, John Bigelow Papers, NYPL; Gideon Welles to the Committee of Arrangements, Apr. 9, 1859, John A. Andrew Papers, MaHS; John Howard, William H. Macfarland, G. N. Johnson et al., "Memorial of the Virginia Colonization Society," *Southern Literary Messenger* 18 (Aug. 1852): 500; *Boston Post,* Sept. 8, 1855. For more on colonization, see Beverly C. Tomek, *Colonization and Its Discontents: Emancipation, Emigration, and Antislavery in Antebellum Pennsylvania* (New York: New York Univ. Press, 2014).

9. James R. Doolittle, "The Character of Thomas Jefferson," n.d. [Apr. 13, 1834], James R. Doolittle Papers, WHS.

10. Whitman quoted in Jonathan H. Earle, *Jacksonian Antislavery and the Politics of Free Soil, 1824-1854* (Chapel Hill: Univ. of North Carolina Press, 2004), 163-64; (Rochester) *Frederick Douglass's Paper,* Jan. 4, 1855.

11. Louisa S. McCord, "Diversity of the Races; Its Bearing upon Negro Slavery," *Southern Quarterly Review,* 2d ser., 3 (Apr. 1851): 403-4; *Richmond Enquirer,* May 9, 1851.

12. George W. Randolph to Joseph C. Cabell, Sept. 23, 1851, Cabell Family Papers, UVA; George W. Randolph to John B. Minor, July 14, 1851, Minor and Wilson Family Papers, UVA; Henry S. Randall, *The Life of Jefferson, in Three Volumes* (New York: Derby & Jackson, 1858), 1:11, 133, 63n2, 58, and 3:328, 498-500.

13. Randall, *Life of Jefferson,* 3:667-68; Merrill D. Peterson, *The Jeffersonian Image in the American Mind* (New York: Oxford Univ. Press, 1960), 151.

14. Randall, *Life of Jefferson,* 3:19n2; Annette Gordon-Reed, *Thomas Jefferson and Sally Hemings: An American Controversy* (Charlottesville: Univ. Press of Virginia, 1997), 2.

15. Henry S. Randall to Theodore Parker, Apr. 18, 1856, Theodore Parker Papers, MaHS; Gordon-Reed, *Jefferson and Hemings,* 81; Winthrop D. Jordan, *White over Black: American Attitudes towards the Negro, 1550-1812* (Chapel Hill: Univ. of North Carolina

Press, 1968), 466; Eugene A. Foster et al., "Jefferson Fathered Slave's Last Child," *Nature* 396 (Nov. 1998): 27-28; Fraser D. Neiman, "Coincidence or Causal Connection? The Relationship between Thomas Jefferson's Visits to Monticello and Sally Hemings's Conceptions," *William & Mary Quarterly,* 3rd ser., 57 (Jan. 2000): 198-210. For more on Ockham's Razor, see Roger Ariew, "Ockham's Razor: A Historical and Philosophical Analysis of Ockham's Principle of Parsimony" (Ph.D. diss., Univ. of Illinois at Urbana-Champaign, 1976).

16. George Frederick Holmes, "A Key to Uncle Tom's Cabin," *Southern Literary Messenger* 19 (June 1853): 322; Virginia Ingraham Burr, ed., *The Secret Eye: The Journal of Ella Gertrude Clanton Thomas, 1848-1889* (Chapel Hill: Univ. of North Carolina Press, 1990), 168; *Charleston Courier,* Mar. 18, 1854; Fanny Trollope, *Domestic Manners of the Americans,* ed. Pamela Neville-Sington (1832; New York: Penguin, 1997), 245-46; *New York National Anti-Slavery Standard,* Aug. 26, 1847.

17. W. M. Corry to Lewis Sanders, Dec. n.d., [1857], Sanders Family Papers, FHS; Arthur P. Hayne to Henry S. Randall, Feb. 15, 1859, Arthur P. Hayne Papers, USC; *Louisville Democrat,* June 2, 1858; Review of Henry S. Randall's *Life of Thomas Jefferson, North American Review* 87 (Oct. 1858): 563; "Notices of New Books," *Southern Literary Messenger* 27 (Apr. 1858): 319; *Memphis Appeal,* May 7, 1858.

18. William W. Freehling, "The Founding Fathers and Slavery," *American Historical Review* 77 (Feb. 1972): 82.

19. Thomas Jefferson, *Notes on the State of Virginia* (1783; Richmond: J. W. Randolph, 1853), 174-75.

20. Sarah Moore Grimké, *An Epistle to the Clergy of the Southern States* (New York: n.p., 1836), 19; *Philadelphia Pennsylvania Freeman,* Mar. 1, 1849; John Boynton to Isaac Boynton, July 4, 1836, Boynton Family Papers, Duane N. Diedrich Collection, UMich.

21. Jefferson, *Notes on Virginia,* 174.

22. Finkelman, *Slavery and the Founders,* 176-77; Northerner living in the South quoted in *New York National Anti-Slavery Standard,* Mar. 19, 1846; *Boston Liberator,* Mar. 13, 1857; *Chicago Tribune,* Oct. 26, 1859.

23. "Slavery in the Virginia Legislature of 1831-'32, (Concluded)," *De Bow's Review* 20 (Apr. 1856): 471a-72a.

24. John Bigelow, Dec. 9, 1843, and Apr. 13, 1851, 1843-53 Diary, John Bigelow Papers, NYPL. For more on how modern historians have treated Jefferson's temporizing on slavery, see Andrew Burstein, *The Inner Jefferson: Portrait of a Grieving Optimist* (Charlottesville: Univ. Press of Virginia, 1995), 279, and Joseph J. Ellis, *American Sphinx: The Character of Thomas Jefferson* (New York: Alfred A. Knopf, 1997), 146, 152.

25. Earle, *Jacksonian Antislavery,* 2, 193; Peter S. Onuf, *Statehood and Union: A History of the Northwest Ordinance* (Bloomington: Indiana Univ. Press, 1987), 110-11; John Bigelow, June 12, 1859, 1859-60 Diary, John Bigelow Papers, NYPL; Chaplain W. Morrison, *Democratic Politics and Sectionalism: The Wilmot Proviso Controversy* (Chapel Hill: Univ. of North Carolina Press, 1967), 17-18; Byron Paine, "Reply to Senator [Isaac P.] Walker," n.d., [1849-50], Byron Paine Papers, WHS; Anthony B. Cleveland, "Speech," n.d., [1848], Anthony B. Cleveland Papers, MaHS.

26. Peter J. Kastor, *The Nation's Crucible: The Louisiana Purchase and the Creation of America* (New Haven, Conn.: Yale Univ. Press, 2004), 51; Gary Wills, *"Negro President":*

*Jefferson and the Slave Power* (Boston: Houghton Mifflin, 2003), 8–9, 2; Robert Pierce Forbes, *The Missouri Compromise and Its Aftermath: Slavery & the Meaning of America* (Chapel Hill: Univ. of North Carolina Press, 2007), 103; Judah P. Benjamin to Lewis Cass, Mar. 19, 1857, Lewis Cass Papers, UMich; J. H. Van Evrie, "Slavery Extension," *De Bow's Review* 15 (July 1853): 5–6.

27. Edward Coles to Martin Van Buren, Oct. 12, 1848, Samuel J. Tilden Papers, NYPL; Thomas Jefferson to Edward Coles, Aug. 25, 1814, in Merrill D. Peterson, ed., *The Portable Thomas Jefferson* (New York: Penguin, 1977), 546; David Brion Davis, *The Problem of Slavery in the Age of Revolution, 1770–1823* (Ithaca, N.Y.: Cornell Univ. Press, 1975), 182; *New York Tribune*, July 7, 1849; *New York National Anti-Slavery Standard*, Oct. 19, 1848; Robert M. Sutton, "Edward Coles and the Constitutional Crisis in Illinois, 1822–1824," *Illinois Historical Journal* 82 (Spring 1989): 33–46. For more on Edward Coles's efforts to keep slavery out of Illinois, see Suzanne Cooper-Guasco, *Confronting Slavery: Edward Coles and the Rise of Anti-Slavery Politics in Nineteenth-Century America* (DeKalb: Northern Illinois Univ. Press, 2013).

28. George Tucker, *The Life of Thomas Jefferson, Third President of the United States* (Philadelphia: Carey, Lea, & Blanchard, 1837) 1:115, 2:502; *Louisville Courier*, Sept. 28, 1849; Mildred Bullitt to John C. Bullitt, June 19, 1849, Bullitt Family Papers—Oxmoor Collection, FHS; P. J. Staudenraus, *The African Colonization Movement, 1816–1865* (New York: Columbia Univ. Press, 1961), 171–72.

29. (Rochester) *North Star*, Dec. 8, 1848; James M. Lucas to John G. Davis, Nov. 21, 1859, John Givan Davis Correspondence, WHS; Eliab P. Mackintire to William Salter, July 28, 1856, Eliab Parker Mackintire Letters, NYPL. The "invention" of the cotton gin was a complex and multifaceted process with Eli Whitney playing the role of technological spy rather than brilliant inventor; Angela Lakwete, *Inventing the Cotton Gin: Machine and Myth in Antebellum America* (Baltimore: Johns Hopkins Univ. Press, 2003).

30. *Charleston Mercury*, May 4, 1853; Alfred Huger to William Porcher Miles, Feb. 18, 1858, William Porcher Miles Papers, UNC; William H. Trescot to Muscoe R. H. Garnett, Nov. 16, 1851, Hunter-Garnett Family Papers, UVA; Peterson, *Jeffersonian Image*, 164–70. Michael O'Brien cautions that Southern skepticism of democracy was not universal in the antebellum South; indeed he argues that it was more applicable to the South in 1900 than in 1840; Michael O'Brien, *Conjectures of Order: Intellectual Life and the American South, 1810–1860* (Chapel Hill: Univ. of North Carolina Press, 2004), 2:782.

31. H. H. Hite to N. Francis Cabell, Apr. 1, 1854, Cabell Family Papers, UVA; John Durant Ashmore to Charles Lanman, n.d., [1859], John Durant Ashmore Papers, USC; Lewis Sanders to J. H. Harney, Feb. 4, 1860, Sanders Family Papers, FHS; Butler quoted in *New York Times*, July 21, 1852.

32. L. W. Crook to Robert M. T. Hunter, Dec. 11, 1859, Robert M. T. Hunter Papers, UVA; John J. Eaton to John A. Burwell, Dec. 9, 1844, Burwell-Guy Family Papers, UMich; William H. Trescot to Muscoe R. H. Garnett, Nov. 16, 1851, Hunter-Garnett Family Papers, UVA.

33. Patrick J. Geary, *The Myth of Nations: The Medieval Origins of Europe* (Princeton, N.J.: Princeton Univ. Press, 2002).

34. "East Room—Independence Hall, Philadelphia," *Ballou's Pictorial Drawing-Room Companion* 9 (Oct. 6, 1855): 213; *Frank Leslie's Illustrated Newspaper,* July 10, 1858.

35. "The City of Washington, No. IV," *United States Magazine* 3 (Oct. 1856): 293; *Louisville Courier,* Mar. 27, 1849; "The Declaration of Independence," *Ballou's Pictorial Drawing-Room Companion* 10 (Feb. 9, 1856): 9; Pauline Maier, *American Scripture: Making the Declaration of Independence* (New York: Knopf, 1998), xi.

36. Frederick Henry Wolcott, Feb. 12, 1850, Frederick Henry Wolcott Diary, vol. 1, NYPL; John M. Read to George Bancroft, Feb. 2, 1853, George Bancroft Papers, MaHS; Zachariah Green, Drafts of Letters, Mar. 6, 1856, and Nov. 6, 1856, Miscellaneous Collections, UMich; newspaper clipping, n.d., [1858], Miscellaneous Collections, UMich.

37. "Revolutionary Relics," *Ballou's Pictorial Drawing-Room Companion* 8 (Jan. 27, 1855): 57; "East Room—Independence Hall," 213; Henry Ashworth, Feb. 13, 1857, Henry Ashworth Travel Diary, USC; W. T. Allen, Sept. 3, 18[52], W. T. Allen Diary, NYPL; George W. Patton, Feb. 10, 1860, George W. Patton Diary, Diaries and Letterbooks Collection, HSP; Charlene Mires, *Independence Hall in American Memory* (Philadelphia: Univ. of Pennsylvania Press, 2002), 102.

38. "Monuments," *Gleason's Pictorial Drawing-Room Companion* 2 (Feb. 28, 1852): 141; "Independence Monument," *Ballou's Pictorial Drawing-Room Companion* 16 (Jan. 8, 1859): 27; *Chicago Tribune,* Jan. 6, 1859; *Washington (D.C.) National Intelligencer,* Oct. 30, 1860.

39. Judith Wellman, *The Road to Seneca Falls: Elizabeth Cady Stanton and the First Women's Rights Convention* (Urbana: Univ. of Illinois Press, 2004), 136; Robert W. Johannsen, ed., *The Lincoln Douglas Debates* (New York: Oxford Univ. Press, 1965), 196-97; Don E. Fehrenbacher, *Slavery, Law, and Politics: The Dred Scott Case in Historical Perspective* (New York: Oxford Univ. Press, 1981), 173-75.

40. William L. Andrews, ed., *From Fugitive Slave to Free Man: The Autobiographies of William Wells Brown* (Columbia: Univ. of Missouri Press, 1993), 88; Henry Bibb, *The Life and Adventures of Henry Bibb, An American Slave,* ed. Charles Heglar (1849; Madison: Univ. of Wisconsin Press, 2001), 17.

41. (Rochester) *Frederick Douglass's Paper,* Mar. 3, 1854; Samuel Wells Leland, June 29, 1858, Samuel Wells Leland Diary, USC. For more on the Liberty Bell, see Gary B. Nash, *The Liberty Bell* (New Haven, Conn.: Yale Univ. Press, 2010).

42. Wendell Phillips to Frederick Douglass, Apr. 22, 1845, in Frederick Douglass, *Narrative of the Life of Frederick Douglass, an American Slave,* ed. Deborah E. McDowell (1845; New York: Oxford Univ. Press, 1999), 13; *Washington (D.C.) National Era,* July 3, 1851.

43. *Louisville Democrat,* July 4, 1858; Melissa Bryant to Peter Bryant, Jan. 1, 1855, Bryant Family Papers, NYPL; emphasis added.

44. *Boston Liberator,* Nov. 28, 1856; John C. Calhoun, "Debate on the Territorial Government of Oregon," June 27, 1848, U.S. Congress, *Congressional Globe,* 30th Cong., 1st sess., 872; Ellis, *American Sphinx,* 54. Even today, Americans read the Declaration in an expansive way that makes that old document responsive to modern concerns and sensibilities; Danielle Allen, *Our Declaration: A Reading of the Declaration in Defense of Equality* (New York: Liveright, 2014).

45. Cassius M. Clay to the editor, Apr. 15, 1852, Cassius M. Clay Papers, FHS; Lincoln quoted in David Brion Davis, *Inhuman Bondage: The Rise and Fall of Slavery in*

*the New World* (New York: Oxford Univ. Press, 2006), 307; *Washington (D.C.) National Era,* June 21, 1847; *New York National Anti-Slavery Standard,* Aug. 5, 1847; *Philadelphia Pennsylvania Freeman,* Nov. 20, 1845; *Salem (Ohio) Anti-Slavery Bugle,* Jan. 15, 1859; *Boston Liberator,* Nov. 28, 1856.

46. William Kauffman Scarborough, ed., *The Diary of Edmund Ruffin,* vol. 1, *Toward Independence, October, 1856-April, 1861* (Baton Rouge: Louisiana State Univ. Press, 1972), 90; Louisa S. McCord, "Diversity of the Races; Its Bearing upon Negro Slavery," *Southern Quarterly Review* 2d ser., 19 (April 1851): 403; "The Doctrine of the Higher Law," *Southern Literary Messenger* 17 (Mar. 1851): 132.

47. *Cincinnati Commercial,* Aug. 25, 1856.

48. *Boston Liberator,* Nov. 28, 1856; Leon F. Litwack, *North of Slavery: The Negro in the Free States, 1790-1860* (Chicago: Univ. of Chicago Press, 1961), 54-57; James G. Birney, "Address in Favor of the Independent Union Party," n.d., [Oct. 1852], James Birney Papers, UMich; Joseph Taper to [Joseph Long], Nov. 11, 1840, in Robert S. Starobin, ed., *Blacks in Bondage: Letters of American Slaves* (Princeton, N.J.: Markus Wiener, 1988), 151; *Sandwich (Canada West [Ontario]) Voice of the Fugitive,* May 21, 1851.

49. Matthew Mason, *Slavery and Politics in the Early American Republic* (Chapel Hill: Univ. of North Carolina Press, 2006), 201, 232; Chancellor Harper, "Memoir on Slavery, Part I," *De Bow's Review* 8 (Mar. 1850): 235; McCord, "Diversity of the Races," 403-4; "The Black Race in North America: Why Was Their Introduction Permitted?" *Southern Literary Messenger* 21 (Nov. 1855): 644.

50. William S. Grayson, "The Inefficiency of the Pews," *Southern Literary Messenger* 25 (May 1857): 321-22; Kenneth M. Stampp, *The Peculiar Institution: Slavery in the Ante-Bellum South* (1956; New York: Vintage, 1989), 102, 108; Samuel W. Cartwright, "The State of Mississippi, Part I," *De Bow's Review* 10 (Feb. 1851): 188, 193.

51. Scarborough, ed., *The Diary of Edmund Ruffin,* 1:90; Albert Taylor Bledsoe, *An Essay on Liberty and Slavery* (Philadelphia: J. B. Lippincott, 1857), 103; Andrew S. Cartwright to James D. B. De Bow, June 5, 1860, James D. B. De Bow Papers, DukeU; "R.," "Liberty and Slavery: Professor Bledsoe," *Southern Literary Messenger* 22 (May 1856): 388; Corydon E. Fuller, July 13, 1858, Corydon E. Fuller Journals, vol. 2, Schoff Civil War Collection, Diaries and Journals, UMich.

52. James Henry Hammond, "Negro Slavery at the South," *De Bow's Review* 7 (Oct. 1849): 295; George Fitzhugh, *Sociology for the South; or, the Failure of Free Society* (Richmond, Va: A. Morris, 1854), 179.

53. Calhoun, "Debate on the Government of Oregon," 872.

54. Ibid.

55. Ibid., 872-73; John C. Calhoun, "A Disquisition on Government and a Discourse on the Constitution of the United States," in Richard K. Crallé, ed., *The Works of John C. Calhoun* (New York: D. Appleton, 1853), 1:57. Although Clyde N. Wilson and Shirley Bright Cook claim that "Calhoun did not make a historical exegesis of what the delegates of the thirteen States had meant in 1776 by 'all men are created equal,'" they are not convincing, especially as Calhoun explicitly rejected that phrase as a pernicious and superfluous abstraction; Clyde N. Wilson and Shirley Bright Cook, eds., *The Papers of John C. Calhoun,* vol. 26, *1848-1849* (Columbia, S.C.: Univ. of South Carolina Press, 2001), xi-xii.

56. J. M. W., "Necessity of the Classics," *Southern Quarterly Review,* 2d ser., 10 (July 1854): 167; Edward J. Pringle, "The People," *Southern Quarterly Review,* 2d ser., 9 (Jan. 1854): 49; "Doctrine of Higher Law," 132; "Lord Macaulay," *Southern Literary Messenger* 31 (Apr. 1860): 249; "The Merchant—His Character, Position, [and] Duties," *De Bow's Review* 4 (Feb. 1847): 96.

57. "Slavery and Freedom," 75; Louisa S. McCord, "Enfranchisement of Woman," *Southern Quarterly Review,* 2d ser., 5 (Apr. 1852): 327; "The Constitution of Virginia," *Southern Quarterly Review,* 2d ser., 12 (Oct. 1855): 366, 382; "Failure of Free Societies," *Southern Literary Messenger* 21 (Mar. 1855): 135; Lord Macaulay," *Southern Literary Messenger* 31 (Apr. 1860): 252; "Campbell's History of Virginia," *Southern Literary Messenger* 31 (Mar. 1860): 213; William A. Link, *Roots of Secession: Slavery and Politics in Antebellum Virginia* (Chapel Hill: Univ. of North Carolina Press, 2003), 13-23; Alfred Huger to William Porcher Miles, Sept. 30, 1858, William Porcher Miles Papers, UNC.

58. John Pettit, "The Nebraska and Kansas Bill—Debate," Mar. 3, 1854, U.S. Congress, *Congressional Globe,* 33rd Cong., 1st sess., Appendix, 310; Rufus Choate to E. W. Farley et al., Aug. 9, 1856, in Samuel Gilman Brown, ed., *The Works of Rufus Choate with a Memoir of His Life* (Boston: Little, Brown, and Company, 1862), 1:215; William E. Gienapp, *The Origins of the Republican Party, 1852-1856* (New York: Oxford Univ. Press, 1987), 335; Lyman Trumbull, "Invasion of Harper's [*sic*] Ferry," Dec. 8, 1859, U.S. Congress, *Congressional Globe,* 36th Cong., 1st sess., 58-59; Eugene H. Berwanger, *The Frontier against Slavery: Western Anti-Negro Prejudice and the Slavery Extension Controversy* (1967; Urbana: Univ. of Illinois Press, 2002), 83-84; Henry Ashworth, Mar. 23, 1857, Travel Diary, Henry Ashworth Papers, USC.

59. John Niven, *John C. Calhoun and the Price of Union* (Baton Rouge: Louisiana State Univ. Press, 1988), 316-17; Stampp, *Peculiar Institution,* 19; Logan McKnight to John C. Bullitt, July 6, 1848, Bullitt Family Papers—Oxnoor Collection, FHS; *Louisville Courier,* July 4, 1848; William Henry Brisbane, Jan. 7, 1848, June 29, 1847-Aug. 26, 1848, Diary, William Henry Brisbane Papers, WHS.

60. Theodore Parker to William H. Herndon, Nov. 17, 1856, Theodore Parker Papers, MaHS; *Lawrence Republican,* May 19, 1859; Samuel Breck, June 19, 1857, Samuel Breck Notebooks, HSP; Lydia Maria Child to William Parker Cutler, July 10, 1862, Lydia Maria Child Papers, UMich; Edward Waldo Emerson, ed., *Lectures and Biographical Sketches by Ralph Waldo Emerson* (Boston: Houghton Mifflin, 1904), 530; Jean V. Matthews, *Rufus Choate: The Law and Civic Virtue* (Philadelphia: Temple Univ. Press, 1980), 222-23; Eliab P. Mackintire to William Salter, Mar. 14, 1857, Eliab Parker Mackintire Letters, NYPL; William Morris Davis to Henry K. Brown, Aug. 21, 1855, William Morris Davis Correspondence, HSP.

61. Akhil Reed Amar, *America's Constitution: A Biography* (New York: Random House, 2005), 384-85; *Constitution of the State of Illinois* (Washington, D.C.: E. De Krafft, 1818), 16; William Goodell to James G. Birney, Apr. 1, 1847, James Birney Papers, UMich.

62. Julian P. Boyd, ed., *The Papers of Thomas Jefferson,* vol. 1, *1760-1776* (Princeton: Princeton Univ. Press, 1950), 426; Davis, *Inhuman Bondage,* 145-46; Wright quoted in *Boston Liberator,* Aug. 13, 1852; *Chicago Tribune,* July 17, 1858.

63. William Campbell Preston to Waddy Thompson, Aug. 28, 1855, Preston Family Papers—Davie Collection, FHS; Antislavery Virginian quoted in *Chicago Tribune,* Aug. 21, 1856.

64. William W. Freehling, *The Road to Disunion,* vol. 1, *Secessionists at Bay, 1776-1854* (New York: Oxford Univ. Press, 1990), 78-79; Clement Eaton, *Freedom of Thought in the Old South* (Durham, N.C.: Duke Univ. Press, 1940), 89-90; Harrison Hale to Artemas Hale, Feb. 3, 1861, Artemas Hale Papers, UMich; Davis, *Inhuman Bondage,* 364n19; Robert Toombs, "Slavery—Its Constitutional Status and Its Influence on Society and on the Colored Race," *De Bow's Review* 20 (May 1856): 582a; "South-Carolina: Her Present Attitude and Future Action," *Southern Quarterly Review,* 2d ser., 4 (Oct. 1851): 295. For more on Bacon's Rebellion, see James D. Rice, *Tales from a Revolution: Bacon's Rebellion and the Transformation of Early America* (New York: Oxford Univ. Press, 2012).

65. DeWitt C. Greenwood to John B. Minor, Aug. 15, 1850, Minor and Wilson Family Papers, UVA; *Richmond Whig,* Nov. 8, 1850; "The South and Her Remedies," *De Bow's Review* 10 (Mar. 1851): 267; Henry A. Wise to Muscoe R. H. Garnett, June 19, 1852, Hunter-Garnett Family Papers, UVA; Elizabeth Fox-Genovese and Eugene D. Genovese, *The Mind of the Master Class: History and Faith in the Southern Slaveholders' Worldview* (New York: Cambridge Univ. Press, 2005), 28.

66. Indiana abolitionist quoted in *Boston Liberator,* Jan. 10, 1851; May quoted in *Boston Liberator,* Nov. 14, 1851; Theodore Parker to Samuel J. May, Sept. 23, 1853, and Theodore Parker to Eliza F. Eddy, Nov. 19, 1859, Theodore Parker Papers, MaHS.

67. Stampp, *Peculiar Institution,* 122-23; Anthony Chase to Jeremiah Hoffman, Aug. 8, 1827, in Starobin, ed., *Blacks in Bondage,* 120-21; Henry to William Gatewood, Mar. 23, 1844, and Jackson Whitney to William Riley, Mar. 18, 1859, in John W. Blassingame, ed., *Slave Testimony: Two Centuries of Letters, Speeches, Interviews, and Autobiographies* (Baton Rouge: Louisiana State Univ. Press, 1977), 48-49, 114-15; M. Thurston to Alvah McCollum, Aug. 21, 1848, M. Thurston Letter, American Travel Collection, UMich.

68. Andrew Burstein, *America's Jubilee, July 4, 1826: A Generation Remembers the Revolution after Fifty Years of Independence* (New York: Knopf, 2001), 255-86; Gordon S. Wood, "The Trials and Tribulations of Thomas Jefferson," in Peter S. Onuf, ed., *Jeffersonian Legacies* (Charlottesville: Univ. Press of Virginia, 1993), 395.

69. *New York National Anti-Slavery Standard,* Jan. 29, 1846, July 26, 1849, and Aug. 26, 1847; *Salem (Ohio) Anti-Slavery Bugle,* Jan. 15, 1859; *Washington (D.C.) National Era,* Jan. 7, 1847.

70. James D. Davidson to Baron & Baskerville, Dec. 19, 1859, James D. Davidson Papers, McCormick Collection, WHS; "Slavery and Freedom," 89; *New Orleans Picayune,* Apr. 11, 1849; Francis Lieber, "Civil Liberty and Self-Government," *Southern Quarterly Review,* 2d ser., 9 (Apr. 1854): 300; "A Few Thoughts on Slavery," *Southern Literary Messenger* 20 (Apr. 1854): 195.

71. *Philadelphia Pennsylvanian,* Aug. 28, 1849; *Memphis Appeal,* July 16, 1856; Hopkins Holsey to Howell Cobb, Dec. 31, 1847, in Ulrich B. Phillips, ed., *The Correspondence of Robert Toombs, Alexander H. Stephens, and Howell Cobb,* in the *Annual Report of the American Historical Association for the Year 1911* (Washington, D.C.: Government Printing Office, 1913), 2:93; W. M. Corry to Lewis Sanders, Mar. 26, 1859, Sanders Family Papers, FHS.

72. J. A. C., "The Rights of the Slave States," *Southern Quarterly Review,* 2d ser., 3 (Jan. 1851): 101.

## 3. GEORGE WASHINGTON

1. Paul K. Longmore, *The Invention of George Washington* (Berkeley: Univ. of California Press, 1988), 210-11; William C. Preston to Francis Lieber, Oct. 20, 1858, Francis Lieber Papers, USC; William S. Pettigrew to James C. Johnston, Nov. 18, 1852, Pettigrew Family Papers, UNC. For more on contemporary militarism in the United States, see Andrew J. Bacevich, *The New American Militarism: How Americans Are Seduced by War* (New York: Oxford Univ. Press, 2005).

2. "Baron Marochetti's Statue of Washington," *Gleason's Pictorial Drawing-Room Companion* 5 (Aug. 13, 1853): 97; John Doyle to Alexander H. H. Stuart, Sept. 20, 1851, Alexander H. H. Stuart Papers, UVA; Eliab P. Mackintire to William Salter, Feb. 22, 1858, Eliab Parker Mackintire Letters, NYPL.

3. Review of Joseph E. Worcester's *Dictionary of the English Language* in *North American Review* 90 (Apr. 1860): 565; Cleland K. Huger Jr., "George Washington," May 13, 1854, Cleland Kinloch Huger Papers, USC. For more on Washington's grace in assuming power, giving it back, and receiving it again, see Gary Wills, *Cincinnatus: George Washington and the Enlightenment* (New York: Doubleday, 1984). For more on how modern Americans—even professional historians—revere him, see Gordon S. Wood, "Was Washington 'Mad for Glory'?" *New York Review of Books* 57 (June 10, 2010): 65-67.

4. Eric L. McKitrick, "Washington the Liberator," *New York Review of Books* 46 (Nov. 4, 1999): 48-49; Jean B. Lee, "Mount Vernon Plantation: A Model for the Republic," in Phillip J. Schwartz, ed., *Slavery at the Home of George Washington* (Mount Vernon, Va.: Mount Vernon Ladies' Association, 2001), 28; Henry Wiencek, *An Imperfect God: George Washington, His Slaves, and the Creation of America* (New York: Farrar, Straus, and Giroux, 2003), 111-12; Raymond A. Bauer and Alice H. Bauer, "Day to Day Resistance to Slavery," *Journal of Negro History* 27 (Oct. 1942): 402-7. Martha Washington actually freed Washington's slaves early rather than give them a perverse incentive to kill her; Gary B. Nash, *The Forgotten Fifth: African Americans in the Age of Revolution* (Cambridge, Mass.: Harvard Univ. Press, 2006), 66.

5. François Furstenberg, *In the Name of the Father: Washington's Legacy, Slavery, and the Making of a Nation* (New York: Penguin, 2006), 83; Peter Kolchin, "Slavery in United States Survey Textbooks," *Journal of American History* 84 (Mar. 1998): 1430; Matthew Dennis, *Red, White, and Blue Letter Days: An American Calendar* (Ithaca, N.Y.: Cornell Univ. Press, 2002), 188; Review of Washington Irving's *Life of George Washington, North American Review* 83 (July 1856): 29; *New York Herald,* Mar. 27, 1848. For more on the management of overseers and slaves, see James O. Breeden, ed., *Advice among Masters: The Ideal in Slave Management in the Old South* (Westport, Conn.: Greenwood Press, 1980).

6. *Memphis Appeal,* Feb. 10, 1855; George Tucker, *The History of the United States from Their Colonization to the End of the Twenty-Sixth Congress, in 1841* (Philadelphia, Pa.: Lippincott, 1856), 99; "The Duties of an Overseer," *De Bow's Review* 18 (Mar. 1855): 339; Kenneth M. Stampp, *The Peculiar Institution: Slavery in the Ante-Bellum South* (1956; New York: Knopf, 1989), 39-40; Wiencek, *Imperfect God,* 110-11, 315-32.

7. *Boston Liberator,* Jan. 1, 1847.

8. Wiencek, *Imperfect God,* 315, 331-34.

9. John Bachelder Pierce to Kitty Pierce, July 5, 1850, John Bachelder Pierce Papers, MaHS; Frederick Douglass, "What to the Slave Is the Fourth of July?: An Address Delivered in Rochester, New York, on 5 July 1852," in John W. Blassingame, ed., *Frederick Douglass Papers, Series One: Speeches, Debates, and Interviews,* vol. 2, *1847-54* (New Haven, Conn.: Yale Univ. Press, 1982), 367; William Lloyd Garrison to J. M. McKim, Nov. 5, 1860, African American History Collection, UMich.

10. *Louisville Courier,* Nov. 13, 1850; *New Orleans Picayune,* Aug. 8, 1854; *Memphis Appeal,* May 25, 1855; *Philadelphia Pennsylvanian,* Oct. 13, 1851; *New York Day Book,* June 6, 1856.

11. *Louisville Courier,* Aug. 6, 1849; William Henry Brisbane, Feb. 22, 1850, Diary, William Henry Brisbane Papers, WHS.

12. "A Few Thoughts on Slavery," *Southern Literary Messenger* 20 (Apr. 1854): 195; "The South and the Union," *De Bow's Review* 10 (Feb. 1851): 160; "Southern School Books," *De Bow's Review* 13 (Sept. 1852): 262; S. D. M., "John Caldwell Calhoun," *Southern Quarterly Review,* 2d ser., 2 (Nov. 1850): 501; John C. Calhoun, "The Compromise," Mar. 4, 1850, U.S. Congress, *Congressional Globe,* 31st Cong., 1st sess., 454; Louisa S. McCord, "Diversity of the Races; Its Bearing upon Negro Slavery," *Southern Quarterly Review,* 2d ser., 3 (Apr. 1851): 393; *Charleston Mercury,* Feb. 27, 1851.

13. James R. Doolittle, "Remarks on the Importance of Celebrating the 4th of July and upon the Dangers of Joining in Denouncing Our Southern Fellow Citizens," July 4, 1837, typescript, James R. Doolittle Papers, WHS; *New York Herald,* Apr. 8, 1851.

14. Parker quoted in *New York National Anti-Slavery Standard,* Jan. 8, 1859; *Philadelphia Pennsylvania Freeman,* May 11, 1848; *Boston Liberator,* Jan. 7, 1859; Stampp, *Peculiar Institution,* 235; Eva Sheppard Wolf, *Race and Liberty in the New Nation: Emancipation in Virginia from the Revolution to Nat Turner's Rebellion* (Baton Rouge: Louisiana State Univ. Press, 2006), 45; Andrew Levy, *First Emancipator: The Forgotten Story of Robert Carter, the Founding Father Who Freed His Slaves* (New York: Random House, 2005), xi, 138, xviii.

15. [John B. Russwurm], "Toussaint L'Ouverture—The Principal Chief in the Revolution of St. Domingo," 4-5, n.d., [1825-26], African American History Collection, UMich.

16. David Brion Davis explains, "Toussaint himself was an *ancien libre* who had owned land and at least one slave," i.e., he was a former slave who owned at least one slave; David Brion Davis, *Inhuman Bondage: The Rise and Fall of Slavery in the New World* (New York: Oxford Univ. Press, 2006), 167.

17. [Russwurm], "Toussaint L'Ouverture," 2-3; David Brion Davis, "He Changed the World," *New York Review of Books* 54 (May 31, 2007): 54-58.

18. Phillips quoted in Thomas Bradford Drew, Mar. 18, 1858, Thomas Bradford Drew Diaries, MaHS; James Brewer Stewart, *Wendell Phillips, Liberty's Hero* (Baton Rouge: Louisiana State Univ. Press, 1986), 184, 199; *Salem (Ohio) Anti-Slavery Bugle,* Dec. 1, 1860; Timothy M. Matthewson, "George Washington's Policy toward the Haitian Revolution," *Diplomatic History* 3 (Summer 1979): 321-22. Matthew J. Clavin finds that this powerful symbol gained resonance during the Civil War when liberated slaves fought for the United States to liberate other slaves; Matthew J. Clavin,

"American Toussaints: Symbol, Subversion, and the Black Atlantic Tradition in the American Civil War," *Slavery & Abolition* 28 (Apr. 2007): 87-113.

19. Alfred Hunt, *Haiti's Influence on Antebellum America: Slumbering Volcano in the Caribbean* (Baton Rouge: Louisiana State Univ. Press, 1988), 85-86, 92-93; Laurent Dubois, *Avengers of the New World: The Story of the Haitian Revolution* (Cambridge, Mass.: Harvard Univ. Press, 2004), 189, 238, 248-49; Madison Smartt Bell, *Toussaint Louverture: A Biography* (New York: Pantheon Books, 2007), 288; Davis, "He Changed the World," 58.

20. Davis, *Inhuman Bondage,* 159; "A Few Thoughts on Slavery," *Southern Literary Messenger* 20 (Apr. 1854): 195; Napoleon Lockett to John B. Minor, Nov. 20, 1860, Minor and Wilson Family Papers, UVA.

21. William Buell Sprague to G. E. Ellis, Apr. 3, 1857, African American History Collection, UMich.

22. Isaac Mervine, May 17, 1838, Isaac Mervine Memorandum Book, Diaries and Letterbooks Collection, HSP; *Boston Post,* June 3, 1854.

23. Dennis, *Red, White, and Blue Days,* 9; *Charleston Courier,* Feb. 22, 1850; David Wyatt Aiken, Feb. 21, 1857, Diary, David Wyatt Aiken Papers, USC; Charles Wister Jr. to Owen J. Wister, Feb. 21, 1849, Owen J. Wister Papers, Wister Family Papers, HSP; Ted Steinberg, *Down to Earth: Nature's Role in American History* (New York: Oxford Univ. Press, 2002), 26. For more on the "Little Ice Age," see Brian Fagen, *The Little Ice Age: How Climate Made History, 1300-1850* (New York: Basic Books, 2000).

24. Virginia Ingraham Burr, ed., *The Secret Eye: The Journal of Ella Gertrude Clanton Thomas, 1848-1889* (Chapel Hill: Univ. of North Carolina Press, 1990), 98; John Hope Franklin, *The Militant South, 1800-1861* (1956; Urbana: Univ. of Illinois Press, 2002), 206-7; Julia Lord Noyes, Feb. 23, 1856, Diary, Julia Lord (Noyes) Loveland Papers, DukeU; Sarah Woolfolk Wiggins, ed., *The Journals of Josiah Gorgas, 1857-1878* (Tuscaloosa: Univ. of Alabama Press, 1995), 27; Caroline A. Dunstan, Feb. 22, 1859, Caroline A. Dunstan Diaries, NYPL; Margaret Cabell Rives to Amélie Louise Rives, Feb. 22, 1848, Rives Family Papers, UVA; William Johnson Taylor, Feb. 22, 1851, William Johnson Taylor Pocket Diaries, Papers of the Jones and Taylor Families, HSP.

25. *Charleston Courier,* Feb. 22, 1850; (New York) *Frank Leslie's Illustrated Newspaper,* Feb. 23, 1856; Thomas Bradford Drew, Apr. 4, 1858, 1858 Diary, Thomas Bradford Drew Diaries, MaHS; Anna Coker to Hannah Ann Coker, Feb. 26, 1849, Papers of the Lide, Coker, and Stout Families, USC; *Charleston Mercury,* Feb. 24, 1852; Matthew Jouett Williams, Feb. 22, 1853, 1852-53 Diary, Matthew Jouett Williams Papers, DukeU.

26. Review of Edward Everett's *Life of George Washington, North American Review* 91 (Oct. 1860): 580; Don Higginbotham, "Introduction: Washington and the Historians," in Don Higginbotham, ed., *George Washington Reconsidered* (Charlottesville: Univ. Press of Virginia, 2001), 5, 11n11; John S. Henderson, "On the Revolution," n.d., [1859], John Steele Henderson Papers, UNC; *Charleston Courier,* Feb. 22, 1849.

27. *Richmond Whig,* May 24, 1850; *Washington (D.C.) National Intelligencer,* Feb. 22, 1848; James D. Davidson, Untitled Speech, Feb. [22], 1855, James D. Davidson Papers, McCormick Collection, WHS.

28. David Outlaw to Emily B. Outlaw, Feb. 22, 1850, David Outlaw Papers, UNC; Howell Cobb to Abaslom H. Chappell et al., Feb. 7, 1851, in Ulrich B. Phillips, ed., *Annual Report of the American Historical Association for the Year 1911,* vol. 2, *The Cor-*

*respondence of Robert Toombs, Alexander H. Stephens, and Howell Cobb* (Washington, D.C.: Government Printing Office, 1913), 221-23; *New Orleans Picayune,* Feb. 22, 1851; Don E. Fehrenbacher, *The Slaveholding Republic: An Account of the United States Government's Relations toward Slavery* (New York: Oxford Univ. Press, 2001), 211-12.

29. Eliab P. Mackintire to William Salter, Feb. 22, 1858, Eliab Parker Mackintire Letters, NYPL; Hannah Robie to Samuel B. Robie, Feb. 22, 1855, Robie-Sewall Family Papers, MaHS.

30. William Henry Holcombe, Feb. 22, 1855, William Henry Holcombe Diary, UNC; William P. Taylor, Feb. 22, 1849, William P. Taylor Account Book, HSP; Benjamin S. Johnston, Feb. 22, 1859, Benjamin S. Johnston Logbook, HSP; Frederick Henry Wolcott, Feb. 22, 1850, Frederick Henry Wolcott Diary, vol. 1, NYPL.

31. Furstenberg, *Name of the Father,* 40; Dennis, *Red, White, and Blue Days,* 180; (New York) *Frank Leslie's Illustrated Newspaper,* Sept. 27, 1856; "Silver Grey, Jr.," Feb. 24, 1851, unidentified newspaper clipping, Alexander H. H. Stuart Papers, UVA.

32. *Boston Herald,* Feb. 22, 1856; H. Holmes to James Gordon Bennett, Jan. 24, 1850, James Gordon Bennett Papers, NYPL; Frank Luther Mott, *American Journalism, 1690-1960* (New York: MacMillan 1962), 339-40.

33. Chalmers Johnson, *The Sorrows of Empire: Militarism, Secrecy, and the End of the American Republic* (New York: Metropolitan Books, 2004), 44; William S. Pettigrew to James C. Johnston, Mar. 7, 1850, Pettigrew Family Papers, UNC; Gilbert Lafayette Strait to James M. Wylie, Apr. 21, 1851, Gaston, Strait, Wylie, and Baskin Families, USC; Robert J. Walker, *An Appeal for the Union* (New York: J. F. Trow, 1856), 1.

34. William Porcher Miles, *Oration Delivered before the Fourth of July Association* (Charleston, S.C.: James S. Burges, 1849), 28; James Kendall to John F. Potter, June 1, 1854, John F. Potter Papers, WHS.

35. Donald S. Spencer, *Louis Kossuth and Young America: A Study of Sectionalism and Foreign Policy, 1848-1852* (Columbia: Univ. of Missouri Press, 1977), 66, 104-6; John Russell Bartlett, *Dictionary of Americanisms: A Glossary of Words and Phrases Usually Regarded as Peculiar to the United States* (Boston: Little, Brown, 1860), 4; William H. Trescot to Muscoe R. H. Garnett, Nov. 7, 1852, Hunter-Garnett Family Papers, UVA; Elizabeth Fox-Genovese and Eugene D. Genovese, *The Mind of the Master Class: History and Faith in the Southern Slaveholders' Worldview* (New York: Cambridge Univ. Press, 2005), 23; Thomas S. Bocock to the Editors of the *Richmond Enquirer,* Feb. 16, 1852, Thomas S. Bocock Papers, UVA.

36. George Bancroft to William B. Reed, Dec. 9, 1859, and George Bancroft to William Gilmore Simms, Jan. 16, 1858, George Bancroft Papers, MaHS; George Custis Parke Washington to James A. Pearce, Sept. 24, 1850, James A. Pearce Papers, MdHS.

37. "Kossuth and Intervention," *Southern Quarterly Review,* 2d ser., 5 (July 1852): 222-23; *New Orleans Picayune,* Feb. 7, 1852; *Memphis Appeal,* Mar. 17, 1858; William Gilmore Simms to George Bancroft, Jan. 7, 1858, George Bancroft Papers, MaHS. For more on the New York Manumission Society, see David N. Gellman, *Emancipating New York: The Politics of Slavery and Freedom, 1777-1827* (Baton Rouge: Louisiana State Univ. Press, 2006), 56-77.

38. Horace Binney, *An Inquiry into the Formation of Washington's Farewell Address* (Philadelphia: J. B. Lippincott, 1859), 170-71. For the argument that Hamilton drafted

the Farewell Address, see Felix Gilbert, *To the Farewell Address: Ideas of Early American Foreign Policy* (Princeton: Princeton Univ. Press, 1961), 124-34. For the argument that Washington drafted the Farewell Address with assistance from Hamilton, see Matthew Spalding and Patrick J. Garrity, *A Sacred Union of Citizens: George Washington's Farewell Address and the American Character* (Lanham, Md.: Rowman & Littlefield, 1996), 47-57.

39. John B. Adger to Jane Ann Smyth, June 18, 1860, Papers of the Adger-Smyth-Flynn Family, USC; Caleb Coker, Aug. 7, [1846], Diary, Caleb Coker Papers, USC; "Sketches of Southern Travel," *Emerson's Magazine* 7 (Nov. 1858): 478; Samuel T. Jones to Mrs. Samuel T. Jones, June 13, 1849, Samuel T. Jones Papers, DukeU; Julia Lord Noyes, May 1, [1855], Diary, Julia Lord (Noyes) Loveland Papers, DukeU; Samuel Wells Leland, [June 30, 1858], Samuel Wells Leland Diary, USC.

40. Catherine Cocks, *Doing the Town: The Rise of Urban Tourism in the United States, 1850-1915* (Berkeley: Univ. of California Press, 2001), 123; E. Kennedy, "Mount Vernon: A Pilgrimage," *Southern Literary Messenger* 18 (Jan. 1852): 53; Thomas Hickling Jr., Feb. 20, 1844, Diary, Hickling-Nye Papers, MaHS; *Proceedings of the American Association for the Advancement of Science* 8 (n.d., 1855), 7-17; Sallie [Bullitt] to John C. Bullitt, June 17, 1849, Bullitt Family Papers—Oxmoor Collection, FHS; George W. Patton, Mar. 2, 1860, George W. Patton Diary, Diaries and Letterbooks Collection, HSP; John Wheeler, Oct. 8, 1859, John Wheeler Diary, UMich.

41. Mary Robertson to John C. Bullitt, Oct. 10, 1843, Bullitt Family Papers—Oxmoor Collection, FHS; David Outlaw to Emily B. Outlaw, Apr. 29, 1850, David Outlaw Papers, UNC.

42. Edith Lukens Letter, Oct. 1, 1850, American Travel Collection, UMich; Henry Ashworth, Apr. 4, 1857, Travel Diary, Henry Ashworth Papers, USC; (Rochester) *Frederick Douglass's Paper,* Mar. 7, 1854, and Oct. 29, 1852; Steven Deyle, *Carry Me Back: The Domestic Slave Trade in American Life* (New York: Oxford Univ. Press, 2005), 7.

43. Leonidas Polk to Sarah Polk, Dec. 1, 1828, Gale and Polk Family Papers, UNC; W. T. Allen, n.d. [Sept. 1853], W. T. Allen Diary, NYPL; Virginia Corbin to Francis P. Corbin, July 2, 1851, Francis Porteous Corbin Papers, NYPL; (New York) *Frank Leslie's Illustrated Newspaper,* May 24, 1856. For more accounts expressing disappointment about the deterioration of Mount Vernon, see Jean B. Lee, ed., *Experiencing Mount Vernon: Eyewitness Accounts, 1784-1865* (Charlottesville: Univ. of Virginia Press, 2007), 143-56.

44. John Wheeler, Oct. 8, 1859, John Wheeler Diary, UMich.

45. *New Orleans Picayune,* Apr. 25, 1848; "Petitions, etc.," April 20, 1848, U.S. Congress, *Congressional Globe,* 30th Cong., 1st sess., 656; *Washington (D.C.) National Intelligencer,* Feb. 26, 1847; *Charleston Courier,* July 19, 1850; "Mount Vernon," *Gleason's Pictorial Drawing-Room Companion* 5 (Aug. 20, 1853): 125; *Charleston Mercury,* June 18, 1853; *Louisville Courier,* July 17, 1849.

46. *Charleston Mercury,* Dec. 2, 1853; Elizabeth R. Varon, *We Mean to Be Counted: White Women & Politics in Antebellum Virginia* (Chapel Hill: Univ. of North Carolina Press, 1998), 4, 125.

47. Varon, *We Mean to Be Counted,* 128-29; Julia Gardiner Tyler to Anna C. O. M. Ritchie, Feb. 11, 1856, Anna Cora Ogden Mowatt Ritchie Papers, UVA; Julie Roy Jeffrey, *The Great Silent Army of Abolitionism: Ordinary Women in the Antislavery Movement*

(Chapel Hill: Univ. of North Carolina Press, 1999), 108-26; James Bullitt to Thomas W. Bullitt, n.d. [Feb., 1859], Bullitt Family Papers—Oxmoor Collection, FHS; "The Birthplace of Washington," *Ballou's Pictorial Drawing-Room Companion* 16 (Mar. 26, 1859): 202; "The Mount Vernon Fund," *Ballou's Pictorial Drawing-Room Companion* 16 (Apr. 23, 1859): 266; Thomas Kelah Wharton, Jan. 12, 1859, Diary, Thomas Kelah Wharton Papers, NYPL; M. R. Fagg to the Tennessee Legislature, Jan. 19, 1861, Papers of the Mt. Vernon [Ladies] Association of Tennessee, Miscellaneous Collections, FHS; (New York) *Frank Leslie's Illustrated Newspaper*, Jan. 1, 1859; "Editor's Table," *Southern Literary Messenger* 28 (Jan./Feb. 1859): 145.

48. Edward P. Alexander, *Museum Masters: Their Museum and Their Influence* (Nashville, Tenn.: American Association for State and Local History, 1983), 182; *New York National Anti-Slavery Standard*, Mar. 11, 1854; *Washington (D.C.) National Intelligencer*, Mar. 15, 1858; Paul A. Varg, *Edward Everett: The Intellectual in the Turmoil of Politics* (Selinsgrove, Pa.: Susquehanna Univ. Press, 1992), 177-79; Ronald F. Reid, *Edward Everett: Unionist Orator* (New York: Greenwood Press, 1990), 80-83.

49. Edward Everett to L. A. Dimock, Dec. 20, 1858, Edward Everett Papers, UVA; Edward Everett to W. C. Ludwig, Oct. 9, 1858, Edward Everett File, Mary L. Suydam Collection, HSP; Edward Everett to Socrates Maupin, Mar. 20, 1856, Letters to Socrates Maupin, UVA; Edward Everett to W. W. Spear, Feb. 10, 1860, Edward Everett File, Simon Gratz Collection: American Literary Duplicates, HSP.

50. *Washington (D.C.) National Intelligencer*, Mar. 15 1858; Louisa H. A. Minor, Mar. 25, 1856, Louisa H. A. Minor Diary, UVA; Mary Brown Askew, Feb. 4, 1858, Mary Brown Askew Diary, Diaries and Letterbooks Collection, HSP; Eliza Gilpin to Albert Sidney Johnston, Feb. 9, 1858, Johnston Family Papers, FHS; Robert Remini, *The House: A History of the House of Representatives* (New York: HarperCollins, 2006), 155.

51. Edward Everett to Mrs. Charles Eames, Apr. 19, 1856, Edward Everett to Robert C. Winthrop, Sept. 18, 1857, and Edward Everett to William H. Trescot, Jan. 17, 1858, Edward Everett Papers, MaHS; Reid, *Edward Everett*, 80-83; William McLaughlin to Alexander H. H. Stuart, Nov. 23, 1857, Alexander H. H. Stuart Papers, UVA; David Wyatt Aiken, Apr. 16, 1858, Diary, David Wyatt Aiken Papers, USC; Jane Petigru North to Jane Caroline North Pettigrew, Apr. 16, 1858, Pettigrew Family Papers, UNC; Alexander, *Museum Masters*, 183.

52. *Charleston Mercury*, July 20, 1857; Oscar Lieber to Francis Lieber, Apr. 24, 1858, Francis Lieber Papers, USC; Pryor and Ruffin quoted in Varon, *We Mean to Be Counted*, 131; Horace Maynard to Edward Everett, Sept. 19, 1857, Edward Everett Papers, MaHS.

53. *Boston Liberator*, May 14, 1858; *New York National Anti-Slavery Standard*, Jan. 8, 1859; Theodore Parker to Caroline C. Thayer, Jan. 10, 1860, Theodore Parker Papers, MaHS; Edward Everett to Mrs. Charles Eames, Apr. 19, 1856, Edward Everett Papers, MaHS. One antebellum reference work defined "Dough-Faces" as "Northern favorers and abettors of negro slavery"; Bartlett, *Dictionary of Americanisms*, 128.

54. "Mount Vernon," *Ballou's Pictorial Drawing-Room Companion* 14 (May 15, 1858): 317; *New York National Anti-Slavery Standard*, Jan. 8, 1859; *Charleston Mercury*, June 18, 1853; *New Orleans Picayune*, May 1, 1858; Daniel R. Hundley, June 8, 1859, Daniel R. Hundley Diary, UMich.

55. Samuel B. Ruggles to Anna Cora Ogden Mowatt Ritchie, Mar. 22, 1856, Samuel B. Ruggles Papers, NYPL; (New York) *Frank Leslie's Illustrated Newspaper,* Nov. 20, 1858; "The Mount Vernon Fund," *Ballou's Pictorial Drawing-Room Companion* 16 (Mar. 5, 1859): 155; *Charleston Mercury,* Apr. 4, 1859; Daniel F. Meader to Edward Everett, Jan. 6, 1859, Edward Everett Papers, MaHS.

56. Alexander, *Museum Masters,* 182-89; Edward Everett to John Pendleton Kennedy, May 17, 1860, John Pendleton Kennedy Papers, MdHS.

57. Review of George Washington Parke Custis's *Recollections and Private Memoirs of Washington, North American Review* 91 (July 1860): 265; "Washington's Head Quarters," *Gleason's Pictorial Drawing-Room Companion* 2 (June 5, 1852): 368; (New York) *Frank Leslie's Illustrated Newspaper,* Feb. 2, 1856; Roger W. Moss, *Historic Houses of Philadelphia: A Tour of the Region's Museum Homes* (Philadelphia: Univ. of Pennsylvania Press, 1998), 5.

58. "Washington's Rock," *Ballou's Pictorial Drawing-Room Companion* 17 (Sept. 24, 1859): 208; "Washington Taking Command at Cambridge," *Ballou's Pictorial Drawing-Room Companion* 9 (July 7, 1855): 1; "The Washington Elm, at Cambridge," *Gleason's Pictorial Drawing-Room Companion* 5 (July 16, 1853): 37; J. G. Jack, "The Cambridge Washington Elm," *Arnold Arboretum Bulletin of Popular Information* 5 (Dec. 10, 1931): 69-71; James W. Hopkins, June 26, 1856, Diary, James Ward Hopkins Papers, USC; Agnes Richardson, Sept. 29, 1859, Agnes Richardson Travel Journal, Notes and Diary 1857-60, John Smythe Richardson Papers, USC. The Washington Elm stood until 1923, when age and Dutch elm disease overwhelmed it.

59. "Washington's Relics," *Ballou's Pictorial Drawing-Room Companion* 9 (July 7, 1855): 4; *Louisville Courier,* Mar. 27, 1849; "The City of Washington," *United States Magazine* 3 (Oct. 1856): 293; Dennis Cooley to [R. Shane], June 1, 1853, Dennis Cooley Papers, DukeU; Samuel T. Jones to Mrs. Samuel T. Jones, June 17, 1849, Samuel T. Jones Papers, DukeU; (New York) *Frank Leslie's Illustrated Newspaper,* Apr. 7, 1860.

60. *Washington (D.C.) National Era,* Oct. 5, 1854; Michael O'Brien, *Conjectures of Order: Intellectual Life and the American South, 1810-1860* (Chapel Hill: Univ. of North Carolina Press, 2004), 1:6-7; Louisa S. McCord, "Diversity of the Races," 393; *Richmond Whig,* Oct. 7, 1848; Tennessean quoted in *Memphis Appeal,* Nov. 10, 1858.

61. "Holidays," *North American Review* 84 (Apr. 1857): 362-63.

## 4. ANTEBELLUM HISTORY WARS OVER THE AMERICAN REVOLUTION

1. Review of E. F. Ellet's *Women of the Revolution, Southern Quarterly Review,* 2d ser., 1 (July 1850): 334; Preston King to Samuel J. Tilden, Oct. 13, 1854, Samuel J. Tilden Papers, NYPL.

2. *Mobile Register,* Nov. 24, 1859; Edward Tabor Linenthal, *Sacred Ground: Americans and Their Battlefields* (Urbana: Univ. of Illinois Press, 1991), 1.

3. Charlotte Baker Hixon, Apr. 18, 1849, "Trip to Aiken, S.C. with Sister Wilder in the Spring of 1849," Charlotte Baker Hixon Papers, USC; *Charleston Mercury,* Mar. 26, 1852; *Washington (D.C.) National Intelligencer,* June 28, 1847; (New York) *Frank Leslie's Illustrated Newspaper,* Mar. 10, 1860, and July 25, 1857.

4. "Events of the Year 1855," *Ballou's Pictorial Drawing-Room Companion* 10 (Feb. 9, 1856): 95; (New York) *Frank Leslie's Illustrated Newspaper,* May 5, 1860, Sept. 8, 1859, and Feb. 13, 1858.

5. Detroit authorities quoted in *Boston Herald,* Aug. 24, 1853; Jon Zug, Nov. 19, 1838, Journal of an Agent of the Pennsylvania Colonization Society, African American History Collection, UMich; white Southerners quoted in *Baltimore Sun,* Aug. 3, 1858; Henry Wiencek, *An Imperfect God: George Washington, His Slaves, and the Creation of America* (New York: Farrar, Straus, and Giroux, 2003), 191-97.

6. Andrew Burstein, *America's Jubilee, July 4, 1826: A Generation Remembers the Revolution after Fifty Years of Independence* (New York: Random House, 2001), 234; Eric Burin, *Slavery and the Peculiar Solution: A History of the American Colonization Society* (Gainesville: Univ. Press of Florida, 2005), 18-19; "Death of the Last Survivor of the Boston Tea Party," *Gleason's Pictorial Drawing-Room Companion* 2 (Mar. 20, 1852): 191; Alfred E. Young, *The Shoemaker and the Tea Party: Memory and the American Revolution* (Boston: Beacon Press, 1999), 180-81. For more on Carroll, see Bradley Brizer, *American Cicero: The Life of Charles Carroll* (Wilmington, Del.: Intercollegiate Studies Institute, 2010).

7. *Boston Herald,* Apr. 1, 1857; Anne Newport Royall to Col. Freeman, Mar. 8, 1837, Miscellaneous Collections, UMich; Sarah J. Purcell, *Sealed with Blood: War, Sacrifice, and Memory in Revolutionary America* (Philadelphia: Univ. of Pennsylvania Press, 2002), 72-73; James G. Austin to the Sec. of State of Connecticut, July 6, 1843, Miscellaneous Collections, UMich; A. G. Saunders to John G. Davis, Dec. 12, 1860, John Givan Davis Correspondence, WHS; J. E. Dow to Noyes Billings, Nov. 4, 1848, Miscellaneous Collections, UMich.

8. *Charleston Courier,* Apr. 2, 1849; *New Orleans Picayune,* July 15, 1849, July 26, 1849; *Richmond Whig,* July 24, 1849; David H. Mattern and Holly C. Shulman, eds., *The Selected Letters of Dolley Payne Madison* (Charlottesville: Univ. Press of Virginia, 2003), 317-25; Alan Nevins and Milton Halsey Thomas, eds., *The Diary of George Templeton Strong,* vol. 1, *Young Man in New York, 1835-1849* (New York: Macmillan, 1952), 334; "Venerable," *Gleason's Pictorial Drawing-Room* 1 (May 31, 1851): 77; "A Relic of the Revolution," *United States Magazine* 1 (July 1854): 79; "Death of Mrs. Alexander Hamilton," *United States Magazine* 1 (Dec. 1854): 234. For more on Dolley Madison, see Catherine Allgor, *A Perfect Union: Dolley Madison and the Creation of the American Nation* (New York: Henry Holt, 2006).

9. *Louisville Courier,* Jan. 15, 1850; *Charleston Courier,* Oct. 25, 1849; Hughes Hillard to Thomas S. Bocock, Oct. 26, 1851, Thomas S. Bocock Papers, UVA; Martha Stanard to William S. Bodley, Feb. 17, 1849, Bodley Family Papers, FHS.

10. Josiah Quincy to William Amory, Sept. 17, 1859, Miscellaneous Collections, UMich; *Baltimore Sun,* June 20, 1854; Southerner quoted in *Louisville Courier,* Nov. 20, 1849.

11. *New Orleans Picayune,* Mar. 28, 1849; *Baltimore Sun,* Feb. 21, 1850.

12. Samuel Breck, Feb. 1, 1847, Samuel Breck Notebooks, HSP; L. I. Anderson to George Bancroft, Oct. 4, 1849, George Bancroft Papers, NYPL; David Hackett Fischer, *Historians' Fallacies: Towards a Logic of Historical Thought* (New York: Harper and Row, 1970), 178; Joseph Garland to [Henry B.] Dawson, Sept. 13, 1858, Miscellaneous Col-

lections, UMich. M. A. DeWolfe Howe reports that Bancroft's ninth volume (1866) precipitated the "War of the Grandfathers" pitting grandsons, who objected to how the historian portrayed the exploits of their ancestors, against each other; M. A. DeWolfe Howe, *The Life and Letters of George Bancroft* (1908; Port Washington, N.Y.: Kennikat Press, 1971), 2:109–12.

13. William H. Prescott to George Bancroft, Feb. 19, 1852, and Apr. 3 1858, George Bancroft Papers, MaHS.

14. John L. DeMoyelles to Samuel J. Tilden, June 30, 1857, Samuel J. Tilden Papers, NYPL; (New York) *Frank Leslie's Illustrated Newspaper,* July 25, 1857; Octavius Wilkie, Daniel Rarenul Jr., and William Y. Paxton to William Porcher Miles, Jan. 9, 1858, William Porcher Miles Papers, UNC.

15. Donald B. Cole and John J. McDonough, eds., *Benjamin B. French, Witness to the Young Republic: A Yankee's Journal, 1828–1870* (Hanover, N.H.: Univ. Press of New England, 2002), 265–66; Mary Elizabeth Boyce, Oct. 4, 1855, Mary Elizabeth Boyce Diary, USC; John Wolcott Phelps, July 28, 1849, Diary, John Wolcott Phelps Papers, NYPL; Frederick Henry Wolcott, Apr. 17, 1850, Frederick Henry Wolcott Diary, NYPL. For more on how modern Americans remember Civil War battlefields, see Jim Weeks, *Gettysburg: Memory, Market, and an American Shrine* (Princeton, N.J.: Princeton Univ. Press, 2003), and Joan M. Zenzen, *Battling for Manassas: The Fifty-Year Preservation Struggle at Manassas National Battlefield Park* (University Park: Pennsylvania State Univ. Press, 1998).

16. Dona Brown, *Inventing New England: Regional Tourism in the Nineteenth Century* (Washington, D.C.: Smithsonian Press, 1997), 107; Ellen Green to Hector Green, Sept. 8, 1843, Green Family Papers, FHS; Edward D. Holton, Aug. 11, 1852, Diary, Edward D. Holton Papers, WHS; Margaret Smith to Lewis Sanders, n.d., [1850], Sanders Family Papers, FHS.

17. Leonard G. Wilson, *Lyell in America: Transatlantic Geology, 1841–1853* (Baltimore: Johns Hopkins Univ. Press, 1998), 147; "Mr. Snooks Discovers the Bunker Hill Monument," *Yankee Doodle* 2 (n.d., 1847): 4; *New York National Anti-Slavery Standard,* June 24, 1847.

18. John B. Lamar to Howell Cobb, June 24, 1846, in Ulrich B. Phillips, ed., *Annual Report of the American Historical Association for the Year 1911,* vol. 2, *The Correspondence of Robert Toombs, Alexander H. Stephens, and Howell Cobb* (Washington, D.C.: Government Printing Office, 1913), 83–84.

19. "Battle Monuments at Lexington and Concord, Mass.," *Ballou's Pictorial Drawing-Room Companion* 8 (May 26, 1855): 336; *Charleston Courier,* Apr. 21, 1841.

20. Tom Engelhardt, *The End of Victory Culture: Cold War America and the Disillusioning of a Generation* (New York: Basic Books, 1995), 4; *Baltimore Sun,* June 19, 1850; John B. Minor to John Davis Minor, Sept. 10, 1851, Minor and Wilson Family Papers, UVA; *New Orleans Picayune,* June 18, 1852.

21. Hugh Swinton Legaré to Robert C. Winthrop, Aug. 7, 1840, Hugh Swinton Legaré Papers, USC; *Charleston Mercury,* Jan. 12, 1849.

22. Julie Roy Jeffrey, *The Great Silent Army of Abolitionism: Ordinary Women in the Antislavery Movement* (Chapel Hill: Univ. of North Carolina Press, 1999), 108–11; Susan Dorr to Ellen Green, Oct. 18, 1840, Green Family Papers, FHS; Southern observer

quoted in *Charleston Courier,* May 3, 1841. For more on the Panic of 1837, see Alasdair Roberts, *America's First Great Depression: Economic Crisis and Political Disorder after the Panic of 1837* (Ithaca, N.Y.: Cornell Univ. Press, 2012).

23. *Charleston Mercury,* July 31, 1854; David Wyatt Aiken, Oct. 2, 1855, David Wyatt Aiken Diary, USC; William Campbell Preston to Waddy Thompson, Aug. 28, 1855, Preston Family Papers—Davie Collection, FHS.

24. *New Orleans Picayune,* Oct. 20, 1854; (New York) *Frank Leslie's Illustrated Newspaper,* May 5, 1860.

25. Anonymous "Wayside Sketches," n.d. [Sept. 1843], American Travel Collection, UMich.

26. John Robinson Todd to Edward Everett, Feb. 16, 1859, Edward Everett Papers, MaHS; H. A. Nearer to George Bancroft, Oct.15, 1858, George Bancroft Papers, MaHS; Eileen Ka-May Chang, *Plain and Noble Garb of Truth: Nationalism & Impartiality in American History, 1784-1860* (Athens: Univ. of Georgia Press, 2008), 154; James Ward Hopkins, June 16, 1857, Diary, James Ward Hopkins Papers, USC; Colin G. Calloway, *The American Revolution in Indian Country: Crisis and Diversity in Native American Communities* (New York: Cambridge Univ. Press, 1995), 272.

27. Donald R. Hickey, *The War of 1812: A Forgotten Conflict* (Urbana: Univ. of Illinois Press, 1989), 1-3; Committee of Arrangements to Charles Wilkes, Aug. 31, 1853, Charles Wilkes Papers, DukeU; (New York) *Frank Leslie's Illustrated Newspaper,* Oct. 16, 1858, and Sept. 15, 1860; Harvey Rice to George Bancroft, Feb. 2, 1860, and Harvey Rice to James R. Briggs, Mar. 31, 1860, George Bancroft Papers, MaHS; Cole and McDonough, eds., *Benjamin B. French,* 333; Usher Parsons to George Bancroft, Oct. 19, 1860, George Bancroft Papers, NYPL.

28. Thomas Kelah Wharton, Jan. 8, 1859, 1858-59 Diary, Thomas Kelah Wharton Papers, NYPL; *New Orleans Picayune,* Jan. 9, 1850, Jan. 7, 1849, and Jan. 8, 1852; *Boston Herald,* Jan. 11, 1851; (New York) *Frank Leslie's Illustrated Newspaper,* Jan. 23, 1858.

29. (New York) *Frank Leslie's Illustrated Newspaper,* Mar. 1, 1856; Franklin A. Hudson, Feb. 8, 1856, Franklin A. Hudson Diaries, vol. 2, UNC; Thomas Kelah Wharton, Feb. 9, 1856, 1855-56 Diary, Thomas Kelah Wharton Papers, NYPL; A. H. Kingman, Mar. 16, 1857, A. H. Kingman Diaries, vol. 3, American Travel Collection, UMich.

30. Julia Marsh Patterson, n.d. [Aug. 1850], Journal of Julia Marsh Patterson, Benjamin C. Yancey Papers, UNC; "Fort McHenry, Baltimore, Maryland," *Ballou's Pictorial Drawing-Room Companion* 9 (Dec. 22, 1855): 389, 397; William Campbell Preston to Waddy Thompson, Sept. 7, 1853, Preston Family Papers—Davie Collection, FHS; *Washington (D.C.) National Intelligencer,* June 1, 1860; *Baltimore Sun,* Aug. 10, 1858.

31. Southerner quoted in *Charleston Courier,* Feb. 25, 1850; *Cincinnati Commercial,* Feb. 26, 1850; *Louisville Democrat,* Feb. 7, 1851; *Memphis Appeal,* Aug. 11, 1858.

32. Parker quoted in Merrill D. Peterson, *The Great Triumvirate: Webster, Clay, and Calhoun* (New York: Oxford Univ. Press, 1987), 481; Thoreau quoted in Albert J. Von Frank, *The Trials of Anthony Burns: Freedom and Slavery in Emerson's Boston* (Cambridge, Mass.: Harvard Univ. Press, 1998), 277; Melissa Bryant to Peter Bryant, July 22, 1854, Bryant Family Papers, NYPL.

33. *Boston Liberator,* Aug. 5, 1859; *Boston Herald,* Mar. 6, 1851. A monument to Crispus Attucks was not erected until 1888 and now stands on the Boston Common.

34. Theodore Parker to George Bancroft, Sept. 10, 1858, George Bancroft Papers, NYPL; Theodore Parker to George Bancroft, Mar. 16, 1858, Theodore Parker Papers, MaHS; George Bancroft, *History of the United States from the Discovery of the American Continent* (Boston: Little and Brown, 1858), 7:421; Lilian Handlin, *George Bancroft: The Intellectual as Democrat* (New York: Harper and Row, 1984), 258. To be fair, Peter Kolchin finds that modern American textbooks tend to discount the important role played by slaves in the American Revolution; Peter Kolchin, "Slavery in United States Survey Textbooks," *Journal of American History* 84 (Mar. 1998): 1428, 1436.

35. Theodore Parker to George Bancroft, Mar. 16, 1858, and George Bancroft to Theodore Parker, Apr. 21, 1858, Theodore Parker Papers, MaHS; Henry Wiencek, *An Imperfect God: George Washington, His Slaves, and the Creation of America* (New York: Farrar, Straus, and Giroux, 2003), 197-218; Saul Cornell, *A Well-Regulated Militia: The Founding Fathers and the Origins of Gun Control in America* (New York: Oxford Univ. Press, 2006), 19, 29, 153-57; George Bancroft, *History of the United States from the Discovery of the American Continent* (Boston: Little and Brown, 1860), 8:44; David Brion Davis, *Inhuman Bondage: The Rise and Fall of Slavery in the New World* (New York: Oxford Univ. Press, 2006), 143-51, 317-20. For more on the service of free blacks and slaves during the Revolutionary War, see Benjamin Quarles, *The Negro in the American Revolution* (Chapel Hill: Univ. of North Carolina Press, 1961), and Alan Gilbert, *Black Patriots and Loyalists: Fighting for Emancipation in the War of Independence* (Chicago: Univ. of Chicago Press, 2012). For more on African Americans before, during, and after the Revolution, see Douglas R. Egerton, *Death or Liberty: African Americans and Revolutionary America* (New York: Oxford Univ. Press, 2009).

36. Douglass quoted in Thomas P. Slaughter, *Bloody Dawn: The Christiana Riot and Racial Violence in the Antebellum North* (New York: Oxford Univ. Press, 1991), 79; Concord Free-Soilers quoted in Von Frank, *Trials of Anthony Burns,* 231.

37. Bibb quoted in *Sandwich (Canada West [Ontario]) Voice of the Fugitive,* Feb. 12, 1851; Mainer quoted in *Boston Herald,* Apr. 21, 1851; Melissa Bryant to Peter Bryant, Apr. 28, 1854, Bryant Family Papers, NYPL; Massachusetts abolitionist quoted in *Boston Liberator,* Mar. 11, 1859.

38. Corydon E. Fuller, July 16, 1857, Corydon E. Fuller Journals, vol. 1, Schoff Civil War Collection, UMich; Theodore Parker to John P. Hale, Feb. 22, 1848, Theodore Parker Papers, MaHS; "In Senate," Dec. 22, 1847, U.S. Congress, *Congressional Globe,* 30th Cong., 1st sess., 62-63.

39. William E. Gienapp, *The Origins of the Republican Party, 1852-1856* (New York: Oxford Univ. Press, 1987), 258; Stone quoted in Charles Theodore Greve, *Centennial History of Cincinnati and Representative Citizens* (Chicago: Biographical Publishing Company, 1904), 1:762-63; Steven Weisenburger, *Modern Medea: A Family Story of Slavery and Child Murder from the Old South* (New York: Hill and Wang, 1998), 74-75; *Boston Liberator,* Nov. 18, 1859.

40. (Rochester) *Frederick Douglass's Paper,* Nov. 9, 1855; J. H. Webb to Samuel Gridley Howe, July 1, 1856, Letters Received by Samuel Gridley Howe, MaHS.

41. New Hampshire newspaper quoted in Leon F. Litwack, *North of Slavery: The Negro in the Free States, 1790-1860* (Chicago: Univ. of Chicago Press, 1961), 119; *Boston Herald,* Feb. 2, 1857. For more on herrenvolk democracy, see George M. Fredrickson,

*White Supremacy: A Comparative Study in American and South African History* (New York: Oxford Univ. Press, 1981).

42. Yancey quoted in Avery O. Craven, *The Growth of Southern Nationalism, 1848-1861* (Baton Rouge: Louisiana State Univ. Press, 1953), 327; William W. Freehling, *The Road to Disunion,* vol. 2, *Secessionists Triumphant, 1854-1861* (New York: Oxford Univ. Press, 2007), 307.

43. Josiah Stoddard Johnston, July 21, 1851, and Apr. 17, 1852, Josiah Stoddard Johnston's Journal, FHS; Review of John P. Kennedy's *Life of Wirt, Southern Quarterly Review,* 2d ser., 1 (Apr. 1850): 210-11. For more on the sectional stereotype of the greedy Yankee, see Joseph A. Conforti, *Imagining New England: Explorations of Regional Identity from the Pilgrims to the Mid-Twentieth Century* (Chapel Hill: Univ. of North Carolina Press, 2001), 151-57.

44. *Louisville Courier,* Dec. 5, 1848; Webster quoted in *Richmond Whig,* June 25, 1850.

45. Buchanan quoted in (New York) *Frank Leslie's Illustrated Newspaper,* July 4, 1857; Leonard L. Richards, *The Slave Power: The Free North and Southern Domination, 1780-1860* (Baton Rouge: Louisiana State Univ. Press, 2000), 197-98.

46. *New Bern (N.C.) Union,* June 27, 1857; David M. Potter, *The Impending Crisis, 1848-1861* (New York: HarperCollins, 1976), 90. For more on Mason, see Robert W. Young, *Senator James Murray Mason: Defender of the Old South* (Knoxville: Univ. of Tennessee Press, 1998).

47. Eliab P. Mackintire to William Salter, June 18, 1857, Eliab P. Mackintire Letters, NYPL; *Boston Herald,* June 16, 1857; Edward Everett to William H. Trescot, July 22, 1857, Edward Everett Papers, MaHS; A. H. Kingman, June 21, 1857, vol. 3, A. H. Kingman Diaries, American Travel Collection, UMich; *Boston Post,* June 22, 1857; Henry A. Wise to Edward Everett, June 25, 1857, Edward Everett Papers, MaHS. In fact, the Fugitive Slave Act of 1850 was designed to undermine the due process protections that many Northern states had provided to alleged fugitives through personal liberty laws. It denied alleged fugitives any opportunity to prove their status. It assumed that all African Americans were fugitive slaves—exactly like the slave codes of the South. Its every provision favored slavemasters; it did not extend even a single protection to alleged slaves; Thomas D. Morris, *Free Men All: The Personal Liberty Laws of the North, 1780-1861* (Baltimore: Johns Hopkins Univ. Press, 1974), 146-47.

48. *Boston Liberator,* Aug. 28, 1857, and June 26, 1857; Thomas Bradford Drew, June 17, 1857, 1857 Diary, Thomas Bradford Drew Diaries, MaHS.

49. South Carolinian quoted in *Charleston Mercury,* June 29, 1854; John W. Gordon, *South Carolina and the American Revolution: A Battlefield History* (Columbia: Univ. of South Carolina Press, 2003), xv; Paul Quigley, "Independence Day Dilemmas in the American South, 1848-1865," *Journal of Southern History* 75 (May 2009): 251; James C. Johnston to William S. Pettigrew, Nov. 9, 1849, Pettigrew Family Papers, UNC; William Gilmore Simms to Henry P. Dale, May 3, [1856?], William Gilmore Simms Papers, USC; William K. Pillsbury to George Bancroft, Aug. 24, 1858, George Bancroft Papers, MaHS.

50. Forefathers' Day speaker quoted in William Way, comp., *History of the New England Society of Charleston, South Carolina, for One Hundred Years, 1819-1919* (Charleston: New England Society of Charleston, 1920), 226-27, 230.

51. "Pulaski Monument, Monument Square, Savannah, Georgia," *Ballou's Pictorial Drawing-Room Companion* 13 (Sept. 5, 1857): 153; "East Room—Independence Hall, Philadelphia," *Ballou's Pictorial Drawing-Room Companion* 9 (Oct. 6, 1855): 213; *Charleston Mercury,* Oct. 3, 1855; (New York) *Frank Leslie's Illustrated Newspaper,* Jan. 24, 1857; Fire-eater quoted in *Charleston Mercury,* June 29, 1854; Octavius Wilkie, Daniel Rarenul Jr., and William Y. Paxton to William Porcher Miles, Jan. 9, 1858, William Porcher Miles Papers, UNC.

52. Gadsden quoted in *Charleston Mercury,* July 9, 1850; Nathaniel Beverly Tucker to John H. Cocke, Feb. 11, 1850, Cocke Family Papers; UVA; Henry A. Washington, "The Virginia Constitution of 1776," *Southern Literary Messenger* 18 (Nov. 1852): 657.

53. Mary Elizabeth Powell to Joseph Nathaniel Allen, July 10, 1858, Joseph Nathaniel Allen Papers, UNC; *New Bern (N.C.) Union,* July 11, 1857; Pauline Maier, *American Scripture: Making the Declaration of Independence* (New York: Knopf, 1998), 172–74.

54. Maier, *American Scripture,* 172–74; John Hope Franklin, *The Militant South, 1800–1861* (1965; Urbana: Univ. of Illinois, 2002), 6; Mecklenburg Declaration defender quoted in *New Bern (N.C.) Union,* July 18, 1857.

55. Bancroft, *History of the United States,* 8:373–74; Hugh B. Grigsby to George Bancroft, June 29, 1857, Thomas Balch to George Bancroft, Sept. 22, 1857, and Henry S. Randall to George Bancroft, Feb. 24, 1858, and Mar. 27, 1858, George Bancroft Papers, MaHS; Henry S. Randall, *Life of Thomas Jefferson: In Three Volumes* (New York: Derby & Jackson, 1858), 3:571, 573.

56. John Hope Franklin believed the dispute was "pointless and fruitless," uncharacteristically missing the very real issues at stake in this public and earnest attempt to fashion sectional identity; John Hope Franklin, "The North, the South, and the American Revolution," *Journal of American History* 62 (June 1975): 22.

57. Elizabeth Fox-Genovese and Eugene Genovese, *Mind of the Master Class: History and Faith in the Southern Slaveholders' Worldview* (Cambridge: Cambridge Univ. Press, 2005), 719; *Charleston Mercury,* July 3, 1856; Franklin, "The North, the South, and the Revolution," 8–9; Nash, *Forgotten Fifth,* 3.

58. *New York Tribune,* Nov. 20, 1841; *Boston Liberator,* July 4, 1856; Byron Paine, "Speech on the Annexation of Texas," n.d., [1845], Byron Paine Papers, WHS.

59. South Carolinian quoted in *Charleston Courier,* Aug. 2, 1850; Review of Kennedy's *Life of Wirt,* 197; *Charleston Mercury,* Aug. 6, 1853; Helen Martin to John C. Bullitt, Nov. 27, 1846, Bullitt Family Papers—Oxmoor Collection, FHS; Virginia Ingraham Burr, ed., *The Secret Eye: The Journal of Ella Gertrude Clanton Thomas, 1848–1889* (Chapel Hill: Univ. of North Carolina Press, 1990), 101.

60. John S. Ezbell, "A Southern Education for Southrons," *Journal of Southern History* 17 (Aug. 1951): 306–11; "Southern School Books," *De Bow's Review* 13 (Sept. 1852): 259; Muscoe R. H. Garnett to William Henry Trescot, Feb. 16, 1851, Hunter-Garnett Family Papers, UVA; *Charleston Mercury,* July 3, 1856. For more on contemporary battles over history textbooks, see Gary B. Nash, Charlotte Crabtree, and Ross E. Dunn, *History on Trial: Culture Wars and the Teaching of the Past* (New York: Knopf, 1997), 114–17, and Carol Sheriff, "Virginia's Embattled Textbooks: Lessons (Learned and Not) from the Centennial Era," *Civil War History* 58 (Mar. 2012): 37–74.

61. "Notices of New Works," *Southern Literary Messenger* 30 (June 1860): 475; Daniel Harvey Hill to James Henley Thornwell, Sept. 21, 1857, James Henley Thornwell Papers, USC; Daniel Harvey Hill, *Elements of Algebra* (Philadelphia: J. P. Lippincott, 1857), iv. It is also not clear what would differentiate "Southern mathematics" from the Northern variety, but the phrase evokes the "Aryan science" of the Nazi regime. For more on the efforts by Hitler to make an "Aryan" or "German" science, see Alan D. Beyerchen, *Scientists under Hitler: Politics and the Physics Community in the Third Reich* (New Haven: Yale Univ. Press, 1977).

62. "South-Carolina: Her Present Attitude and Future Action," *Southern Quarterly Review,* 2d ser., 4 (Oct. 1851): 295; *Charleston Mercury,* Aug. 6, 1853.

63. Solon Robinson, "Negro Slavery at the South," *De Bow's Review* 6 (Sept. 1849): 206; "Progress and Resources of the Southern States," *De Bow's Review* 10 (Jan. 1851): 83-84, emphasis added; Georgian quoted in William W. Freehling, *The Road to Disunion,* vol. 1, *Secessionists at Bay, 1776-1854* (New York: Oxford Univ. Press, 1990), 133-34; Matthew F. Maury, "The Commercial Prospects of the South," *Southern Literary Messenger* 17 (Nov. 1851): 697; Eva Sheppard Wolf, *Race and Liberty in the New Nation: Emancipation in Virginia from the Revolution to Nat Turner's Rebellion* (Baton Rouge: Louisiana State Univ. Press, 2006), 43-47; Stephen T. Whitman, *The Price of Freedom: Slavery and Manumission in Baltimore and Early National Maryland* (Lexington: Univ. Press of Kentucky, 1997), 93.

64. "Southern Slavery and Its Assailants," *De Bow's Review* 15 (Nov. 1853): 488.

65. William J. Rivers to William E. Martin, Aug. 17, 1859, George Bancroft Papers, MaHS; "Canaan Identified with the Ethiopian," *Southern Quarterly Review,* 1st ser., 2 (Oct. 1842): 360; *New Orleans Picayune,* July 28, 1848; Virginian quoted in Drew Gilpin Faust, ed., *The Ideology of Slavery: Proslavery Thought in the Antebellum South, 1830-1860* (Baton Rouge: Louisiana State Univ. Press, 1981), 59; Alfred Hunt, *Haiti's Influence on Antebellum America: Slumbering Volcano in the Caribbean* (Baton Rouge: Louisiana State Univ. Press, 1988), 89-91. In 1776 Jamaican slaves took inspiration from the American Revolution and plotted their own revolt a fact that escaped the notice of American abolitionists and slavemasters; Seymour Drescher, *Abolition: A History of Slavery and Antislavery* (Cambridge: Cambridge Univ. Press, 2009), 123.

66. *Richmond Whig,* Oct. 7, 1849; "The South and the Union," *De Bow's Review* 10 (Feb. 1851): 160; Franklin, *Militant South,* 5-9; K. Jack Bauer, *The Mexican War, 1846-1848* (New York: Macmillan, 1974), 72.

67. Kenneth S. Greenberg, *Honor & Slavery: Lies, Duels, Noses, Masks, Dressing as a Woman, Gifts, Strangers, Humanitarianism, Death, Slave Rebellions, The Proslavery Argument, Baseball, Hunting, and Gambling in the Old South* (Princeton, N.J.: Princeton Univ. Press, 1996), 7-9; David Outlaw to Emily B. Outlaw, Feb. 27, 1850, David Outlaw Papers, UNC; R. L. Scott to Benjamin C. Yancey, Mar. 17, 1855, Benjamin C. Yancey Papers, UNC; Hickey, *War of 1812,* 258-68; Robert V. Remini, *The House: The History of the House of Representatives* (New York: HarperCollins, 2006), 151-52; Craven, *Growth of Southern Nationalism,* 317.

68. David Herbert Donald, William E. Gienapp, Michael D. Pierson, and Manisha Sinha miss this underlying dispute. (David Herbert Donald, *Charles Sumner and the*

*Coming of the Civil War* [New York: Knopf, 1960], 284-86.) William E. Gienapp, "The Crime against Sumner: The Caning of Charles Sumner and the Rise of the Republican Party," *Civil War History* 25 (Sept. 1979): 218-45; Michael D. Pierson, "'All Southern Society Is Assailed by the Foulest Charges': Charles Sumner's 'The Crime Against Kansas' and the Escalation of Republican Anti-Slavery Rhetoric," *New England Quarterly* 68 (Dec. 1995): 531-57; and Manisha Sinha, "The Caning of Charles Sumner: Slavery, Race, and Ideology in the Age of the Civil War," *Journal of the Early Republic* 23 (Summer 2003): 233-62). John Hope Franklin noted that Sumner's "The Crime against Kansas" speech reiterated charges that slavery undermined Southern arms during the Revolutionary War and "led to the well-known episode, the caning of Sumner on the Senate floor by Butler's cousin, Representative Preston Brooks," and Bertram Wyatt-Brown as well as William L. Welch concur; John Hope Franklin, *A Southern Odyssey: Travelers in the Antebellum North* (Baton Rouge: Louisiana State Univ. Press, 1976), 234; Bertram Wyatt-Brown, *Yankee Saints and Southern Sinners* (Baton Rouge: Louisiana State Univ. Press, 1985), 198; William L. Welch, "Lorenzo Sabine and the Assault on Sumner," *New England Quarterly* 65 (June 1992): 299-302).

69. Franklin, "The North, the South, and the Revolution," 10-11; *Charleston Mercury,* July 21, 1856; *New York National Anti-Slavery Standard,* June 14, 1856; Laurence M. Keitt, "Defense of South Carolina," July 14, 1856, U.S. Congress, *Congressional Globe,* 34th Cong., 1st sess., 833, 834, 839.

70. Franklin, *Southern Odyssey,* 239-42; Fox-Genovese and Genovese, *Mind of the Master Class,* 33; *Charleston Mercury,* Nov. 28, 1856, and Dec. 1, 1856; William Gilmore Simms to James Chesnut Jr., Dec. 16, 1856, William Porcher Miles Papers, UNC; *New York Express* quoted in *Salem (Ohio) Anti-Slavery Bugle,* Nov. 22, 1856; Bertram Wyatt-Brown, *Southern Honor: Ethics and Behavior in the Old South* (New York: Oxford Univ. Press, 1982), 34-35.

71. John S. Preston to George Bancroft, Dec. 17, 1855, George Bancroft Papers, MaHS; *Charleston Mercury,* May 24, 1855, and Nov. 27, 1856; R., "Liberty and Slavery: Professor Bledsoe," *Southern Literary Messenger* 23 (May 1856): 387.

72. Handlin, *George Bancroft,* 261; Ralph Waldo Emerson to George Bancroft, May 24, 1858, George Bancroft to Joseph Johnson, Dec. 20, 1855, and Thomas Balch to George Bancroft, Sept. 22, 1857, George Bancroft Papers, MaHS; Peter Kolchin, *American Slavery, 1619-1877,* rev. ed. (New York: Hill and Wang, 2003), 70; George Bancroft to William Porcher Miles, Jan. 3, 1860, William Porcher Miles Papers, UNC; William J. Rivers to George Bancroft, Dec. 8, 1856, George Bancroft Papers, NYPL; Bancroft, *History of the United States,* 8:44, 225, 322-23, 373-74; Nash, *Forgotten Fifth,* 33; Davis, *Inhuman Bondage,* 150-51.

73. William C. Preston to Francis Lieber, Dec. 19, 1858, Francis Lieber Papers, USC; George Fitzhugh, "Mr. Bancroft and the 'Inner Light,'" *De Bow's Review* 29 (Nov. 1860): 607, 599-600.

74. *Cincinnati Commercial,* Aug. 2, 1850; "Battle of Cowpens," *Ballou's Pictorial Drawing-Room Companion* 11 (Nov. 8, 1856): 301; Lewis Cass to William Porcher Miles, Sept. 19, 1858, and James Dixon to William Porcher Miles, Sept. 11, 1858, William Porcher Miles Papers, UNC.

75. Isaac E. Morse to Nathan Appleton, Dec. 3, 1845, Appleton Family Papers, MaHS; "The State of Mississippi, Part I," *De Bow's Review* 10 (Feb. 1851): 193; Daniel Webster, "Second Reply to Hayne," in Charles M. Wiltse and Alan R. Berolzheimer, eds., *The Papers of Daniel Webster: Speeches and Formal Writings*, vol. 1, *1800–1833* (Hanover, N.H.: Univ. Press of New England 1986), 326; Joseph Johnston to George Bancroft, Dec. 26, 1855, George Bancroft Papers, MaHS; "The South and the Union," *De Bow's Review* 10 (Feb. 1851): 161.

76. Review of Charles Francis Adams's *The Works of John Adams, North American Review* 85 (July 1857): 22; Jim Piecuch, *Three Peoples, One King: Loyalists, Indians, and Slaves in the Revolutionary South, 1775–1782* (Columbia: Univ. of South Carolina Press, 2008), 132–49; *Charleston Mercury,* May 17, 1859; "Eᴜᴛᴀᴡ" quoted in *Charleston Mercury,* May 3, 1859.

77. E. C. Herrick to George Bancroft, June 20 1851, George Bancroft Papers, MaHS; John S. Henderson, "On the Revolution," [n.d., 1859], John Steele Henderson Papers, UNC.

78. George M. Fredrickson, "America's Original Sin," *New York Review of Books* 51 (Mar. 25, 2004): 34; *Washington (D.C.) National Era,* Aug. 5, 1847.

79. Correspondent quoted in *Memphis Appeal,* Nov. 10, 1858.

80. Robert J. Walker, *An Appeal for the Union* (New York: J. F. Trow, 1856), 15.

## 5. FINISHING WHAT THE FOUNDERS STARTED

1. Michael A. Morrison, *Slavery and the American West: The Eclipse of Manifest Destiny and the Coming of the Civil War* (Chapel Hill: Univ. of North Carolina Press, 1997), 134; Elizabeth Fox-Genovese and Eugene D. Genovese, *The Mind of the Master Class: History and Faith in the Southern Slaveholders' Worldview* (New York: Cambridge Univ. Press, 2005), 26.

2. *New York Tribune,* Nov. 19, 1851; *Salem (Ohio) Anti-Slavery Bugle,* Sept. 20, 1851; *Dover Delaware State Reporter,* Dec. 4, 1855.

3. Charles Lowell to George Bancroft, Mar. 16, 1853, George Bancroft Papers, NYPL; Arthur Zliversmit, *The First Emancipation: The Abolition of Slavery in the North* (Chicago: Univ. of Chicago Press, 1967), 113–15; George J. Bryan to George Bancroft, June 29, 1858, George Bancroft Papers, MaHS; Gary B. Nash and Jean Soderlund, *Freedom by Degrees: Emancipation in Pennsylvania and Its Aftermath* (New York: Oxford Univ. Press, 1991), 100–106; David Brion Davis, *Inhuman Bondage: The Rise and Fall of Slavery in the New World* (New York: Oxford Univ. Press, 2006), 155.

4. *New Orleans Picayune,* July 8, 1854; *Sandwich (Canada West [Ontario]) Voice of the Fugitive,* Mar. 12, 1851; *Salem (Ohio) Anti-Slavery Bugle,* May 22, 1858.

5. James G. Birney to Theodore Parker, Oct. 27, 1848, James Birney Papers, UMich; *Providence Post,* Mar. 19, 1853; Robert Toombs, "Slavery—Its Constitutional Status, and Its Influence on Society and the Colored Race," *De Bow's Review* 20 (May 1856): 582.

6. *Salem (Ohio) Anti-Slavery Bugle,* Sept. 20, 1851; Davis, *Inhuman Bondage,* 152; *New York Tribune,* Sept. 1, 1852.

7. V. Wright Kingsley to James R. Doolittle, Jan. 8, 1860, James R. Doolittle Papers, WHS; C. H. Winslow to John A. Andrew, Dec. 23, 1860, John A. Andrew Papers, MaHS; Salmon P. Chase to B. B. Musser and George F. Williams, June 17, 1854, William K. Bixby Papers, MHM.

8. *Chillicothe (Ohio) Scioto Gazette,* Mar. 20, 1850; *Providence Post,* May 3, 1853.

9. Jim M. Douglas to E. B. Douglas, Apr. 12, 1842, Jim M. Douglas Papers, Miscellaneous Collections, FHS; George J. Bryan to George Bancroft, June 29, 1858, George Bancroft Papers, MaHS; James Manney to the Editors of the *Republic,* n.d. [Dec. 1849], James Manney Letterbook, Transcripts, UNC.

10. *New York Tribune,* June 8, 1853.

11. Edgar J. McManus, *Black Bondage in the North* (Syracuse: Syracuse Univ. Press, 1973), 160-79; William W. Freehling, *The Road to Disunion,* vol. 1, *Secessionists at Bay, 1776-1854* (New York: Oxford Univ. Press, 1990), 132-33; *Dover Delaware State Reporter,* Dec. 4, 1855; *Philadelphia Pennsylvanian,* Dec. 20, 1849.

12. Ruth N. Hastings to Ruth W. Hastings and Mary Anne Hastings, Aug. 12, 1852, Ruth N. Hastings Letters, UMich; *Philadelphia Pennsylvania Freeman,* Nov. 13, 1851; Freehling, *Road to Disunion,* vol. 1, 134.

13. "Southern Slavery and Its Assailants," *De Bow's Review* 15 (Nov. 1853): 486; *New York Day Book,* Feb. 7, 1857.

14. Stephen F. Miller, "The North and the South in Regard to Slavery," *De Bow's Review* 10 (Jan. 1851): 84; William B. Napton, n.d., [Mar.] 1855, Diary Typescripts, pp. 148, William B. Napton Papers, MHM; *Salem (Ohio) Anti-Slavery Bugle,* Sept. 20, 1851; *Washington (D.C.) National Era,* Feb. 4, 1847.

15. Thomas B. Lincoln to Artemas Hale, Dec.11, 1860, Artemas Hale Papers, UMich; John Minor Botts to Anna Ella Carroll, Dec. 29, 1859, Anna Ella Carroll Letters, MdHS.

16. John Lothrop Motley to William Gray, Feb. 27, 1862, John Lothrop Motley Letters, MaHS; Frank V. Winston to John B. Minor, Mar. 10, 1860, Minor and Wilson Family Papers, UVA.

17. William S. Pettigrew to James L. Petigru, n.d., [May] 1860, Pettigrew Family Papers, UNC; Jacob Brown to Anna Ella Carroll, Oct. 26, 1859, Anna Ella Carroll Letters, MdHS.

18. John H. Graham, Feb. 4, 1861, John H. Graham Journals, vol. 1, UMich.

19. Jane Caroline North Pettigrew to Charles L. Pettigrew, Nov. 17, 1860, Pettigrew Family Papers, UNC; John Steele Henderson to Mr. and Mrs. Archibald Henderson, Apr. 21, 1861, John Steele Henderson Papers, UNC; Rogene A. Scott to Hannah Scott Warren, Dec. 25, 1860, Scott Family Papers, UNC; Lundsford P. Yandell Jr. to Lundsford P. Yandell Sr., Dec. 23, 1860, Yandell Family Papers, FHS; Henry Campbell Davis to Mrs. Henry Campbell Davis, Dec. 21, 1860, Henry Campbell Davis Letters, USC; Thomas Kelah Wharton, Dec. 21, 1860, and Jan. 26, 1861, Diary 1860-61, Thomas Kelah Wharton Papers, NYPL.

20. *New York Herald,* Oct. 30, 1860; *New York National Anti-Slavery Standard,* Dec. 1, 1860.

21. John Bigelow to Mr. Hargreaves, Nov. 10, 1860, John Bigelow Papers, NYPL.

22. J. David Hacker estimates that the Civil War's body count exceeded 750,000

combatants; J. David Hacker, "A Census-Based Count for Civil War Dead," *Civil War History* 57 (Dec. 2011): 338.

23. William Davidson Harris to J. Morrison Harris, June 4, 1861, J. Morrison Harris Papers, MdHS; Alexander H. Stephens to [unknown], Nov. 25, 1860, in Ulrich B. Phillips, ed., *Annual Report of the American Historical Association for the Year 1911,* vol. 2, *The Correspondence of Robert Toombs, Alexander H. Stephens, and Howell Cobb* (Washington, D.C.: Government Printing Office, 1913), 504-5; Jason O. Harrison to William S. Bodley, Nov. 27, 1860, Bodley Family Papers, FHS.

24. *Washington (D.C.) National Intelligencer,* May 10, 1860; Mrs. Robert Cunningham to Ann Pamela Cunningham, Apr. 10-11, 1860, Ann Pamela Cunningham Papers, USC; Edward Everett to J. S. Hilliard, Aug. 4, 1860, Edward Everett Papers, MaHS; M. L. [Pearsen?] to Ann Eliza Mills, Mar. 18, 1861, Bryan and Leventhorpe Family Papers, UNC.

25. *New York National Anti-Slavery Standard,* July 7, 1860; *Washington (D.C.) National Intelligencer,* July 6, 1860; *Boston Liberator,* June 29, 1860, and Oct. 19, 1860.

26. Thomas Bradford Drew, July 4, 1861, 1860-65 Diary, Thomas Bradford Drew Diaries, MaHS; James H. Campbell to Juliet Campbell, July 4, 1861, James Hepburn Campbell Papers, UMich; Thaddeus W. Swank, July 4, 1861, Thaddeus W. Swank Civil War Diary, MdHS.

27. John Steele Henderson to Mrs. Archibald Henderson, Mar. 31, 1861, John Steele Henderson Papers, UNC; Beth G. Crabtree and James W. Patton, eds., *"Journal of a Secesh Lady": The Diary of Catherine Ann Devereux Edmonston, 1860-1866* (Raleigh, N.C.: Division of Archives and History, 1979), 63; Joseph C. Sitterson, *The Secession Movement in North Carolina* (Chapel Hill: Univ. of North Carolina Press, 1939), 237.

28. Theodore Parker to Eliza F. Eddy, Nov. 19, 1859, Theodore Parker Papers, MaHS; *Boston Liberator,* Apr. 26, 1861.

29. John T. Dye to Richard Nickman Kewitt, Feb. 1, 1862; William S. Bodley to A. Burwell, Nov. 22, 1860, Bodley Family Papers, FHS; William S. Pettigrew to J. Johnston Pettigrew, Nov. 2, 1860, Pettigrew Family Papers, UNC.

30. William Porcher Miles to George Bancroft, Feb. 6, 1860, and Charles F. Mayer to George Bancroft, Feb. 2, 1861, George Bancroft Papers, MaHS; "Editor's Table," *Southern Literary Messenger* 31 (Feb. 1860): 157.

31. George Bancroft to Dean Milman, Aug. 15, 1861, George Bancroft Papers, NYPL; Edward Everett to J. S. Hilliard, June 1, 1860, Edward Everett Papers, MaHS.

32. *Richmond Enquirer,* Aug. 6, 1861; Henry Calvin Conner to Ellen Conner, Dec. 19, 1861, Henry Calvin Conner Papers, USC; John H. Graham, Mar. 4, 1861, John H. Graham Journals, vol. 1, UMich.

33. *Boston Liberator,* Jan. 11, 1861; Thomas Bradford Drew, Apr. 19, 1861, 1860-65 Diary, Thomas Bradford Drew Diaries, MaHS; James H. Campbell to Juliet Campbell, June 19, 1862, James Hepburn Campbell Papers, UMich.

# Select Bibliography

PRIMARY SOURCES

MANUSCRIPTS
William L. Clements Library, University of Michigan, Ann Arbor, Mich. (UMich)
  African American History Collection
  American Travel Collection
  Birney, James, Papers
  Boynton Family Papers
  Burwell-Guy Family Papers
  Campbell, James Hepburn, Papers
  Cass, Lewis, Papers
  Child, Lydia Maria, Papers
  Fuller, Corydon E., Journals
  Graham, John H., Journals
  Hale, Artemas, Papers
  Hastings, Ruth N., Letters
  Hundley, Daniel R., Diary
  Kingman, A. H., Diaries
  Miscellaneous Collections
  Wheeler, John, Diary

Filson Historical Society, Louisville, Ky. (FHS)
  Bodley Family Papers
  Bullitt Family Papers—Oxmoor Collection
  Clay, Cassius M., Papers
  Green Family Papers

Johnston, Josiah Stoddard, Journal
Johnston Family Papers
Mount Vernon [Ladies'] Association of Tennessee, Miscellaneous, Collections, Papers
Preston Family Papers—Davie Collection
Sanders Family Papers
Yandell Family Papers

Historical Society of Pennsylvania, Philadelphia, Pa. (HSP)
Askew, Mary Brown, Diary
Breck, Samuel, Notebooks
Davis, William Morris, Correspondence
Dealy, Dennis F., Papers
Gratz, Simon, Collection: American Literary Duplicates
Jones and Taylor Families, Papers
Johnston, Benjamin S., Logbook
Mervine, Isaac, Memorandum Book
Patton, George W., Diary
Suydam, Mary L., Collection
Taylor, William P., Account Book
Wister Family Papers

Maryland Historical Society, Baltimore, Md. (MdHS)
Carroll, Anna Ella, Letters
Harris, J. Morrison, Papers
Jacobs, Curtis W., Diary and Account Book
Kennedy, John Pendleton, Papers
Pearce, James A., Papers
Swank, Thaddeus W., Civil War Diary

Massachusetts Historical Society, Boston, Mass. (MaHS)
Andrew, John A., Papers
Appleton Family Papers
Bancroft, George, Papers
Cleveland, Anthony B., Speech
Drew, Thomas Bradford, Diaries
Everett, Edward, Papers
Hickling-Nye Papers
Howe, Samuel Gridley, Letters Received by
Lawrence, Amos Adams, Papers
Motley, John Lothrop, Letters
Parker, Theodore, Papers
Pierce, John Bachelder, Papers
Robie-Sewall Family Papers

Missouri History Museum, St. Louis, Mo. (MHM)
   Bixby, William K., Papers
   Napton, William B., Papers

New York Public Library, New York City, N.Y. (NYPL)
   Allen, W. T., Diary
   Bancroft, George, Papers
   Bennett, James Gordon, Papers
   Bigelow, John, Papers
   Bryant Family Papers
   Corbin, Francis Porteous, Papers
   Dunstan, Caroline A., Diaries
   Mackintire, Eliab Parker, Letters
   Phelps, John Wolcott, Papers
   Raymond, Henry J., Papers
   Ruggles, Samuel B., Papers
   Tilden, Samuel J., Papers
   Wharton, Thomas Kelah, Papers
   Wolcott, Frederick Henry, Diary

Rubenstein Rare Book & Manuscript Library, Duke University, Durham, N.C. (DukeU)
   Cooley, Dennis, Papers
   De Bow, James D. B., Papers
   Jones, Samuel T., Papers
   Loveland, Julia Lord (Noyes), Papers
   Wilkes, Charles, Papers
   Williams, Matthew Jouett, Papers

Albert and Shirley Small Special Collections Library, University of Virginia, Charlottesville, Va. (UVA)
   Bocock, Thomas S., Papers
   Cabell Family Papers
   Cocke Family Papers
   Everett, Edward, Papers
   Gordon Family Papers
   Hunter, Robert M. T., Papers
   Hunter-Garnett Family Collection
   Maupin, Socrates, Letters to
   Minor, Louisa H. A., Diary
   Minor and Wilson Family Papers
   Ritchie, Anna Cora Ogden Mowatt, Papers
   Rives Family Papers
   Stuart, Alexander H. H., Papers

South Caroliniana Library, University of South Carolina, Columbia, S.C. (USC)
    Adger-Smyth-Flynn Family Papers
    Aiken, David Wyatt, Papers
    Ashmore, John Durant, Papers
    Ashworth, Henry, Papers
    Boyce, Mary Elizabeth, Diary
    Coker, Caleb, Papers
    Conner, Henry Calvin, Papers
    Cunningham, Ann Pamela, Papers
    Davis, Henry Campbell, Letters
    Gaston, Strait, Wylie, and Baskin Families Papers
    Glass Family Papers
    Hayne, Arthur P., Papers
    Hixon, Charlotte Baker, Papers
    Hopkins, James Ward, Papers
    Huger, Cleland Kinloch, Papers
    Legaré, Hugh Swinton, Papers
    Leland, Samuel Wells, Diary
    Lide, Coker, and Stout Families Papers
    Lieber, Francis, Papers
    Richardson, John Smythe, Papers
    Simms, William Gilmore, Papers
    Thornwell, James Henley, Papers
    Watts, Beauford Taylor, Papers
    Williams-Chestnut-Manning Families Papers

Southern Historical Collection, University of North Carolina, Chapel Hill, N.C. (UNC)
    Allen, Joseph Nathaniel, Papers
    Bryan and Leventhorpe Family Papers
    Bynum, John Bowen, Papers
    Gale and Polk Family Papers
    Henderson, John Steele, Papers
    Holcombe, William Henry, Diary
    Hudson, Franklin A., Diaries
    Manney, James, Letterbook
    Miles, William Porcher, Papers
    Outlaw, David, Papers
    Perkins, John, Papers
    Pettigrew Family Papers
    Scott Family Papers
    Tripp, William Henry and Araminta Guilford, Papers
    Yancey, Benjamin C., Papers

Wisconsin Historical Society, University of Wisconsin, Madison, Wis. (WHS)
  Brisbane, William Henry, Papers
  Davidson, James D., Papers, McCormick Collection
  Davis, John Givan, Correspondence
  Doolittle, James R., Papers
  Holton, Edward D., Papers
  Paine, Byron, Papers
  Potter, John F., Papers


NEWSPAPERS
*Baltimore Sun*
*Boston Herald*
*Boston Liberator*
*Boston Post*
*Charleston Courier*
*Charleston Mercury*
*Chicago Tribune*
*Chillicothe (Ohio) Scioto Gazette*
*Cincinnati Commercial*
*Dover Delaware State Reporter*
*Hartford Courant*
*Lawrence Republican*
*Louisville Courier*
*Louisville Democrat*
*Memphis Appeal*
*Mobile Register*
*New Bern (N.C.) Union*
*New Orleans Picayune*
New York Day Book
(New York) *Frank Leslie's Illustrated Newspaper*
*New York Herald*
*New York National Anti-Slavery Standard*
*New York Times*
*New York Tribune*
*Philadelphia Pennsylvania Freeman*
*Philadelphia Pennsylvanian*
*Providence Post*
*Richmond Enquirer*
*Richmond Whig*
(Rochester) *Frederick Douglass's Paper*
*Rochester North Star*
*Salem (Ohio) Anti-Slavery Bugle*
*Sandwich (Canada West [Ontario]) Voice of the Fugitive*

St. Louis Missouri Democrat
Washington (D.C.) National Era
Washington (D.C.) National Intelligence

PERIODICALS
*Ballou's Pictorial Drawing-Room Companion*
*De Bow's Review*
*Emerson's Magazine*
*Gleason's Pictorial Drawing-Room Companion*
*New Englander and Yale Review*
*North American Review*
*Proceedings of the American Association for the Advancement of Science*
*Southern Literary Messenger*
*Southern Quarterly Review*
*United States Magazine*
*Yankee Doodle*

BOOKS AND PAMPHLETS
Bancroft, George. *History of the United States from the Discovery of the American Continent.* 10 vols. Boston: Little and Brown, 1834-75.

Bartlett, John Russell. *Dictionary of Americanisms: A Glossary of Words and Phrases Usually Regarded as Peculiar to the United States.* Boston: Little, Brown, 1860.

Blassingame, John W., ed. *Slave Testimony: Two Centuries of Letters, Speeches, Interviews, and Autobiographies.* Baton Rouge: Louisiana State University Press, 1977.

Bibb, Henry. *The Life and Adventures of Henry Bibb, an American Slave.* Edited by Charles Heglar. Madison: University of Wisconsin Press, 2001. Published 1849 by the author.

Binney, Horace. *An Inquiry into the Formation of Washington's Farewell Address.* Philadelphia: J. B. Lippincott, 1859.

Bledsoe, Albert Taylor. *An Essay on Liberty and Slavery.* Philadelphia: J. P. Lippincott, 1857.

Botts, John Minor. *The Great Rebellion: Its Secret History, Rise, Progress, and Disastrous Failure.* New York: Harper & Brothers, 1866.

Breeden, James O., ed. *Advice among Masters: The Ideal in Slave Management in the Old South.* Westport, Conn.: Greenwood Press, 1980.

Brown, William Wells. *From Fugitive Slave to Free Man: The Autobiographies of William Wells Brown.* Edited by William L. Andrews. Columbia: University of Missouri Press, 1993.

Calhoun, John C. *The Papers of John C. Calhoun.* Edited by Clyde N. Wilson et al. 28 vols. Columbia: University of South Carolina Press, 1959-2003.

———. *The Works of John C. Calhoun.* Edited by Richard K. Crallé. New York: D. Appleton, 1853.

Choate, Rufus. *The Works of Rufus Choate with a Memoir of His Life.* Edited by Samuel Gilman Brown. 2 vols. Boston: Little, Brown, and Company, 1862.

Cromwell, Oliver, and Thomas Carlyle, eds. *Complete Works of Thomas Carlyle.* Vol. 4, *Critical and Miscellaneous Essays.* New York: P. F. Collier, 1901.

Curtis, George William. *Orations and Addresses of George William Curtis.* Edited by Charles Eliot Norton. New York: Harper and Brothers, 1894.

Douglass, Frederick. *Frederick Douglass Papers.* Edited by John W. Blassingame. 5 vols. New Haven, Conn.: Yale University Press, 1979-92.

———. *Narrative of the Life of Frederick Douglass, an American Slave.* Edited by Deborah E. McDowell. New York: Oxford University Press, 1999. First published 1845 by the Anti-Slavery Office.

Edmondston, Catherine Ann Devereux. *"Journal of a Secesh Lady": The Diary of Catherine Ann Devereux Edmondston, 1860-1866.* Edited by Beth G. Crabtree and James W. Patton. Raleigh, N.C.: Division of Archives and History, 1979.

Emerson, Ralph Waldo. *Lectures and Biographical Sketches by Ralph Waldo Emerson.* Edited by Edward Waldo Emerson. Boston: Houghton Mifflin, 1904.

Faust, Drew Gilpin, ed. *The Ideology of Slavery: Proslavery Thought in the Antebellum South, 1830-1860.* Baton Rouge: Louisiana State University Press, 1981.

Fitzhugh, George. *Sociology for the South; Or, The Failure of Free Society.* Richmond, Va.: A. Morris, 1854.

French, Benjamin Brown. *Witness to the Young Republic: A Yankee's Journal, 1828-1870.* Edited by Donald B. Cole and John J. McDonough. Hanover, N.H.: University Press of New England, 2002.

Garnett, Muscoe, R. H. *An Address Delivered before the Society of Alumni of the University of Virginia.* Charlottesville, Va.: O. S. Allen, 1850.

Gorgas, Josiah. *The Journals of Josiah Gorgas, 1857-1878.* Edited by Sarah Woolfolk Wiggins. Tuscaloosa: University of Alabama Press, 1995.

Grimké, Sarah Moore. *An Epistle to the Clergy of the Southern States.* New York: n.p., 1836.

Hammond, James Henry. *Secret and Sacred: The Diaries of James Henry Hammond, a Southern Slaveholder.* Edited by Carol K. Bleser. New York: Oxford University Press, 1988.

Hill, Daniel Harvey. *Elements of Algebra.* Philadelphia: J. P. Lippincott, 1857.

Jefferson, Thomas. *Notes on the State of Virginia.* Richmond, Va.: J. W. Randolph, 1853. First published 1783 by John Stockdale.

———. *The Papers of Thomas Jefferson.* First Series. Edited by Julian Boyd. 33 vols. Princeton, N.J.: Princeton University Press, 1950-2006.

———. *The Portable Thomas Jefferson.* Edited by Merrill D. Peterson. New York: Penguin, 1977.

Johannsen, Robert W., ed. *The Lincoln Douglas Debates.* New York: Oxford University Press, 1965.

Keeler, William Frederick. *Aboard the U.S.S. Florida, 1863-65: The Letters of Paymaster William Frederick Keeler, U.S. Navy, to His Wife, Anna.* Edited by Robert W. Daly. New York: Arno Press, 1980.

Lee, Jean B., ed. *Experiencing Mount Vernon: Eyewitness Accounts, 1784-1865.* Charlottesville: University of Virginia Press, 2007.

Madison, Dolley Payne. *The Selected Letters of Dolley Payne Madison.* Edited by David H. Mattern and Holly C. Shulman. Charlottesville: University of Virginia Press, 2003.

Miles, William Porcher. *Oration Delivered before the Fourth of July Association.* Charleston, S.C.: James S. Burges, 1849.

Phillips, Ulrich B., ed. *Annual Report of the American Historical Association for the Year 1911.* Vol. 2, *The Correspondence of Robert Toombs, Alexander H. Stephens, and Howell Cobb.* Washington, D.C.: Government Printing Office, 1913.

Pillsbury, Parker. *Acts of the Anti-Slavery Apostles.* Concord, N.H.: Clague, Wegman, Schlicht, 1883.

Randall, Henry S. *The Life of Jefferson: In Three Volumes.* New York: Derby & Jackson, 1858.

Rives, William C. *Letter from the Hon. William C. Rives to a Friend, on the Important Questions of the Day.* Richmond, Va.: Whig Book and Job Office, 1860.

Ruffin, Edmund. *The Diary of Edmund Ruffin.* Edited by William Kauffman Scarborough. 2 vols. Baton Rouge: Louisiana State University Press, 1972-77.

Starobin, Robert S., ed. *Blacks in Bondage: Letters of American Slaves.* Princeton, N.J.: Markus Wiener, 1988.

Strong, George Templeton. *The Diary of George Templeton Strong.* Edited by Allan Nevins and Milton Halsey Thomas. 4 vols. New York: Macmillan, 1952.

Temple, Oliver P. *East Tennessee and the Civil War.* Cincinnati, Ohio: R. Clarke Company, 1899.

Thomas, Ella Gertrude Clanton. *The Secret Eye: The Journal of Ella Gertrude Clanton Thomas, 1848-1889.* Edited by Virginia Ingraham Burr. Chapel Hill: University of North Carolina Press, 1990.

Trollope, Fanny. *Domestic Manners of the Americans.* Edited by Pamela Neville-Sington. New York: Penguin, 1997. First published 1832 by Whittaker, Treacher, & Co.

Tucker, George. *The Life of Thomas Jefferson, Third President of the United States.* 2 vols. Philadelphia: Carey, Lea, & Blanchard, 1837.

———. *The History of the United States from Their Colonization to the End of the Twenty-Sixth Congress, in 1841.* 3 vols. Philadelphia: Lippincott, 1856-58.

Walker, Robert J. *An Appeal for the Union.* New York: J. F. Trow, 1856.

Webster, Daniel. *The Papers of Daniel Webster.* Edited by Charles M. Wiltse and Alan R. Berolzheimer. 13 vols. Hanover, N.H.: University Press of New England, 1974-89.

Winthrop, Robert C. *A Memoir of Robert C. Winthrop.* 2d ed. Edited by Robert C. Winthrop Jr. Boston: Little, Brown, and Company, 1897.

Wright, Joshua G. *An Oration Delivered in the Methodist Episcopal Church, Wilmington, N.C. on the Fourth of July, A.D. 1851.* Wilmington, N.C.: "Herald" Book and Job Office, 1851.

GOVERNMENT DOCUMENTS

Calhoun, John C. "Debate on the Territorial Government of Oregon." June 27, 1848. U.S. Congress, *Congressional Globe,* 30th Congress, 1st Session, 868-73.

———. "The Compromise." March 4, 1850. U.S. Congress, *Congressional Globe,* 31st Congress, 1st Session, 451-55.

*Constitution of the State of Illinois.* Washington, D.C.: E. De Krafft, 1818.

Hale, John P. "In Senate." December 22, 1847. U.S. Congress, *Congressional Globe,* 30th Congress, 1st Session, 62-63.

Keitt, Laurence M. "Defense of South Carolina." July 14, 1856. U.S. Congress, *Congressional Globe,* 34th Congress, 1st Session, Appendix, 833-39.

"Petitions, etc." April 20, 1848. U.S. Congress, *Congressional Globe,* 30th Congress, 1st Session, 656.

Pettit, John. "The Nebraska and Kansas Bill—Debate." March 3, 1854. U.S. Congress, *Congressional Globe,* 33rd Congress, 1st Session, Appendix, 310-11.

Toombs, Robert Toombs. "Relation of the States." February 20, 1860. U.S. Congress, *Congressional Globe,* 36th Congress, 1st Session, 838.

Trumbull, Lyman. "Invasion of Harper's [*sic*] Ferry." December 8, 1859. U.S. Congress, *Congressional Globe,* 36th Congress, 1st Session, 53-65.


SECONDARY SOURCES

JOURNAL ARTICLES

Bauer, Raymond A., and Alice H. Bauer. "Day to Day Resistance to Slavery." *Journal of Negro History* 27 (October 1942): 388-419.

Clavin, Matthew J. "American Toussaints: Symbol, Subversion, and the Black Atlantic Tradition in the American Civil War." *Slavery & Abolition* 28 (April 2007): 87-113.

Conlin, Michael F. "The Dangerous *Isms* and the Fanatical *Ists:* Antebellum Conservatives in the South and the North Confront the Modernity Conspiracy." *Journal of the Civil War Era* 4 (June 2014): 205-33.

Crider, Jonathan B. "De Bow's Revolution: The Memory of the American Revolution in the Politics of the Sectional Crisis, 1850-1861." *American Nineteenth Century History* 10 (September 2009): 317-32.

Davis, David Brion. "He Changed the World." *New York Review of Books* 54 (May 31, 2007): 54-58.

Degler, Carl N. "Thesis, Antithesis, Synthesis: The South, the North, and the Nation." *Journal of Southern History* 53 (February 1987): 3-18.

Eaton, Clement. "The Resistance of the South to Northern Radicalism." *New England Quarterly* 8 (June 1935): 215-31.

Ezbell, John S. "A Southern Education for Southrons." *Journal of Southern History* 17 (August 1951): 303-27.

Franklin, John Hope. "The North, the South, and the American Revolution." *Journal of American History* 62 (June 1975): 5-23.

Fredrickson, George M. "America's Original Sin." *New York Review of Books* 51 (March 25, 2004): 34-36.

Freehling, William W. "The Founding Fathers and Slavery." *American Historical Review* 77 (February 1972): 81-93.

Foster, Eugene A., et al. "Jefferson Fathered Slave's Last Child." *Nature* 396 (November 1998): 27-28.

Gienapp, William E. "The Crime against Sumner: The Caning of Charles Sumner and the Rise of the Republican Party." *Civil War History* 25 (September 1979): 218-45.

Jack, J. G. "The Cambridge Washington Elm." *Arnold Arboretum Bulletin of Popular Information* 5 (December 10, 1931): 69-71.

Kolchin, Peter. "Slavery in United States Survey Textbooks." *Journal of American History* 84 (March 1998): 1425-38.

Matthewson, Timothy M. "George Washington's Policy toward the Haitian Revolution." *Diplomatic History* 3 (Summer 1979): 321-36.

McKitrick, Eric L. "Washington the Liberator." *New York Review of Books* 46 (November 4, 1999): 48-49.

Morgan, Edmund S. "The Other Founders." *New York Review of Books* 52 (September 22, 2005): 41-43.

Neiman, Fraser D. "Coincidence or Causal Connection? The Relationship between Thomas Jefferson's Visits to Monticello and Sally Hemings's Conceptions." *William & Mary Quarterly*, 3rd ser., 57 (January 2000): 198-210.

Pierson, Michael D. "'All Southern Society Is Assailed by the Foulest Charges': Charles Sumner's 'The Crime against Kansas' and the Escalation of Republican Anti-Slavery Rhetoric." *New England Quarterly* 68 (December 1995): 531-57.

Quigley, Paul. "Independence Day Dilemmas in the American South, 1848-1865." *Journal of Southern History* 75 (May 2009): 235-66.

Sheriff, Carol. "Virginia's Embattled Textbooks: Lessons (Learned and Not) from the Centennial Era." *Civil War History* 58 (March 2012): 37-74.

Sinha, Manisha. "The Caning of Charles Sumner: Slavery, Race, and Ideology in the Age of the Civil War." *Journal of the Early Republic* 23 (Summer 2003): 233-62.

Sutton, Robert M. "Edward Coles and the Constitutional Crisis in Illinois, 1822-1824." *Illinois Historical Journal* 82 (Spring 1989): 33-46.

Tewell, Jeremy J. "Assuring Freedom to the Free: Jefferson's Declaration and the Conflict over Slavery." *Civil War History* 58 (March 2012): 75-96.

Welch, William L. "Lorenzo Sabine and the Assault on Sumner." *New England Quarterly* 65 (June 1992): 299-302.

Wood, Gordon S. "The Greatest Generation." *New York Review of Books* 48 (March 29, 2001): 17-22.

———. "Was Washington 'Mad for Glory?'" *New York Review of Books* 57 (June 10, 2010): 65-67.

BOOK CHAPTERS

Ayers, Edward L. "What We Talk about When We Talk about the South." In *All over the Map: Rethinking American Regions,* edited by Edward L. Ayers and Peter S. Onuf, 62-83. Baltimore, Md.: Johns Hopkins University Press, 1996.

Conlin, Michael F. "'All Men Are *Born Free and* Equal': The Radicalization of the Declaration of Independence by Slaves, Abolitionists, Slavemasters, and Doughfaces, 1840-1861." In *"And the War Came": Essays on the Coming of the Civil War,* edited by John R. Neff. Jackson: University Press of Mississippi, forthcoming.

Higginbotham, Don. "Introduction: Washington and the Historians." In *George Washington Reconsidered,* edited by Don Higginbotham, 1-12. Charlottesville: University Press of Virginia, 2001.

Hobsbawm, Eric. "Introduction: Inventing Traditions." In *The Invention of Tradition,* edited by Eric Hobsbawm and Terrence Ranger, 1-14. Cambridge: Cambridge University Press, 1992.

Lee, Jean B. "Mount Vernon Plantation: A Model for the Republic." In *Slavery at the Home of George Washington,* edited by Phillip J. Schwartz, 13-45. Mount Vernon, Va.: Mount Vernon Ladies' Association, 2001.

Sellers, Charles Grier, Jr. "Introduction." In *The Southerner as American,* edited by Charles Grier Sellers Jr., v-ix. Chapel Hill: University of North Carolina Press, 1960.

Wainright, Nicholas B. "The Age of Nicholas Biddle, 1825-1841." In *Philadelphia: A 300-Year History,* edited by Russell F. Weigley et al., 258-306. New York: W. W. Norton, 1982.

Wood, Gordon S. "The Trials and Tribulations of Thomas Jefferson." In *Jeffersonian Legacies,* edited by Peter S. Onuf, 395-417. Charlottesville: University Press of Virginia, 1993.


BOOKS

Alexander, Edward P. *Museum Masters, Their Museum, and Their Influence.* Nashville, Tenn.: American Association for State and Local History, 1983.

Allen, Danielle. *Our Declaration: A Reading of the Declaration in Defense of Equality.* New York: Liveright, 2014.

Allgor, Catherine. *A Perfect Union: Dolley Madison and the Creation of the American Nation.* New York: Henry Holt, 2006.

Amar, Akhil Reed. *America's Constitution: A Biography.* New York: Random House, 2005.

Anderson, Benedict. *Imagined Communities: Reflections on the Origin and Spread of Nationalism.* Rev. ed. New York: Verso, 1991.

Ayers, Edward L. *In the Presence of Mine Enemies: War in the Heart of America, 1859-1863.* New York: W. W. Norton, 2003.

Bacevich, Andrew J. *The New American Militarism: How Americans Are Seduced by War.* New York: Oxford University Press, 2005.

Bauer, K. Jack. *The Mexican War, 1846-1848.* New York: Macmillan, 1974.

Beeman, Richard R. *Patrick Henry: A Biography.* New York: McGraw-Hill, 1974.

Bell, Madison Smartt. *Toussaint Louverture: A Biography.* New York: Pantheon Books, 2007.

Bennett, William J. *America: The Last Best Hope.* Vol. 1, *From the Age of Discovery to a World at War.* Nashville, Tenn.: Nelson Current, 2006.

Berlin, Ira. *Slaves without Masters: The Free Negro in the Antebellum South.* New York: Random House, 1974.

Berwanger, Eugene H. *The Frontier against Slavery: Western Anti-Negro Prejudice and the Slavery Extension Controversy.* Urbana: University of Illinois Press, 2002. First published 1967 by University of Illinois Press.

Beyerchen, Alan D. *Scientists under Hitler: Politics and the Physics Community in the Third Reich.* New Haven, Conn.: Yale University Press, 1977.

Blacklett, Richard J. M. *Running a Thousand Miles for Freedom.* Baton Rouge: Louisiana State University Press, 1999.

Bowman, Shearer Davis. *At the Precipice: Americans North and South during the Secession Crisis.* Chapel Hill: University of North Carolina Press, 2010.

Brizer, Bradley Brizer. *American Cicero: The Life of Charles Carroll.* Wilmington, Del.: Intercollegiate Studies Institute, 2010.

Brown, Dona. *Inventing New England: Regional Tourism in the Nineteenth Century.* Washington, D.C.: Smithsonian Press, 1997.

Bruce, Philip Alexander. *History of the University of Virginia, 1819-1919: The Lengthened Shadow of One Man.* New York: Macmillan, 1921.

Burin, Eric. *Slavery and the Peculiar Solution: A History of the American Colonization Society.* Gainesville: University Press of Florida, 2005.

Burstein, Andrew. *America's Jubilee, July 4, 1826: A Generation Remembers the Revolution after Fifty Years of Independence.* New York: Knopf, 2001.

———. *The Inner Jefferson: Portrait of a Grieving Optimist.* Charlottesville: University Press of Virginia, 1995.

Calloway, Colin G. *The American Revolution in Indian Country: Crisis and Diversity in Native American Communities.* New York: Cambridge University Press, 1995.

Camp, Stephanie M. H. *Closer to Freedom: Enslaved Women & Everyday Resistance in the Plantation South.* Chapel Hill: University of North Carolina Press, 2004.

Chambers, Thomas A. *Memories of War: Visiting Battlegrounds and Bonefields in the Early American Republic.* Ithaca, N.Y.: Cornell University Press, 2012.

Chang, Eileen Ka-May. *Plain and Noble Garb of Truth: Nationalism & Impartiality in American History, 1784-1860.* Athens: University of Georgia Press, 2008.

Cobb, James C. *Away Down South: A History of Southern Identity.* New York: Oxford University Press, 2005.

Cocks, Catherine. *Doing the Town: The Rise of Urban Tourism in the United States, 1850-1915.* Berkeley: University of California Press, 2001.

Colaiaco, James A. *Frederick Douglass and the Fourth of July.* New York: Palgrave Macmillan, 2007.

Conforti, Joseph A. *Imagining New England: Explorations of Regional Identity from the Pilgrims to the Mid-Twentieth Century.* Chapel Hill: University of North Carolina Press, 2001.

Cooper-Guasco, Suzanne. *Confronting Slavery: Edward Coles and the Rise of Anti-Slavery Politics in Nineteenth-Century America.* DeKalb: Northern Illinois University Press, 2013.

Cornell, Saul. *A Well-Regulated Militia: The Founding Fathers and the Origins of Gun Control in America.* New York: Oxford University Press, 2006.

Crackel, Theodore J. *West Point: A Bicentennial History.* Lawrence: University Press of Kansas, 2002.

Craven, Avery O. *The Growth of Southern Nationalism, 1848-1861.* Baton Rouge: Louisiana State University Press, 1953.

Criblez, Adam. *Parading Patriotism: Independence Day Celebrations in the Urban Midwest, 1826-1876.* New York: New York University Press, 2014.

Davis, David Brion. *Inhuman Bondage: The Rise and Fall of Slavery in the New World.* New York: Oxford University Press, 2006.

———. *The Problem of Slavery in the Age of Revolution, 1770-1823.* Ithaca, N.Y.: Cornell University Press, 1975.

Dennis, Matthew. *Red, White, and Blue Letter Days: An American Calendar.* Ithaca, N.Y.: Cornell University Press, 2002.

Deyle, Steven. *Carry Me Back: The Domestic Slave Trade in American Life.* New York: Oxford University Press, 2005.

Donald, David Herbert. *Charles Sumner and the Coming of the Civil War*. New York: Knopf, 1960.

Drescher, Seymour. *Abolition: A History of Slavery and Antislavery*. Cambridge: Cambridge University Press, 2009.

Dubois, Laurent. *Avengers of the New World: The Story of the Haitian Revolution*. Cambridge, Mass.: Harvard University Press, 2004.

Earle, Jonathan H. *Jacksonian Antislavery and the Politics of Free Soil, 1824-1854*. Chapel Hill: University of North Carolina Press, 2004.

Eaton, Clement. *Freedom of Thought in the Old South*. Durham, N.C.: Duke University Press, 1940.

Egerton, Douglas R. *Death or Liberty: African Americans and Revolutionary America*. New York: Oxford University Press, 2009.

Ellis, Joseph J. *American Sphinx: The Character of Thomas Jefferson*. New York: Alfred A. Knopf, 1997.

Engelhardt, Tom. *The End of Victory Culture: Cold War America and the Disillusioning of a Generation*. New York: Basic Books, 1995.

Escott, Paul D. *After Secession: Jefferson Davis and the Failure of Confederate Nationalism*. Baton Rouge: Louisiana State University Press, 1978.

Essah, Patience. *A House Divided: Slavery and Emancipation in Delaware, 1638-1865*. Charlottesville: University Press of Virginia, 1996.

Fagen, Brian. *The Little Ice Age: How Climate Made History, 1300-1850*. New York: Basic Books, 2000.

Faust, Drew Gilpin. *The Creation of Southern Nationalism: Ideology and Identity in the Civil War South*. Baton Rouge: Louisiana State University Press, 1988.

Fehrenbacher, Don E. *Slavery, Law, and Politics: The Dred Scott Case in Historical Perspective*. New York: Oxford University Press, 1981.

———. *The Slaveholding Republic: An Account of the United States Government's Relations toward Slavery*. New York: Oxford University Press, 2001.

Finkelman, Paul. *Slavery and the Founders: Race and Liberty in the Age of Jefferson*. 2d ed. Armonk, N.Y.: M. E. Sharpe, 2001.

Fischer, David Hackett . *Historians' Fallacies: Towards a Logic of Historical Thought*. New York: Harper and Row, 1970.

Fleche, Andre M. *The Revolution of 1861: The American Civil War in the Age of Nationalist Conflict*. Chapel Hill: University of North Carolina Press, 2012.

Foner, Eric. *Free Soil, Free Labor, Free Men: The Ideology of the Republican Party before the Civil War*. Rev. ed. New York: Oxford University Press, 1995.

———. *The Story of American Freedom*. New York: W. W. Norton, 1998.

Forbes, Robert Pierce. *The Missouri Compromise and Its Aftermath: Slavery & the Meaning of America*. Chapel Hill: University of North Carolina Press, 2007.

Fox-Genovese, Elizabeth, and Eugene D. Genovese. *The Mind of the Master Class: History and Faith in the Southern Slaveholders' Worldview*. Cambridge: Cambridge University Press, 2005.

Franklin, John Hope. *A Southern Odyssey: Travelers in the Antebellum North*. Baton Rouge: Louisiana State University Press, 1976.

———. *The Militant South, 1800-1861.* Urbana: University of Illinois Press, 2002. First published 1956 by Belknap Press of Harvard University Press.

Frederickson, George M. *White Supremacy: A Comparative Study in American and South African History.* New York: Oxford University Press, 1981.

Freehling. Alison Goodyear. *Drift toward Dissolution: The Virginia Slavery Debate of 1831-1832.* Baton Rouge: Louisiana State University Press, 1982.

Freehling, William W. *The Road to Disunion.* Vol. 1, *Secessionists at Bay, 1776-1854.* New York: Oxford University Press, 1990.

———. *The Road to Disunion.* Vol. 2, *Secessionists Triumphant, 1854-1861.* New York: Oxford University Press, 2007.

———. *Prelude to Civil War: The Nullification Controversy in South Carolina, 1816-1836.* New York: Oxford University Press, 1965.

Furstenberg, François. *In the Name of the Father: Washington's Legacy, Slavery, and the Making of a Nation.* New York: Penguin, 2006.

Gallagher, Gary. *The Confederate War: How Popular Will, Nationalism, and Military Strategy Could Not Stave Off Defeat.* Cambridge, Mass.: Harvard University Press, 1997.

Geary, Patrick J. *The Myth of Nations: The Medieval Origins of Europe.* Princeton, N.J.: Princeton University Press, 2002.

Gellman, David N. *Emancipating New York: The Politics of Slavery and Freedom, 1777-1827.* Baton Rouge: Louisiana State University Press, 2006.

Genovese, Eugene D. *Roll, Jordan, Roll: The World the Slaves Made.* New York: Vintage, 1976. First published 1972 by Pantheon.

Gienapp, William E. *The Origins of the Republican Party, 1852-1856.* New York: Oxford University Press, 1987.

Gilbert, Alan. *Black Patriots and Loyalists: Fighting for Emancipation in the War of Independence.* Chicago: University of Chicago Press, 2012.

Gilbert, Felix. *To the Farewell Address: Ideas of Early American Foreign Policy.* Princeton, N.J.: Princeton University Press, 1961.

Goldfield, David. *Still Fighting the Civil War: The American South and Southern History.* Baton Rouge: Louisiana State University Press, 2002.

Gordon, John W. *South Carolina and the American Revolution: A Battlefield History.* Columbia: University of South Carolina Press, 2003.

Gordon-Reed, Annette. *Thomas Jefferson and Sally Hemings: An American Controversy.* Charlottesville: University Press of Virginia, 1997.

Grant, Susan-Mary. *North over South: Northern Nationalism and American Identity in the Antebellum Era.* Lawrence: University Press of Kansas, 2000.

Greenberg, Kenneth S. *Honor & Slavery: Lies, Duels, Noses, Masks, Dressing as a Woman, Gifts, Strangers, Humanitarianism, Death, Slave Rebellions, the Proslavery Argument, Baseball, Hunting, and Gambling in the Old South.* Princeton, N.J.: Princeton University Press, 1996.

Greenfield, Liah. *Nationalism: Five Roads to Modernity.* Cambridge, Mass.: Harvard University Press, 1992.

Greve, Charles Theodore. *Centennial History of Cincinnati and Representative Citizens.* 2 vols. Chicago: Biographical Publishing Company, 1904.

Griffin, Larry J., and Don H. Doyle, eds. *The South as an American Problem*. Athens: University of Georgia Press, 1995.

Grimsted, David. *American Mobbing, 1828-1861: Toward Civil War*. New York: Oxford University Press, 1998.

Handlin, Lilian. *George Bancroft: The Intellectual as Democrat*. New York: Harper and Row, 1984.

Hickey, Donald R. *The War of 1812: A Forgotten Conflict*. Urbana: University of Illinois Press, 1989.

Hobsbawm, Eric, and Terrence Ranger, eds. *The Invention of Tradition*. Cambridge: Cambridge University Press, 1992.

Hofstadter, Richard. *The Paranoid Style in American Politics and Other Essays*. New York: Knopf, 1965.

Howe, M. A. DeWolfe. *The Life and Letters of George Bancroft*. Port Washington, N.Y.: Kennikat Press, 1971. First published 1908 by C. Scribner's Sons.

Hunt, Alfred. *Haiti's Influence on Antebellum America: Slumbering Volcano in the Caribbean*. Baton Rouge: Louisiana State University Press, 1988.

Jeffrey, Julie Roy. *The Great Silent Army of Abolitionism: Ordinary Women in the Antislavery Movement*. Chapel Hill: University of North Carolina Press, 1999.

Jennings, Thelma. *The Nashville Convention: Southern Movement for Unity, 1848-1851*. Memphis, Tenn.: Memphis State University Press, 1980.

Johannsen, Robert W. *Stephen A. Douglas*. Urbana: University of Illinois Press, 1997. First published 1973 by Oxford University Press.

Johnson, Chalmers. *The Sorrows of Empire: Militarism, Secrecy, and the End of the American Republic*. New York: Metropolitan Books, 2004.

Jordan, Winthrop D. *Tumult and Silence at Second Creek: An Inquiry into a Civil War Slave Conspiracy*. Rev. ed. Baton Rouge: Louisiana State University Press, 1995.

———. *White over Black: American Attitudes towards the Negro, 1550-1812*. Chapel Hill: University of North Carolina Press, 1968.

Kachun, Mitch. *Festivals of Freedom: Memory and Meaning in African American Emancipation Celebrations, 1808-1915*. Amherst: University of Massachusetts Press, 2003.

Kahler, Gerald E. *The Long Farewell: Americans Mourn the Death of George Washington*. Charlottesville: University of Virginia Press, 2008.

Kammen, Michael. *A Machine That Would Go of Itself: The Constitution in American Culture*. New York: Alfred A. Knopf, 1986.

Kastor, Peter J. *The Nation's Crucible: The Louisiana Purchase and the Creation of America*. New Haven, Conn.: Yale University Press, 2004.

Kennedy, Randall. *Nigger: The Strange Career of a Troublesome Word*. New York: Pantheon, 2003.

Kerr-Ritchie, J. R. *Rites of August First: Emancipation Day in the Black Atlantic World*. Baton Rouge: Louisiana State University Press, 2007.

Kolchin, Peter. *American Slavery, 1619-1877*. Rev. ed. New York: Hill and Wang, 2003.

Lakwete, Angela. *Inventing the Cotton Gin: Machine and Myth in Antebellum America*. Baltimore, Md.: Johns Hopkins University Press, 2003.

Leepson, Marc. *Saving Monticello: The Levy Family's Epic Quest to Rescue the House That Jefferson Built*. New York: Free Press, 2001.

Levy, Andrew. *First Emancipator: The Forgotten Story of Robert Carter, the Founding Father Who Freed His Slaves.* New York: Random House, 2005.

Linenthal, Edward Tabor. *Sacred Ground: Americans and Their Battlefields.* Urbana: University of Illinois Press, 1991.

Linenthal, Edward T., and Tom Engelhardt, eds. *History Wars: The Enola Gay and Other Battles for the American Past.* New York: Henry Holt, 1996.

Link, William A. *Roots of Secession: Slavery and Politics in Antebellum Virginia.* Chapel Hill: University of North Carolina Press, 2003.

Litwack, Leon F. *North of Slavery: The Negro in the Free States, 1790-1861.* Chicago: University of Chicago Press, 1961.

Longmore, Paul K. *The Invention of George Washington.* Berkeley: University of California Press, 1988.

Maier, Pauline. *American Scripture: Making the Declaration of Independence.* New York: Knopf, 1998.

Martin, James K. *Benedict Arnold, Revolutionary Hero: An American Warrior Reconsidered.* New York: New York University Press, 1997.

Martin, Jonathan D. *Divided Mastery: Slave Hiring in the American South.* Cambridge, Mass.: Harvard University Press, 2004.

Mason, Matthew. *Slavery and Politics in the Early American Republic.* Chapel Hill: University of North Carolina Press, 2006.

Masur, Louis P. *1831: Year of Eclipse.* New York: Hill and Wang, 2001.

Matthews, Jean V. *Rufus Choate: The Law and Civic Virtue.* Philadelphia: Temple University Press, 1980.

McCardell, John. *The Idea of a Southern Nation: Southern Nationalists and Southern Nationalism, 1830-1860.* New York: W. W. Norton, 1979.

McManus, Edgar J. *Black Bondage in the North.* Syracuse, N.Y.: Syracuse University Press, 1973.

Meade, Robert Douthat. *Patrick Henry, Practical Revolutionary.* Philadelphia: Lippincott, 1969.

Merriam, George Spring. *The Negro and the Nation: A History of American Slavery and Enfranchisement.* New York: Henry Holt, 1906.

Minardi, Margot. *Making Slavery History: Abolitionism and the Politics of Memory in Massachusetts.* New York: Oxford University Press, 2010.

Mires, Charlene. *Independence Hall in American Memory.* Philadelphia: University of Pennsylvania Press, 2002.

Moore, Glover. *The Missouri Controversy, 1819-1821.* Lexington: University of Kentucky Press, 1953.

Morris, Thomas D. *Free Men All: The Personal Liberty Laws of the North, 1780-1861.* Baltimore, Md.: Johns Hopkins University Press, 1974.

Morrison, Chaplain W. *Democratic Politics and Sectionalism: The Wilmot Proviso Controversy.* Chapel Hill: University of North Carolina Press, 1967.

Morrison, Michael A. *Slavery and the American West: The Eclipse of Manifest Destiny and the Coming of the Civil War.* Chapel Hill: University of North Carolina Press, 1997.

Moss, Roger W. *Historic Houses of Philadelphia: A Tour of the Region's Museum Homes.* Philadelphia: University of Pennsylvania Press, 1998.

Mott, Frank Luther. *American Journalism, 1690-1960.* New York: MacMillan, 1962.

Nagel, Paul C. *One Nation Indivisible: The Union in American Thought, 1776-1861.* New York: Oxford University Press, 1964.

Nash, Gary B. *The Forgotten Fifth: African Americans in the Age of Revolution.* Cambridge, Mass.: Harvard University Press, 2006.

———. *The Liberty Bell.* New Haven, Conn.: Yale University Press, 2010.

Nash, Gary B., Charlotte Crabtree, and Ross E. Dunn. *History on Trial: Culture Wars and the Teaching of the Past.* New York: Alfred A. Knopf, 1997.

Nash, Gary B., and Jean Soderlund. *Freedom by Degrees: Emancipation in Pennsylvania and Its Aftermath.* New York: Oxford University Press, 1991.

Niven, John. *John C. Calhoun and the Price of Union: A Biography.* Baton Rouge: Louisiana State University Press, 1988.

O'Brien, Michael. *Conjectures of Order: Intellectual Life and the American South, 1810-1860.* 2 vols. Chapel Hill: University of North Carolina Press, 2004.

Onuf, Peter S. *Statehood and Union: A History of the Northwest Ordinance.* Bloomington: Indiana University Press, 1987.

Peterson, Merrill D. *The Great Triumvirate: Webster, Clay, and Calhoun.* New York: Oxford University Press, 1987.

———. *The Jeffersonian Image in the American Mind.* New York: Oxford University Press, 1960.

Piecuch, Jim. *Three Peoples, One King: Loyalists, Indians, and Slaves in the Revolutionary South, 1775-1782.* Columbia: University of South Carolina Press, 2008.

Phillips, Ulrich Bonnell. *The Life of Robert Toombs.* New York: Macmillan, 1913.

Potter, David M. *The Impending Crisis, 1848-1861.* New York: HarperCollins, 1976.

Purcell, Sarah J. *Sealed with Blood: War, Sacrifice, and Memory in Revolutionary America.* Philadelphia: University of Pennsylvania Press, 2002.

Quarles, Benjamin. *The Negro in the American Revolution.* Chapel Hill: University of North Carolina Press, 1961.

Quigley, Paul. *Shifting Grounds: Nationalism and the American South, 1848-1865.* New York: Oxford University Press, 2012.

Rable, George C. *Civil Wars: Women and the Crisis of Southern Nationalism.* Urbana: University of Illinois Press, 1989.

Reid, Ronald F. *Edward Everett: Unionist Orator.* New York: Greenwood Press, 1990.

Remini, Robert V. *The House: A History of the House of Representatives.* New York: HarperCollins, 2006.

Rice, James D. *Tales from a Revolution: Bacon's Rebellion and the Transformation of Early America.* New York: Oxford University Press, 2012.

Richards, Leonard L. *"Gentlemen of Property and Standing": Anti-Abolition Mobs in Jacksonian America.* New York: Oxford University Press, 1970.

———. *The Slave Power: The Free North and Southern Domination, 1780-1860.* Baton Rouge: Louisiana State University Press, 2000.

Roberts, Alasdair. *America's First Great Depression: Economic Crisis and Political Disorder after the Panic of 1837.* Ithaca, N.Y.: Cornell University Press, 2012.

Roberts, Timothy Mason. *Distant Revolutions: 1848 and the Challenge to American Exceptionalism.* Charlottesville: University of Virginia Press, 2009.

Russell, Jeffery Burton. *Lucifer: The Devil in the Middle Ages.* Ithaca, N.Y.: Cornell University Press, 1984.

Sanford, Charles B. *The Religious Life of Thomas Jefferson.* Charlottesville: University Press of Virginia, 1984.

Schwartz, Barry. *George Washington: The Making of an American Symbol.* New York: Free Press, 1987.

Sewall, Richard H. *John P. Hale and the Politics of Abolition.* Cambridge, Mass.: Harvard University Press, 1965.

Sinclair, William A. *The Aftermath of Slavery: A Study of the Condition and Environment of the American Negro.* Boston: Small, Maynard, 1905.

Sitterson, Joseph C. *The Secession Movement in North Carolina.* Chapel Hill: University of North Carolina Press, 1939.

Slaughter, Thomas P. *Bloody Dawn: The Christiana Riot and Racial Violence in the Antebellum North.* New York: Oxford University Press, 1991.

Smokin, Fred. *Unquiet Eagle: Memory and Desire in the Idea of American Freedom, 1815-1860.* Ithaca, N.Y.: Cornell University Press, 1967.

Spalding, Matthew, and Patrick J. Garrity. *A Sacred Union of Citizens: George Washington's Farewell Address and the American Character.* Lanham, Md.: Rowman & Littlefield, 1996.

Spencer, Donald S. *Louis Kossuth and Young America: A Study of Sectionalism and Foreign Policy, 1848-1852.* Columbia: University of Missouri Press, 1977.

Stampp, Kenneth M. *America in 1857: A Nation on the Brink.* New York: Oxford University Press, 1990.

——. *The Peculiar Institution: Slavery in the Ante-Bellum South.* New York: Vintage, 1989. First published 1956 by Alfred A. Knopf.

Staudenraus, P. J. *The African Colonization Movement, 1816-1865.* New York: Columbia University Press, 1961.

Steinberg, Ted. *Down to Earth: Nature's Role in American History.* New York: Oxford University Press, 2002.

Stewart, James Brewer. *Wendell Phillips: Liberty's Hero.* Baton Rouge: Louisiana State University Press, 1986.

Stovall, Pleasant A. *Robert Toombs: Statesman, Speaker, Soldier, Sage.* New York: Cassell Publishing Company, 1892.

Sydnor, Charles S. *The Development of Southern Sectionalism, 1819-1848.* Baton Rouge: Louisiana State University Press, 1948.

Tallant, Harold D. *Evil Necessity: Slavery and Political Culture in Antebellum Kentucky.* Lexington: University Press of Kentucky, 2003.

Thompson, William Y. *Robert Toombs of Georgia.* Baton Rouge: Louisiana State University Press, 1966.

Tomek, Beverly C. *Colonization and Its Discontents: Emancipation, Emigration, and Antislavery in Antebellum Pennsylvania.* New York: New York University Press, 2014.

Travers, Len. *Celebrating the Fourth: Independence Day and the Rites of Nationalism in the Early Republic.* Amherst: University of Massachusetts Press, 1997.

Urofsky, Melvin I. *The Levy Family and Monticello, 1834-1923: Saving Thomas Jefferson's House.* Charlottesville: Thomas Jefferson Association, 2002.

Varg, Paul A. *Edward Everett: The Intellectual in the Turmoil of Politics.* Selinsgrove, Pa.: Susquehanna University Press, 1992.

Varon, Elizabeth R. *We Mean to Be Counted: White Women & Politics in Antebellum Virginia.* Chapel Hill: University of North Carolina Press, 1998.

Von Frank, Albert J. *The Trials of Anthony Burns: Freedom and Slavery in Emerson's Boston.* Cambridge, Mass.: Harvard University Press, 1998.

Wallace, Mike. *Gotham: A History of New York City to 1898.* New York: Oxford University Press, 1999.

Way, William. *History of the New England Society of Charleston, South Carolina, for One Hundred Years, 1819–1919.* Charleston, S.C.: New England Society of Charleston, 1920.

Weeks, Jim. *Gettysburg: Memory, Market, and an American Shrine.* Princeton, N.J.: Princeton University Press, 2003.

Weisenburger, Steven. *Modern Medea: A Family Story of Slavery and Child Murder from the Old South.* New York: Hill and Wang, 1998.

Wellman, Judith. *The Road to Seneca Falls: Elizabeth Cady Stanton and the First Women's Rights Convention.* Urbana: University of Illinois Press, 2004.

Whitman, Stephen T. *The Price of Freedom: Slavery and Manumission in Baltimore and Early National Maryland.* Lexington: University Press of Kentucky, 1997.

Wiencek, Henry. *An Imperfect God: George Washington, His Slaves, and the Creation of America.* New York: Farrar, Straus, and Giroux, 2003.

Wills, Gary. *Cincinnatus: George Washington and the Enlightenment.* Garden City, N.Y.: Doubleday, 1984.

———. *"Negro President": Jefferson and the Slave Power.* Boston: Houghton Mifflin, 2003.

Wilson, Barry. *Benedict Arnold: A Traitor in Our Midst.* Montreal: McGill-Queen's University Press, 2001.

Wilson, Leonard G. *Lyell in America: Transatlantic Geology, 1841–1853.* Baltimore, Md.: Johns Hopkins University Press, 1998.

Wilson, Major. *Space, Time, and Freedom: The Quest for Nationality and the Irrepressible Conflict, 1815–1861.* Westport, Conn.: Greenwood Press, 1974.

Wolf, Eva Sheppard. *Race and Liberty in the New Nation: Emancipation in Virginia from the Revolution to Nat Turner's Rebellion.* Baton Rouge: Louisiana State University Press, 2006.

Wyatt-Brown, Bertram. *Honor and Violence in the Old South.* New York: Oxford University Press, 1986.

———. *Yankee Saints and Southern Sinners.* Baton Rouge: Louisiana State University Press, 1985.

Young, Alfred E. *The Shoemaker and the Tea Party: Memory and the American Revolution.* Boston: Beacon Press, 1999.

Young, Robert W. *Senator James Murray Mason: Defender of the Old South.* Knoxville: University of Tennessee Press, 1998.

Zaborney, John J. *Slaves for Hire: Renting Enslaved Laborers in Antebellum Virginia.* Baton Rouge: Louisiana State University Press, 2012.

Zelinsky, Wilbur. *Nation into State: The Shifting Symbolic Foundations of American Nationalism.* Chapel Hill: University of North Carolina Press, 1988.

Zenzen, Joan M. *Battling for Manassas: The Fifty-Year Preservation Struggle at Manassas National Battlefield Park.* University Park: Pennsylvania State University Press, 1998.

Zilversmit, Arthur. *The First Emancipation: The Abolition of Slavery in the North.* Chicago: University of Chicago Press, 1967.

UNPUBLISHED PH.D. DISSERTATION

Ariew, Roger. "Ockham's Razor: A Historical and Philosophical Analysis of Ockham's Principle of Parsimony." Ph.D. diss., University of Illinois at Urbana-Champaign, 1976.

# Index

abolitionists: Bunker Hill Monument symbolism and, 1-8 (*see also* Bunker Hill); defined, 12-15; Harpers Ferry Raid by, 2, 67, 108, 126, 157, 159; on Jefferson as slave owner, 41-42, 47-52 (*see also* Jefferson, Thomas); on sex between slave owners and slaves, 45; on Washington as slave owner, 78-79 (*see also* Washington, George); women abolitionists and Fourth of July commemoration, 30. *See also* American Revolution; Declaration of Independence; Independence Day (Fourth of July); Secession Crisis; slavery

Adams, John, 44, 69

Adams, John Quincy (U.S. Representative), 113

agriculture, slavery in Southern states and, 51, 150

Aiken, David Wyatt, 118

Alexander, Joseph McKnit, 132

Allen, W. T., 54, 95

American Colonization Society, 51

*American Loyalists, The* (Sabine), 134

American Revolution, 106-45; American Revolution battles commemorated, 115-19; Fourth of July commemoration and, 18-22, 29; monuments to, 1-8, 106-8, *107;* Newburgh Con-

spiracy (March 15, 1783), 102, *103;* Northern and Southern portrayals of, 133-45; overview, 16-17; sectional tension about battles of, 122-33; veterans and families honored for, 108-14; War of 1812 and, 119-21; Washington and, 72-75, *73,* 85, 86, 102-4, *103, 104,* 105

Anderson, Benedict, 11

*Anti-Slavery Bugle,* 58, 82, 147, 148-49, 150, 153

Appleton, Nathan, 6

Ashmore, John Durant, 52

Ashworth, Henry, 64, 94

Attucks, Crispus, 123

*Ballou's Pictorial Drawing-Room Companion:* on American Revolution, 109, 121, 142; "Civic Heroes of the American Revolution," *38;* on Declaration of Independence, 53, 54, 55; on Mount Vernon, 100, 101; "Washington's Rock, Somerset County, New Jersey," *194*

Baltimore, Pratt Street Riot in, 161, 162

*Baltimore Sun,* 113, 117

Bancroft, George: on American Revolution, 141-42, 144; on Declaration of Independence, 54, 157; on Farewell Address (Washington), 91; *History*